EXISTENTIALISM
AND EXCESS

EXISTENTIALISM AND EXCESS

The Life and Times of Jean-Paul Sartre

GARY COX

BLOOMSBURY ACADEMIC

LONDON • NEW YORK • OXFORD • NEW DELHI • SYDNEY

BLOOMSBURY ACADEMIC
Bloomsbury Publishing Plc
50 Bedford Square, London, WC1B 3DP, UK
1385 Broadway, New York, NY 10018, USA

BLOOMSBURY, BLOOMSBURY ACADEMIC and the Diana logo
are trademarks of Bloomsbury Publishing Plc

First published in paperback in Great Britain 2019

First published in 2016

Cover design by Catherine Wood
Cover image: Photo by Fritz Eschen / ullstein bild via Getty Images

ISBN: HB: 978-1-4742-3533-4
PB: 978-1-3500-6657-1
ePDF: 978-1-4742-3534-1
eBook: 978-1-4742-3535-8

Typeset by Fakenham Prepress Solutions, Fakenham, Norfolk NR21 8NN

To find out more about our authors and books visit
www.bloomsbury.com and sign up for our newsletters.

'What? A great man? I always see only the actor of his own ideal.'

(Friedrich Nietzsche, *Beyond Good and Evil*)

CONTENTS

ACKNOWLEDGEMENTS

Many thanks to a host of Sartre scholars without whose extensive knowledge of Sartre's life and work this biography would have been impossible. Particular thanks to Annie Cohen-Solal and Ronald Hayman whose marvellously vast and detailed biographies, *Jean-Paul Sartre: A Life* and *Writing Against: A Biography of Sartre*, were my main guiding lights throughout. I am also indebted to Sartre himself, not only for living the life that is the subject of this book, but for documenting many parts of it while transforming other parts into literature. Lastly, I am deeply indebted to Sartre's great companion, Simone de Beauvoir, who wrote even more about him in her epic autobiography and elsewhere than he wrote about himself.

GLOSSARY OF ABBREVIATIONS

EDC   European Defence Community

ENS   École Normale Supérieure

FLN   Front de libération nationale

M22M   Mouvement du 22 mars

OAS   Organisation de l'armée secrète

PCF   Parti communiste français

RDR   Rassemblement démocratique révolutionnaire

1

Genius

Who is Jean-Paul Sartre? As this book will reveal, this question was one Sartre spent much of his life trying to answer, alongside more general philosophical questions such as, 'What is a person?' and more specific, practical questions such as, 'When will Castor arrive?' and 'Where is my pipe tobacco?'

In his book, *Existentialism and Humanism*, Sartre said, 'There is no genius other than that which is expressed in works of art' (*Existentialism and Humanism*, p. 41). In short, 'Genius is as genius does', or even, to employ a central existentialist maxim, 'To be is to do.' Sartre was a genius, not because he was what modern educators label 'gifted and talented' – although he was certainly exceptionally gifted and talented – but because of what he *did*, because of the many exceptional works of philosophy and literature he produced in the seventy-four years and ten months he lived.

His life itself was a work of art too. An extraordinary life, as you will see, even from this relatively brief summary of it: one of those lives that makes you wonder how the person concerned fitted it all in.

True, Sartre lived in interesting times, but then everyone does. Interesting things kept on happening to Sartre largely because he made them happen. He said, 'In life, a man commits himself, draws his own portrait and there is nothing but that portrait. No doubt this thought may seem comfortless to one who has not made a success of his life. On the other hand, it puts everyone in a position to understand that reality alone is reliable' (*Existentialism and Humanism*, p. 42). Sartre was a real go-getter, almost always extremely enthusiastic about what he was doing and always extremely busy. It helped that he possessed phenomenal stamina and energy.

Reflecting on his many achievements, Sartre refused to view them as the product of a gift. In his 1964 autobiography, *Words,* he said: 'Where would be the anguish, the ordeal, the temptation resisted, even the merit, if I had gifts?' (*Words*, p. 117). In his view, his achievements were not the consequence of his total linguistic fluency or the outcome of his astonishing capacity to generate and organize highly complex, abstract and original thoughts. His achievements, he insisted, were entirely the product of a supreme conjuring trick, a lifelong mission to create himself, the Sartre brand, out of nothing. He did not write because he was special; he was special because he wrote. 'I have never seen myself as the happy owner of a "talent": my one concern was to save myself – nothing in my hands, nothing in my pockets – through work and faith' (*Words*, p. 158).

These lines from the final paragraph of *Words* echo a passage from his 1953 play, *Kean*. Kean, the great Shakespearean actor, who is nothing more than the parts he plays and whose genius lies entirely in his *performances*, says: 'I live from day to day in a fabulous imposture. Not a farthing, nothing in my hands, nothing in my pockets, but I need only snap my fingers to summon spirits of the air' (*Kean*, Act 2, p. 31).

The subject of this book is *how* Sartre made himself out of nothing, or at most, out of not much more than his diminutive 153 centimetres of height, his few pounds of flesh, his one good eye, his indomitable will, his severe workaholism and a little help from his very special friends.

All half-decent biographies strive to get the basic facts straight – names, dates and so on – but every biography is also inevitably a biographer's own idiosyncratic view of a person. As well as being a novelist, playwright and philosopher, Sartre was also very much a biographer. His biographies of Baudelaire, Genet and Flaubert are very much his impression of these people, just as his autobiography *Words* is very much his impression of himself – Sartre's take on Sartre, Sartre's search for Sartre.

This biography, then, is very much my take on Sartre, my search for Sartre. Though I already knew him quite well before, my view of him changed and developed considerably as I wrote this book, and will continue to change and develop into the future as I think more about him. And of course, the impression you form of him in reading this book, despite my various efforts to sway your opinion, will not be the same as mine, perhaps not even similar. And so it goes.

Where does the truth of a person lie? Does it lie anywhere? As Sartre argues, we constantly invent, interpret and reinterpret ourselves as we live. We also constantly invent, interpret and reinterpret others by thinking, talking and writing about them, both while they are alive and after they die. Perhaps that is all any of us are, an ongoing exercise in invention and interpretation undertaken by ourselves and others, until such time as we are dead *and* forgotten. People are impossible to entirely pin down, that is what makes them so fascinating.

Sartre has been dead since 15 April 1980. His remains lie in Montparnasse Cemetery, Paris, alongside those of his great companion and intellectual sparring partner, Simone de Beauvoir, who joined him there in 1986. But he is certainly not forgotten. He tried his damnedest not to be forgotten, to immortalize himself.

It was always his ultimate ambition from childhood to be a great, dead, French writer, the Voltaire of the twentieth century.

He strained every sinew to inspire people to think about him and his ideas, to keep his memory and legacy alive, to recognize his relevance to our times and to all times. And here we are, doing just that.

2

Stowaway Traveller

Jean-Paul Sartre was born in Paris on 21 June 1905. To think of Sartre is to think of Paris. For his many fans, to think of Paris is to think of Sartre. They haunt one another. Sartre was a Parisian through and through, always most at home in the city. He did not spend his entire life in Paris but he always gravitated back there. For his entire life, even when he was not in Paris, he was somehow in orbit around Paris. 'Every man has his natural place; it is not pride or worth that settles its height: childhood decides everything. Mine is a sixth floor in Paris with a view of the rooftops' (*Words*, p. 40).

He was the son of a diminutive, ailing, naval officer, Jean-Baptiste, and a tall, educated, bored, bourgeois girl, Anne-Marie Schweitzer. They married in Paris on 5 May 1904, and a little over a year later the baby boy they nicknamed Poulou sprang into the world, much adored by everyone, including his father who was bitterly disappointed to be absent from the birth. Stationed off Crete, tied to a career in the navy he no longer cared for or had the strength to fulfil, Jean-Baptiste was suffering from a combination of enterocolitis and tuberculosis.

Sent home to Paris to rest and recuperate, Jean-Baptiste finally made it back to his wife and son in November 1905. He delighted in the healthy, laughing baby but his ecstasy could not restore his health. Repeated extensions of sick leave on half pay carried him through to May 1906, when he decided to move his family and his furniture to his small home town of Thiviers in the Aquitaine region of southwest France.

Everyone said the country air would do him good. It did not. His family rallied round, helping to nurse him and to tend and entertain the infant. During the hot, difficult summer, Jean-Baptiste began to realize the stark truth. By the evening of 17 September 1906 he was dead.

Sartre junior was less than fifteen months old when Sartre senior died. Not surprisingly, Sartre had no direct recollection of his father. 'Jean-Baptiste had denied me the pleasure of meeting him. Even today, I am amazed how little I know about him' (*Words*, p. 15). As he had no acquaintance with his father, he held, quite sensibly, that his father played no positive role in shaping him, though he was certainly his father's double physically. If anything, Sartre considered his true father to be himself. Sartre was profoundly interested in what makes a person, and his autobiography, *Words*, is an exercise in *existential psycho-analysis* that shows how the child is the father of the man.

Sartre was not particularly interested in his father, his father's family or his father's town of Thiviers. He was once given a copy of his family tree, which he barely glanced at before binning, as if to say, 'It ain't where you're from, it's where you're at.' He had more interesting and important things to read and write.

He viewed his father from a Freudian perspective: considered the absence of a father's oppressive will upon the development of his character. Unlike most boys, unlike Flaubert for example, Sartre was spared having to carry the weight of his father's expectations on his back and was free to enter into a more intimate and equal relationship with his mother. He was glad he did not have a father and was deeply upset when his mother married again in 1917.

Mother and son were close, more like brother and sister. Sartre makes clear his deep and abiding affection for his mother, even if, like most boys with their mothers, he took her completely for granted. Something that he made up to her in later years.

The young widow found herself living among her in-laws in provincial France with no reason to stay. Thiviers only reminded her of Jean-Baptiste's suffering. Immediately after the funeral on 21 September 1906, Anne-Marie and her son took a carriage to Limoges and then a train to Paris. Their destination was the house of her parents at Meudon in the Paris suburbs.

The Schweitzers originated from the Alsace-Lorraine region of northeast France, adjacent to Germany. They had been a wealthy and respectable dynasty of teachers for many generations, except for Sartre's great-grandfather, Philippe-Chrétien. He became a grocer and then, after choosing to live in Germany, Mayor of Pfaffenhofen from 1875 to 1886. As well as Sartre's grandfather, Charles, Philippe-Chrétien's five children included the pious Louis. He became a church minister and fathered the theologian and missionary, Albert Schweitzer, winner of the 1952 Nobel Prize for Peace. Sartre called Albert, born in 1875, 'uncle' rather than 'cousin' because of their significant age difference.

Reviving the family tradition, Charles qualified as a teacher, choosing French Citizenship in 1872 after the Franco-Prussian War. Before moving to Paris, he married Louise Guillemin while teaching in Macon.

The room Sartre and his mother shared in her father's house was condescendingly known as 'the children's room'. Though her parents dutifully took her back when she lost her husband, they never quite forgave her for marrying a man who had the indecency to die young. 'Families naturally prefer widows to unmarried mothers, but only just' (*Words*, p. 14).

Treated like a child and a servant, a dual role she accepted without complaint, Anne-Marie was shown far less respect and consideration than her son, who was doted on, at least by his grandfather. Sartre's grandmother, Louise, was withdrawn and cynical and singularly unimpressed by the boy's pretensions.

Everyone, even Louise, was deeply concerned when, in 1909 at the age of four, the boy permanently lost 90 per cent of the vision in his right eye. A cold caught at the seaside led to an eye infection which in turn led to leucoma, an opacity of the cornea. Thus Sartre acquired his famous, much caricatured squint. Far from disturbing his childhood happiness his affliction merely increased the amount of pampering he enjoyed. He was not, however, without ill will towards at least one of the adults who mollycoddled him.

Sartre explores with great insight and humour the complex relationship he had with his grandfather. He clearly resented Charles' attitude towards his mother and there is no indication of any real affection for this stiff, respectable, conceited, overbearing member of the protestant bourgeoisie who was educated but narrow minded, who loved books but despised writers, who claimed to love the poor but could not tolerate them under his roof.

Cuttingly, Sartre tells how Charles, advancing in years, seized upon the child as a gift from heaven, an indicator of the sublime and a solace to his fear of death. As the wider family noted, young Poulou, with his abundant golden curls, had turned the old man's head.

As Sartre readily acknowledges, Charles was the biggest single influence on his early intellectual development. Charles took charge of his grandson's academic and moral education, allowing him almost unlimited access to his extensive if conservative library. This library became Sartre's childhood playground. 'I began my life as I shall no doubt end it: among books' (*Words*, p. 28).

Desperate to decipher the mysteries of his grandfather's dusty volumes, he soon taught himself to read and immediately began exploring words as other children explore woodlands, finding ideas more real than objects. With few real friends due to his insufferable precociousness and presumed fragile health, his playmates became great dead writers. He fused them with their works: Corneille was leather backed and smelt of glue while Flaubert was small and clothbound.

The two parts of *Words* are 'Reading' and 'Writing', and Sartre tells how his younger self soon made the leap from the former to the latter. More in keeping with the pursuits of an 'ordinary' child, he read comic book adventure stories alongside his reading of the classics. These influenced his earliest efforts with the pen. His early novels were trashy, globetrotting tales of heroes and villains with contrived plots that he poured out without re-reading them. His mother loved them and copied them out, although most are now lost. Charles disapproved and would not look at them except to correct the spelling.

Sartre says he was not fascinated by what he wrote once the ink had dried but by the act of writing itself that allowed him both to create heroes and to create himself, the writer, as a hero. He was struck by the respect writers received (from all but his grandfather), the gratitude they inspired and the immortality and omnipresence they achieved. 'At the age of eight ... I embarked on a simple but insane operation which altered the course of my life: I unloaded on to the writer the consecrated powers of the hero' (*Words*, p. 106).

He tells of being bowled over by the story of Charles Dickens' arrival in New York. A dense crowd brimming with expectation, mouths open, caps waving, massed on the quay as Dickens' ship approached. 'To be so wildly acclaimed, men of letters, I thought, must have to tackle the worst of dangers and render the most distinguished services to humanity' (*Words*, p. 106).

Sartre's doting family treated him as a necessity, as a being that was meant to be, but the precocious child was never quite convinced that he was a necessary being. Instead, he felt vague and insubstantial, pointless, even superfluous. Sartre later gave the same feelings to Lucien Fleurier, the central character of his short story, *The Childhood of a Leader*. '"What am I, *I* ...?" There was this fog rolling back on itself, indefinite. "I!"' (*The Childhood of a Leader*, p. 99).

Sartre saw himself as travelling on a train without a ticket: travelling through life without justification for his absurd existence, troubled by a ticket inspector that was also himself. 'Stowaway traveller, I had fallen asleep on the seat and the ticket-inspector was shaking me. "Your ticket!" I was forced to admit that I had not got one' (*Words*, p. 70). Realizing that he had no ticket, that nobody had or could have given him a ticket, he asked himself at an unusually early age how he was to justify his presence on life's train.

One of the abiding themes of Sartre's philosophy is that there is nothing that a person *is* in the mode of being it. Whatever a person is, he must *choose* to be it, he must constantly strive through his actions to *be* what he is without ever being able to fully and finally become it. A chair, for example, is what it is, a *being-in-itself*. But a person, a *being-for-itself*, can only ever aim at or play at being a banker, a waiter, a writer and so on. The ever-present possibility of an alternative choice of himself prevents him from simply *being* a banker, a waiter or a writer – a writer-*thing*.

From the age of just seven Sartre chose writing as his ticket to life and his reason to be. His choice to be a writer was his *fundamental choice* of himself, a choice that influenced all his subsequent choices and so shaped his entire life and personality.

I was born from writing: before that, there only a reflection in a mirror. From my first novel, I knew that a child had entered the palace of mirrors. By writing, I existed,

I escaped from the grown-ups; but I existed only to write and
if I said: me – that meant the me who wrote.

(*Words*, p. 97)

Sartre claims in *Words* that it was his desire for heroic immortality as a writer, set alongside his childhood dismissal of
Christian notions of salvation and the afterlife, that motivated
his actions above all else. Sartre deliberately set out from
childhood to create himself as a genius, as a great writer, through
sustained hard work and unflinching self-belief. Constantly
making himself a writer through the act of writing enabled
Sartre to maintain an illusion of substance and purpose that
effectively kept at bay those disturbing childhood feelings of
pointlessness and superfluity.

He maintained this grand illusion so well by his efforts,
believed so strongly in his vocation, in his capacity to achieve
his destiny, that as a young man he was, unlike his friends,
untroubled by fears of an untimely death. 'I had forearmed
myself against accidental death, that was all; the Holy Ghost had
commissioned a long-term work from me, so he had to give me
time to complete it' (*Words*, pp. 123–4).

In 1911, the family moved from Meudon to the Rue Le Goff in
central Paris, near the Luxembourg Gardens and the Sorbonne.
Charles had founded an institute of modern languages there in
order to fund his retirement.

Charles now dedicated much of his time to the education of his spoilt but extremely bright grandson. He found his protégé a joy to teach, foisting upon him so many nineteenth-century ideas that Sartre later joked, 'I started off with an eighty-year handicap' (*Words*, pp. 41–2).

3

Exile

Sartre received little public education until the age of ten, when, in 1915, he entered the Lycée Henri IV, close to his home. This step was not a rude awakening, but one was soon to come for the bookish, pampered, pompous child. In 1917, Anne-Marie married the hated Joseph Mancy, shattering forever her son's fairy-tale kingdom.

For Anne-Marie, it meant an end to being a disrespected, grown-up girl in the house of her parents, and liberation from certain legal rights that her in-laws had over her son. Mancy, a level-headed man of science, a shallow, narrow-minded bourgeois, brought her financial security and the status and relative independence of a married woman. For Sartre, it meant competition for his beloved mother's affections, subordination to a practical man with no patience for the lad's nonsense, a move to La Rochelle, a seaport on the Bay of Biscay, and worst of all, a new and daunting school.

He was twelve years old, on the verge of being a teenager. His idyllic childhood – the one he made the subject of *Words* – was well and truly over. It was time to enter the real world. Time to grow up fast.

Up to this point in his life, Sartre's *being-for-others* – a concept that later played such a central role in his philosophy – had been an almost exclusively positive affair. To exist for others had been to exist for adults who adored him. He later asserted that the essence of all human relationships is conflict and, most famously, that 'Hell is other people!' (*In Camera*, p. 223). His first real taste of conflict, his first real experience of the demon Other, as opposed to the comic book conflicts and comical villains he was familiar with, was at the public school in La Rochelle.

The boys at La Rochelle were particularly aggressive, full of hatred for the Germans, angry that the Great War had taken away their fathers. They were easily tempted to violence, and pompous Poulou with his smart-arsed ways and his minia-turized Parisian pretentions was an obvious target.

It is too easy for a biographer to say at this point that Sartre was bullied mercilessly, and to then make that one of the main forces that shaped his character. Let us say then that he received his fair share of the meanness and contempt that his angry, unsophisticated, provincial classmates dispensed so liberally in all directions. Let us say that he was no more bullied than many a child who survives the mass company of other children largely intact. And let us even pick on him a little ourselves and say that to some extent it did him good, providing a much-needed and long overdue antidote to his narcissism.

For a time, he bought the superficial goodwill of his classmates with expensive chocolates, the money stolen from Anne-Marie. He was soon found out and as a consequence had, for the first time in his life, to add the genuine contempt of his family to the thoughtless scorn of his peers.

He concocted tall stories about himself in an effort to impress, but these only earned him a reputation as a fibber. The only thing that won him some grudging respect from the other boys was his ability to correct his professors when they slipped up on some minor academic point, but a know-all child is never popular with other children.

As the months became years he began to keep himself to himself. He began to avoid wasting energy on fools and to keep his mouth shut when it was wise to do so. He joined all the libraries of the town and concentrated on his writing. In short, he began to mature.

He endured La Rochelle and Joseph Mancy, who had inflicted La Rochelle upon him, until he was fifteen, when, mercifully, he was finally released from exile. In the autumn of 1920, he was allowed to return to his spiritual home of Paris where he took up his rightful place among the young intellectual elite of France.

He never had much to say about the La Rochelle years afterwards. Understandably, he had no fondness for the place. Nonetheless, the town honours him to this day, having named a large avenue after him.

Apart from serving as a bitter antidote to his narcissism, La Rochelle, a seaport unnerved by the shadows of war, gave him an early insight into a troubled wider world. He returned to Paris less self-obsessed and more self-reliant. Though hardly an outsider, he had tasted a little of what it was to be an outsider, and he knew what it meant to suffer injustice at the hands of others. Injustice is always at the hands of others.

The seeds of rebellion had been planted. He had begun to hate the bourgeoisie, as typified, in his mind, by Mancy. He hated their smug narrow-mindedness and lack of imagination, their sense of entitlement and belief in their own necessity. This abiding hatred would influence him in his choice of lifestyle and come to characterize much of his philosophy. As Annie Cohen-Solal writes, 'The adolescent emerged out of the war years fatherless, classless, a bastard of sorts, and an avant-gardist – in short, well-prepared to face the coming era' (*Jean-Paul Sartre: A Life*, pp. 46–7).

4

Very Heaven

It was undoubtedly a good thing for Sartre's personal development that he did not return to Paris to live with grand-père and grand-mère. He was re-enrolled in the Lycée Henri IV as a boarder, visiting his grandparents only on Sunday mornings after singing in the choir. He renewed friendships interrupted when he was twelve, most notably with Paul Nizan.

Sartre and Nizan would become their school and college double act for the next several years, 'Nitre and Sarzan', playing pranks and dispensing their satirical wit in all directions. Nizan, who unlike Sartre was in a hurry to grow up, was soon to have several stories, poems and essays published in magazines, thus providing Sartre with a model for his own literary ambitions.

The emphasis at Henri IV was on academic excellence and competition, and Sartre took to it like a duck to water. His reading was a little behind the curve – not enough Proust in the mix – but he soon caught up and was soon able to discuss Swann at break times as though Proust's hero was one of his personal friends.

His intelligence and wit, no longer scorned but admired, flourished, and he soon constructed a formidable public image on the basis of it. He was his image, the roles he played. There was and never would be any such thing as a private Sartre, as opposed to a public Sartre. To throw oneself entirely into one's role, to realize to the full one's *being-in-situation*, that was now and would forever remain the Sartre way, the authentic way, the way that avoids bad faith.

Then as now, the area around the Boulevard Saint-Michel, close to the Luxembourg Gardens, is replete with schools, colleges and universities, most famously the mighty Sorbonne. This education agglomeration encourages competition, innovation, a meeting of minds, networking. Sartre and his classmates could literally see what challenged them, what they aspired to, etched around them in stone. The next step up, the Lycée Louis-le-Grand, was within spitting distance of Henri IV, and the ultimate destination of the meritocratic École Normale Supérieure (ENS), one of France's leading centres for the study of philosophy and related subjects, was just a few hundred yards away to the south.

Examinations were the keys that unlocked these august edifices and Sartre and his little gang of super-geek swats turned those keys with enthusiasm as they moved relentlessly up the

Parisian educational ladder to win their places at France's top school.

Sartre was reading widely, every avant-garde book he could lay his hands on. In his mind he was already Nietzsche's superman, only Nizan was allowed to be his equal. He was already a novelist, he had been a novelist for years, but what he wanted to be was a famous novelist, a giant figure like Dickens or Proust.

At Louis-le-Grand he studied philosophy under the tiny, crippled, influential figure of Professor Colonna d'Istria, who introduced him to the ideas of Henri Bergson. Sartre read Bergson's *Time and Free Will* for an essay on duration and became hooked. He discovered in Bergson an almost perfect description of his own consciousness and the way he experienced it. He became fascinated by Bergson's distinction between divisible, scientific time and the continuous temporal flow that is intuitively experienced by consciousness and is central to psychic life.

In studying Bergson, Sartre first discovered the key idea of *temporality*: the idea that time and consciousness are intimately related. He would later refine his understanding of this idea through his studies of Edmund Husserl and Martin Heidegger, themselves influenced by Bergson, eventually placing it at the core of his own philosophy of mind.

Sartre's eclecticism, his rather directionless dilettantism, ended with the advent of Bergson. Bergson inspired Sartre to consider himself a philosopher first and foremost. He knew straightaway he had an aptitude for the subject and that there was a great deal he could contribute to it. Like so many of the brightest minds down through the centuries, he felt that only the study of philosophy could truly absorb, occupy and challenge his restless intellect.

He did not, however, as a consequence of falling in love with philosophy, abandon his earlier aspirations to be a writer of fiction. Confronted by a choice between philosophy and fiction he could not bring himself to abandon either, so he chose to excel at both and to amalgamate them whenever possible. Each would be made to serve the purposes of the other. He would eventually write philosophical works rich in descriptions of real life that in places read like literary fiction. He would write short stories, novels and plays that are truly philosophical.

In the late summer of 1924, Colonna d'Istria wrote to Nizan congratulating his philosophy lads on gaining their places at the ENS. He was confident that they would become part of a group of 'new philosophers' destined to have dazzling careers shaping a new age with their intellects. He was not wrong.

In 1924, the ENS was a dingy, squalid place inside, and the students were slovenly, with little regard for personal hygiene. In contrast, their minds were bright and razor-sharp and they adhered to a strong work ethic. As is ever the student way, however, they always strove to appear as though they were achieving their goals effortlessly. 'Genius is as genius does not need to do.'

Having used the school gymnasium to develop thick muscles for boxing and wrestling, little Sartre became tough little Sartre, robust Sartre, if not quite ripped Sartre. He had boundless energy and personal strength, the capacity to push himself mercilessly, to work hard and play hard hour after busy hour, week in week out. He remained like this, at full throttle, for decades. He was proud and self-confident. He told his friend, Daniel Lagache, 'I want to be the man who knows most about everything,' and he meant it.

He devoured at least half a dozen books every week, always seeking his own angles, his own theories and philosophies. He did far more work than was required to gain certificates in History of Philosophy, General Philosophy, Psychology, Logic, Ethics and Sociology. It was all one to him. He began to surpass his teachers in knowledge, finding he could no longer test his ideas against theirs.

He had to put his questions directly to the great masters: Plato, Aristotle, Descartes and Kant. He trawled their works for a response. Only Paul Nizan and Raymond Aron could keep up with him. Aron in particular became Sartre's main intellectual sparring partner, remaining so until Simone de Beauvoir appeared on the scene. Aron was, arguably, second only to de

Beauvoir as the most significant *personal* philosophical influence of Sartre's life.

Sartre, Nizan and Aron became devotees of the powerful Cartesian method of systematic doubt, the approach of academic scepticism. If in doubt throw it out, in the hope of discovering or formulating something else that stands up to the most rigorous scrutiny. Though much of Sartre's philosophy of mind was constructed in opposition to Descartes, he would always honour Descartes by proudly describing himself for his entire career as a post-Cartesian.

Sartre became an almost legendary figure among his peers. A legend in his own lunchtime. He made a major contribution to the ENS satirical reviews, which became more biting and cruel under his influence. One review in which Sartre played a central role was even attended by the three times Prime Minister of the French Third Republic, Edouard Herriot, an old boy of the ENS.

Sartre wrote sketches and songs, performed, sang, played the piano, all for the purpose of mocking the establishment, especially the college principal, Gustave Lanson. A false beard and a fake Legion of Honour transformed Sartre into the spitting image of Lanson. Sartre despised Lanson as the self-appointed custodian of the French language, the author of an influential manual on how to teach French literature. Sartre's sustained ridicule of Lanson so tarnished the grandee's public image as presented in the popular press that by 1927 he was obliged to resign as principal.

Sartre loved to mock the establishment, to subvert and play pranks, and he had developed, like most students, broadly left-wing sympathies, but he was not, back then, a serious political animal. He loosely aligned himself with various political causes, but resisted being defined by any of them. He was and would always be too much of a freethinker to toe any party line for long. He was only ever really happy politically to be defined by what he was against. Hence his stormy relationship with the Parti communiste français (PCF) in later years. He was often a PCF 'fellow traveller' but never a fully paid-up, card-carrying member.

Nizan, for his part, became a fully paid-up, card-carrying member of the PCF at an early age. In 1926, he went travelling: to England, the Middle East, North Africa. Shocked by what he saw of European imperialism, he came back a changed man: more serious, more mature, a disciple of the Marxist faith. He was now inclined to see the proceedings of the ENS as the antics of privileged, bourgeois intellectuals killing time at the expense of poor, downtrodden workers.

Nizan married Henriette Alphen on Christmas Eve 1927 and was soon seen, horror of existential horrors, pushing a pram in the Luxembourg Gardens. Sartre and he remained friends but the Nitre-Sarzan double act was well and truly over. With Nizan all but gone, Sartre was ready for a new central relationship in his life.

5

Castor

By the late 1920s, Sartre had already had several affairs with women. The earliest was a childhood romance that continued into adolescence with his first cousin, Annie Lannes, the daughter of his father's sister. They spent their summer vacations together in Thiviers, and for the rest of the year exchanged letters and gifts. Sartre looked after Annie in Paris when she came to study there for a short while. According to one account she was Sartre's double, terrorizing her professors with her cleverness and confidence. She died of tuberculosis in 1925 at the age of nineteen. Sartre later named the heroine of his first novel *Nausea* after her.

Never one to miss an opportunity – life is for the living after all – Sartre began another affair at Annie's funeral, with Simone Jollivet, the daughter of a sister of Annie's father. Tall, elegant, blue eyed and blonde, her father a Toulouse pharmacist, she was the only person at the funeral who was not a provincial bore.

An immodest Toulouse socialite, she became an actress and playwright and the mistress of the actor, theatre manager and director, Charles Dullin.

With Sartre by far the keener of the two, their on-off relationship lasted for three years and generated an extensive correspondence – almost all of Sartre's personal relationships generated an extensive correspondence. Sartre was proud to have her on his arm at an ENS dance, where she wore a daring dress, but her willingness to flirt with him and little more seems to have given him more grief than joy. She is said to have once scandalized and excited the bookish Sartre and Nizan by offering them a lampshade made from a pair of her panties.

After Jollivet, perhaps on the rebound from Jollivet, Sartre even became engaged to the cousin of a fellow student. He saw little of her as she lived in Lyon and the relationship, such as it was, ended when her parents declined to give their daughter's hand in marriage. Sartre was briefly melancholic but relieved. Part of the reason for their refusal was that Sartre had failed his exams.

Many incredible things happened to Sartre in his life, yet this mere failure of exams in 1928 still stands out as one of the most remarkable. Surely, of all people, Sartre was the least capable of failing written examinations. The explanation was simple and familiar. His answers were so daring and original that he failed to fulfil the strict examination criteria. He drifted from answering the questions he was asked. Like many a brilliant student before and since he disappeared up his own personal gum tree.

His failure meant that he lost his ENS room on the Rue d'Ulm and had to decamp to a room at the Cité Universitaire. He does not appear to have been overly bothered by the setback, but importantly he decided to accept Aron's advice to set his great originality aside for a while: to play the game and give safe answers that fitted the strict examination criteria.

While attending courses at the Sorbonne, and swatting and cramming in the Bibliothèque Nationale for his next exams, scheduled for June 1929, Sartre noticed a serious young woman that he described to friends as charming and pretty but horribly dressed.

Simone de Beauvoir was born in Paris on 9 January 1908, making her two and a half years younger than Sartre. Her petit bourgeois family, having lost most of its wealth shortly after World War I, stretched its means to send her to a top convent school. A deeply religious child, who even contemplated becoming a nun, she experienced a crisis of faith in her early teens that transformed her into a lifelong atheist.

After studying mathematics at the Institut Catholique, Paris, and literature and languages at the Institut Saint-Marie, Paris, she studied philosophy at the Sorbonne. She also sat in on lectures at the ENS in preparation for the *agrégation* in philosophy that served to provide a national ranking of France's brightest students – a tough series of examinations that tripped even Sartre at the first hurdle. De Beauvoir undertook the *agrégation* a year earlier than required. The Sorbonne had only recently started admitting women and she was only the ninth woman to graduate from there. Times were changing and she would do more than almost any other woman of her century to compel them to change further.

She and Sartre moved in the same circles, were both intensely interested in philosophy and had both heard how brainy the other was, so it was inevitable they would eventually meet. Sartre's friend, René Maheu (aka André Herbaud), knew her first and nicknamed her Castor – 'castor' being French for 'beaver'. The nickname stuck and became Sartre's pet name for her for the rest of his life.

As de Beauvoir tells in *Memoirs of a Dutiful Daughter*, the first volume of her vast and brilliant autobiography, 'Sartre wanted to make my acquaintance; he had suggested meeting me one evening in the near future' (*Memoirs of a Dutiful Daughter*, p. 331). The suggestion, seconded by Nizan, was made to Maheu who duly invited de Beauvoir to join Sartre's little gang.

Maheu could not make the meeting, and not wanting Sartre to monopolize de Beauvoir in his absence, he persuaded her to send along her sister, Hélène (aka Poupette), instead. Poupette went along, making some excuse that her sister had been called away to the country. Poupette and Sartre spent a pleasant enough evening together but conversation dried up, just about the only time in Sartre's life this ever happened. Poupette reported back that Sartre was not as special as Maheu made him out to be.

According to de Beauvoir, her first proper meeting with Sartre occurred when Maheu invited her to revise philosophy in Sartre's filthy, book- and cigarette-encrusted room at the Cité Universitaire. The comrades were counting on her to help them with Leibniz. 'I was feeling a bit scared when I entered Sartre's room; there were books all over the place, cigarette ends in all the corners and the air was thick with tobacco smoke. Sartre greeted me in a worldly manner; he was smoking a pipe' (*Memoirs of a Dutiful Daughter*, p. 334).

During this first meeting they discussed metaphysics: she nervously, he enthusiastically. Her confidence quickly grew as they began to see more and more of each other. Sartre's little gang agreed that she may have dressed horribly but she was certainly one of them when it came to brains.

According to some in their circle at that time, de Beauvoir somewhat over-romanticizes the first few meetings between herself and Sartre, giving the impression that it was all love at first sight. 'Sartre corresponded exactly to the dream-companion I had longed for since I was fifteen: he was the double in whom I found all my burning aspirations raised to the pitch of incandescence' (*Memoirs of a Dutiful Daughter*, p. 345). The young de Beauvoir was fond of seeing herself as Maggie Tulliver in George Eliot's novel, *The Mill on the Floss*: a deprived heroine desperate for life to become more intellectually and emotionally stimulating.

Is that how de Beauvoir really remembered it, or does she allow herself a little too much dramatic licence? Certainly, with Sartre and de Beauvoir, life and literature often merged, not least because they often deliberately contrived to transform their lives into literature. In writing about them their biographers are often tempted to follow their example and do the same. It is unavoidable. In Sartre's words, or those of his alter ego, Antoine Roquentin, 'This is what I have been thinking: for the most commonplace event to become an adventure, you must – and this is all that is necessary – start *recounting* it' (*Nausea*, p. 61).

What is not in doubt is that 1929 saw the start of one of the most famous, enduring and intellectually fruitful relationships in history. Socrates and Plato, Boswell and Johnson, Simon and Garfunkel, Bill and Hillary, Sartre and de Beauvoir. A legendary meeting of minds.

Sartre having decided to play the game, the results of the June exams were perhaps never in doubt: Sartre first of seventy-six candidates, with de Beauvoir second. It was a very close run thing, the jury debating who should get first place. De Beauvoir was the youngest student to take the exams and Sartre's standing was significantly boosted by his dazzling oral lesson, 'Psychology and Logic'. Maybe the jury felt they owed him one, having failed him the first time, and de Beauvoir should really have come first. We will probably never know.

At this point, some commentators, particularly those whose knowledge of philosophy is far surpassed by their desire to discover scandals where none exist, enter an uninformed debate as to which of the two was really the greatest thinker. Claims based largely on bizarre, highly selective readings of certain texts are made along the lines that Sartre took all his ideas from de Beauvoir and put them forward as his own, or de Beauvoir took all her ideas from Sartre and put them forward as her own. Such claims are inspired by various prejudices about what the relationship between a male and female philosopher must inevitably be like, or they are simply a product of indolence in face of the effort required to understand the subtleties of a very special intellectual association and working relationship.

The best way to dismiss the nonsense and gain a proper understanding of the intellectual relationship between de Beauvoir and Sartre is to view it in its historical context. De Beauvoir and Sartre inherited the same philosophical tradition in the same place at the same time, a time of great social and political change between two world wars. From the moment they met they shared and developed the ideas of Descartes, Kant, Hegel, Marx, Freud and others that they were learning as students, testing these ideas against their shared reality and using them to explain it.

Who first thought what is a silly game to play when considering de Beauvoir and Sartre, although it is a game that some commentators are all too fond of playing. Precisely because they were such fiercely independent thinkers, they were never reluctant to exchange thoughts and opinions with each other. There was a constant interplay and refinement of ideas between them. Each philosopher was constantly the midwife of the other's thoughts and as a result each greatly influenced the philosophical ideas and personal and political values of the other.

They did not, of course, always agree. They disagreed with each other frequently and with a passion, but this disagreement was always a respectful, ultimately constructive debate that sought to thrash out thesis and antithesis so as to produce a synthesis of ideas that could be accommodated within the body of existentialist and later on Marxist and feminist thought.

Sartre and de Beauvoir would be the first to agree that they were absolute equals. Or if they were not to begin with, Sartre being a little older, they soon became equals. De Beauvoir tells in *Memoirs of a Dutiful Daughter* that when she first met Sartre he knew more philosophy than she did and could wipe the floor with her in an argument. He was by far the most intelligent person she had ever met: the only person she ever knew that she did not find less intelligent than herself. The absolute equality of their great intellects was the main basis of their great and enduring love for one another.

What is undoubtedly true is that without her influence, Sartre's philosophical contribution would have been different and less impressive. But this is also undoubtedly true the other way around.

The exams finally over, they took it easy for a while, at least by their standards. Delighting in each other's company, they drifted around Paris, endlessly discussing philosophy, psychology and literature. De Beauvoir became so laid back, at least by her standards, that Sartre joked she now only wanted to be a housewife.

They knew that their tranquillity could not last, that the freedom of their student days was over and adult responsibilities loomed. Sartre faced a period of compulsory military service and had already applied for a lecturing post in Japan to follow it. He was looking to avoid having to take up some miserable school teaching post in the French provinces. De Beauvoir was also on course to take up a provincial teaching post, but she decided to postpone the move and remain in Paris while Sartre did his military service.

Knowing they would soon be apart for considerable periods of time, they came to a very modern arrangement regarding their relationship. They would try to see each other as frequently as possible and their relationship would constitute 'necessary love'. But they would both also enjoy 'contingent love': relationships with other people. Anything other than a commitment to polygamy would be an affront to the freedom they valued so highly. Looking back, Sartre confessed that this assertion of his right to enjoy a variety of women was slightly ridiculous as women were not exactly chasing him at the time.

Though subject to various stresses and strains, this arrangement served them reasonably well for decades until Sartre's death in 1980 finally ended their 'marriage of true minds' (Shakespeare, *Sonnet 116*). They considered actual marriage only once, early in their relationship, as an act of expediency: married couples were entitled to teaching posts at the same school. Rejecting marriage even as a solution to practical problems however, they formulated the truly existentialist view that wedlock is basically a bourgeois institution that seeks to bind people into an intimate association that ought, instead, to be freely chosen day by day.

Lovers, they thought, should resist the false security offered by marriage vows and material entanglements and accept that the love they currently enjoy is based, and can only be based, on nothing more than the freedom of the Other. To live like this may well be a source of great anxiety, but anxiety is the price of freedom. The true existentialist would rather endure anxiety than seek in bad faith to impose artificial and stifling limits on his own freedom and his lover's freedom simply for the sake of his peace of mind.

Sartre began his military service at the fort of Saint-Cyr near Versailles before being transferred to a barracks near Tours, a one- to two-hour train journey from Paris and his beloved Castor, who had started writing a novel to occupy herself in his absence. He was trained to use meteorological equipment. De Beauvoir tells us in *The Prime of Life*, the second volume of her autobiography, that when she first visited him, 'He had not resigned himself to the stupidity of military life, nor to wasting eighteen months: he was still furious' (*The Prime of Life*, p. 28). They were both anti-militarists.

He appears, however, to have had no real problem coping with army discipline and soon settled into a routine. His enduring complaint was of boredom which he sought to stave off by writing. He would find himself back in military uniform just nine years later, deploying meteorological equipment, and it would no longer be a training exercise.

During his military service he learned that his next planned move, a lecturing job in Tokyo, had fallen through. A school teaching job in the provinces now beckoned, and on 1 March 1931, he was duly assigned to the Lycée François Ier in Le Havre, northwest France, to cover for a teacher who had suffered a nervous breakdown. The star of the ENS, who had shown so much promise, found himself in provincial exile once more. He was twenty-five years old.

Fortunately, it was only a few months to the long summer holiday, much of which he and de Beauvoir spent on a low-budget tour of Spain. By October of that year, she, now twenty-three years old, was assigned to a teaching post in Marseilles, southeast France. The authorities had placed them in opposite corners of a massive country. They would rendezvous in Paris whenever they could and sustain their 'necessary love' in between with an endless exchange of letters.

De Beauvoir loved Marseilles and certainly, in true existentialist style, she made the most of her time there. She tells in *The Prime of Life* how she was struck by the light, heat and energy of the place even before she left the train station. Moreover, she was struck by a delicious sense of her own freedom. Never in her life had she been so free. 'Hitherto I had been closely dependent upon other people, who had laid down rules and objectives for me; and now this wonderful piece of luck had come my way. Here no one was aware of my existence' (*The Prime of Life*, p. 88).

We leave her there, making her way in the bright Mediterranean sunshine, as we head north to colder, duller climes, to a far drearier-looking port on the often grim northwest coast of France.

6

Le Havre

The Le Havre years were an important period of personal and philosophical development for Sartre. Though publishers rejected his early manuscripts and the easy fame he had naively expected as an undergraduate eluded him, he continued to refine and develop his ideas. No longer the student show-off and prankster surrounded by bright young things he became more serious and more genuinely introspective.

The atmosphere of Le Havre pervaded his moods. The coastal light and the sea breeze made the filthy slums, the seedy red light district, the huge, stark windswept docks and the smart bourgeois district above the cliffs with its villas, gardens and churches, emerge with excruciating sharpness. Le Havre became Bouville, the town in which Sartre's astonishing first novel, *Nausea*, is set.

The insight Sartre indulged and pondered during his solitary walks, the anxious realization that reality is inexorable and overwhelming, yet elusive, unnecessary, contingent and superfluous, became *the nausea*, the terrifying and loathsome ontological revelation that lies at the heart of the novel.

Sartre first outlined his ideas on contingency as early as 1926 while studying Nietzsche. He continued incubating these ideas during his military service and they went with him to Le Havre in the form of an ever-increasing collection of notes and passages he nicknamed his 'factum on contingency', 'factum' being a term he and Nizan had adopted to describe any form of ruthless analysis.

Nausea is set in 1932, and it was from late 1931 onwards that the factum, by absorbing the character and detail of Sartre's new situation, began to grow into something resembling the novel we know today. The work became Sartre's constant companion for six years as no fewer than three successive complete versions underwent continuous revision and refinement, always under the scrupulous eye of de Beauvoir.

He poured his thoughts and experiences into the work while at the same time ruthlessly cutting anything that struck him or de Beauvoir as unnecessary. The result is a highly polished and refined text, Sartre's most accomplished work of fiction, possibly his greatest work of all. *Nausea* is a stylistic masterpiece that achieves a seamless marriage of fiction and philosophy: a *tour de force* that advances a distinctive and profound philosophical vision without ever falling short of being a pure and genuine novel. It is, as many commentators including Iris Murdoch have noted, a rare example of a truly *philosophical novel*.

There are no wasted words in *Nausea*. As a result, even its English translation has a sublime, poetic quality reminiscent of T. S. Eliot at his best. 'What kind of book is *La Nausée*?' asks Iris Murdoch in *Sartre: Romantic Rationalist*, concluding that 'It seems more like a poem or an incantation than a novel' (p. 19).

> I liked yesterday's sky so much, a narrow sky, dark with rain, pressing against the window-panes like a ridiculous, touching face. This sun isn't ridiculous, quite the contrary. On everything I love, on the rust in the yards, on the rotten planks of the fence, a miserly, sensible light is falling, like the look you give, after a sleepless night, at the decisions you made enthusiastically the day before, at the pages you wrote straight off without a single correction.
>
> (*Nausea*, p. 27)

Le Havre, of course, was not all or even largely the tragic, romantic life of the poet-philosopher, the man alone, seeking to speak to the world from the depths of his isolation. Sartre was there to school teach, to be forced into the company of others week after week, subjected to their myriad expectations, obliged to carry out a regular and demanding day job that he could not afford to give up. He threw himself into it, as he threw himself into almost everything, with great enthusiasm.

He was friendly and informal with his students, encouraging them to be independent thinkers and to take responsibility for their actions. He inspired them with his own love of ideas and, with the addition of personal stories and anecdotes, made his teaching of logic, psychology, ethics and metaphysics thoroughly entertaining and accessible.

Only a few years older than the oldest of them, certainly for the first couple of years, he socialized with them, singing bawdy songs at their beach picnics. Most remarkable, by today's standards, he allowed them to smoke in class. He was a cool teacher, down with the kids, which made him an object of suspicion to the school authorities, though they had to admit that his subject knowledge was vast and that his students' grades were excellent.

He put two fingers up to the Le Havre bourgeoisie early on. At the annual prize-giving ceremony where he, as the youngest teacher, was obliged to give the opening speech, he dispensed with polite formalities as he spoke directly to his students over the heads of their stuffy parents. His topic was the wonders of the new, widely disapproved of, art form of cinema.

Even more scandalous, 'the anarchist' – as he was called by supporters and detractors alike – deliberately took a room at the sleazy Hotel Printania in the lower, slum part of town, overlooking the power station and the rail yard. This in preference to the higher, respectable, bourgeois district, where a teacher and a graduate of the ENS was expected to live.

He fed off the vibrancy of the lower town, with its docks, brothels, bars and cafés, as though he himself was plugged directly into the unceasing buzz of the power station. Cafés became his office and would always be his favourite workplace from then on. The life of cafés, their ceaseless comings and goings, their clatter and chatter, did not distract him. Rather, along with the constant stimulation of coffee, beer, cigarettes and pipe tobacco, café life always served to drive his restless, unceasing pen.

Apart from teaching youngsters and writing his own material, the ever-busy Sartre undertook a detailed study of literature, the fruits of which he delivered in the form of monthly lectures at the Lyre Havraise hall. Serious but relaxed, constantly inter-acting with his literature-loving audience, he explored the work of writers largely unknown in France at that time: Virginia Woolf, James Joyce, Aldous Huxley, John Dos Passos and William Faulkner.

His choice of writers reflected the profound interest he and de Beauvoir had developed in contemporary English, Irish and American literature – somewhat in preference to most contem-porary French literature. His own fictional writing was to be heavily influenced by the non-linear storytelling and stream of consciousness methods that these writers employed. Many of their techniques were new and cutting edge, as was Sartre's analysis of them, analysis that formed the basis of critically acclaimed articles of literary criticism that he published in *La Nouvelle Revue Française* towards the end of the 1930s.

To keep himself fit, Sartre even ran his own fight club at the Charles Porta gymnasium. Its members included students and several of the cooler teachers – the English teacher, the PE teacher: the usual suspects. Using punch bags and skipping ropes, the muscular little philosopher trained them all to box. That was Sartre, always up for a fight, always primed and ready.

Sartre always taught in the same classroom at the Lycée François Ier, the philosophy room, a little removed from the other classrooms, as philosophy rooms often are, to avoid the contamination of free thought spreading to the more conventional students. After he died, Le Havre honoured him by naming the road outside his philosophy room, Rue Jean-Paul Sartre. And so another provincial town that hosted him for a while further immortalized his name by marrying it with its infrastructure. Unlike La Rochelle, however, Sartre was, in the words of de Beauvoir, 'quite fond of Le Havre' (*The Prime of Life*, p. 119). But then, the times he spent in those two not dissimilar places were very different.

7

Apricot Cocktails

The main perk of being a teacher is undoubtedly the holidays. In June 1932, while his students sat their exams, Sartre spent ten wonderful days in Marseilles soaking up the sun as de Beauvoir showed him all the sites she had come to love, so that he would come to love them too.

Soon after, they made a second excursion to Spain to visit the places they had not managed to visit the previous year. They were keen to travel and had a vague notion that in time they would visit every corner of the world. Travel certainly became a key feature of their relationship from then on.

De Beauvoir did not return to Marseilles at the end of the summer. As much as she loved Marseilles, she belonged to the north, and was pleased to have been assigned a teaching post in Rouen, roughly half way between her twin poles of Sartre and Paris.

When interviewed by leading Sartre biographer, Annie Cohen-Solal, Sartre's former students at Le Havre vividly recalled how he would often rush away at the end of the last lesson of the day to catch the train to Rouen to visit his mysterious woman. The Le Havre to Rouen train ran on to Paris so it was easy for them to travel into their beloved city together, which they often did.

Picture their simple delight as Sartre pulls into Rouen, book in hand, pipe in mouth, grinning, and de Beauvoir jumps aboard and kisses him, the rendezvous having been meticulously arranged at their previous meeting, or by letter, or on one of those cranky but perfectly serviceable 1930s telephones.

In the spring of 1933, one such excursion was arranged for the purpose of meeting up with Aron, who was visiting Paris from Berlin. Aron was on a year's sabbatical in Berlin studying the philosophy of Husserl at the French Institute. At this legendary meeting, now a cornerstone of Sartre folklore, at the Bec de Gaz on the Rue Montparnasse, where de Beauvoir recalls that they drank apricot cocktails and Aron that they drank only beer, the three began discussing Husserl's phenomenology: the philosophical examination and description of phenomena as they appear to consciousness.

Sartre's philosophical thinking had reached something of an impasse. He was still working away at his factum on contingency at every opportunity, but to really move forward with it, to really begin to formulate his own particularly Sartrean philosophy, he needed an approach that by-passed old-fashioned idealist and realist claims and allowed him to affirm 'both the supremacy of reason and the reality of the visible world as it appears to our senses' (*The Prime of Life*, p. 135). In a famous passage about the legendary meeting, de Beauvoir writes:

> Aron said, pointing to his glass: 'You see, my dear fellow, if you are a phenomenologist, you can talk about this cocktail and make philosophy out of it!' Sartre turned pale with emotion at this. Here was just the thing he had been longing to achieve for years – to describe objects just as he saw and touched them, and extract philosophy from the process.
>
> (*The Prime of Life*, p. 135)

Sartre wasted no time. He purchased Emmanuel Lévinas' *The Theory of Intuition in Husserl's Phenomenology* on the Boulevard Saint-Michel and started reading the uncut pages as he walked along. There was some material in the book about contingency but to Sartre's relief, Husserl, born in 1859, had not already had the same thoughts as Sartre on the subject.

Sartre began to make an in-depth study of Husserl. He read everything Husserl had written and hardly studied another philosopher for the next six years. Husserl became Sartre's biggest single philosophical influence, both directly and through his influence on his student, Heidegger, whom Sartre also studied closely later on.

One of Sartre's first major publications, *The Transcendence of the Ego: A Sketch for a Phenomenological Description*, is effectively his thesis on Husserl, in which he endorses certain aspects of Husserl's theory of the relationship between consciousness and the world while criticizing others. It is an ambitious book in which he first formulates the theory of consciousness that lies at the heart of his later works.

Following that momentous meeting at the Bec de Gaz, Sartre became hooked on phenomenology. It was as though he had found a drug, an enduring stimulant, the catalyst that truly launched him as a philosopher in a clear and single-minded direction. Phenomenology would form the backbone of his own philosophy. He would remain true to it for the rest of his career, endlessly refining and developing it through the medium of essays, vast philosophical treatises, short stories, novels, plays, biographies and even film scripts, into a stunningly comprehensive and penetrating theory of the human condition.

Sartre and Aron hatched an excellent plan. Sartre would apply to replace Aron at the French Institute in Berlin in the autumn of 1933, and Aron would cover Sartre's teaching job in Le Havre. This arrangement suited both of them perfectly. Aron needed a job when his time in Berlin ended and Sartre was keen to take a break from the heavily timetabled routine of school teaching. He was impatient to throw himself into an exhaustive, full-time study of Husserl in that distinguished philosopher's own country.

The top 1929 graduate of France's best school submitted his proposal. It was duly accepted. Sartre was heading to Germany to study the best of its philosophy – there are so many great German philosophers – while the worst of its politics was coming to the boil.

There were still a few months of school to get through and the long summer holiday to enjoy before Sartre resumed the student life he loved so much. At the end of the Le Havre academic year his students got him extremely drunk and took him to a local brothel. It was Sartre's first experience of brothels and he was too drunk to remember much about it, although, according to his close friend Jacques-Laurent Bost, he claimed afterwards to have been carried upstairs on the back of a sturdy whore.

Having visited Spain the previous two summers, he and de Beauvoir decided to explore Italy instead, partly attracted by the cheap, countrywide train travel that Mussolini was offering to draw visitors to the Exhibition of the Fascist Revolution in Rome. They spent most of their time in Florence and only a few days in Rome.

The capital was in the grip of fascist fever. Fascist posters and slogans were everywhere and cocky, thuggish blackshirts claimed right of way on the pavements. The two lovers attempted to wander the streets of the Eternal City until dawn but they were hassled by blackshirt patrols and ordered back to their hotel.

As a youngster, Sartre had assumed he would be a famous writer by the age of twenty-eight. By the age of twenty-eight he was still, basically, a provincial schoolteacher, and even if there was a lot more to him than that, he was certainly not famous. Like every sad, persistent academic pen-pusher he had had a few papers published, but nothing that was recognized as particularly significant at the time.

To make matters worse, a further dent to his ego, his contemporaries were stealing a march on him. Nizan was about to have his first novel published, *Antoine Bloyé*, and was running for political office as a communist. Meanwhile, Aron, a fluent German speaker, had already taught at the University of Cologne. Shortly after exchanging places with Sartre, Aron would publish his first two books.

Sartre recognized, then, that his sabbatical in Berlin offered a golden opportunity to catch up. It was time to break the back of various current projects and begin others. He dedicated himself to weaving together the various philosophical and literary threads that he had been spinning for years into a substantial and coherent theory with the legs to run on to fame and glory. Always a tireless worker, he imposed a schedule upon himself that was gruelling even by his extreme standards.

In the morning he would read and critique Husserl, with

the modest aim of permanently redefining the parameters of phenomenology. In the afternoon he would wrestle with his ever-present, ever-changing, factum on contingency. If there was any time left in the day, he would attempt to read Heidegger in the original German. Unfortunately, he struggled with Heidegger's tortuous vocabulary, a familiar enough problem even to those attempting to read Heidegger in translation.

In the evening he would relax by intensely discussing his ideas with fellow postgraduates over a pipe or three, a stein of German beer and a large bratwurst. His knowledge and under-standing was not the only thing he fattened while in Germany.

Sartre has been widely criticized for not taking up his pen against the Nazis at that time. He had the contacts and could, for example, have submitted powerful articles to French newspapers describing the scenes he undoubtedly witnessed or heard about. In addition to the same far-right swagger he and de Beauvoir had encountered in Italy, there were mass demonstrations by swastika-waving fanatics, disturbingly nationalistic speeches and book burnings. Jews were being threatened and insulted and their property expropriated. An older Sartre would have spoken out, blazing with clear, forceful, persuasive indignation, but this relatively young Sartre was not yet a political animal.

As an unapologetically self-centred individualist preoc-cupied by the idea of the man alone, Sartre was romantically opposed to politics as a feature of group behaviour. He had chosen not to follow Nizan to the far left. Far left, far right, it was all collective fanaticism, undignified herd mentality. He had not yet accepted the truth of the claim that if one is not actively against something then one is effectively for it. Arguably, he had a moral obligation to actively take sides which, in 1933–34, he ignored.

Then again, his critics have the benefit of hindsight. He did not know what the Nazis were about to become, the greater atrocities they would soon commit. There was a widespread complacency among intellectuals about Adolf Hitler. They fooled themselves that his influence was declining. Surely, such an absurd little man – his 'infantile face, the face of a human fly' (*The Reprieve*, p. 61) – could not last. Such an essentially absurd regime could not last. The German people would wake up.

On a more mundane level, Sartre was in Germany for the specific purpose of occupying an intellectual ivory tower. He spent long hours studying and most of his leisure time socializing with a small group of French postgraduates. With accommodation and regular meals provided, he and his associates were institutionalized guests of the French Institute. What student, single-mindedly absorbed by student life, really knows or cares what is happening in the news? Contemporary Germany was a mere backdrop easily ignored. Cohen-Solal summarizes matters well when she says, 'It was not contemporary Germany that drew them there, but some writer of the *Sturm und Drang*, or some nineteenth-century philosopher' (*Jean-Paul Sartre: A Life*, p. 99).

Sartre's focus was the best of German philosophy, not the worst of German politics. Had he spent his time criticizing Hitler rather than analysing Husserl, he may not have become a great philosopher, the great Sartre, the great champion of individual freedom and responsibility, and so Hitler would have done yet more damage to humankind. Maybe this is not such a strong argument, as even with his busy schedule, Sartre could have found time to say something.

He spent Christmas and New Year 1933–34 in France, but at Easter de Beauvoir visited him in Berlin. As theirs was an open relationship he told her of his liking for German women. He had not actually managed to seduce any as the language barrier robbed him of his main weapon, leaving him with nothing but his intriguing ugliness. De Beauvoir lingered beyond the end of the school holiday, perhaps to keep an eye on him, and he abandoned plans to stay another year.

Sartre left Berlin in June 1934, the month of his twenty-ninth birthday, just weeks before Hitler became absolute dictator of Germany following the death of President Hindenburg. Sartre was still not launched as an important writer and philosopher, and it would be some time yet before his career took off, but the launch pad was constructed and he had plotted a direction of travel.

8

Ostraconophobia

Back to Le Havre. Back to the tedium of the chalkface. He would be thirty next birthday. The start of another school year after the freedoms of Berlin and the long summer break soon instilled in him an uncharacteristic pessimism. In their darkest moments, he and de Beauvoir would sit in cafés in Le Havre and Rouen pondering their life and worrying that nothing new would ever happen to them. Were they now sticks-in-the-mud, serving life sentences as provincial schoolteachers with only the holidays to look forward to? They would get drunk and argue until they reached the conclusion that if they were stuck, it was their own fault. Their destiny was nowhere else but in their own hands.

Sartre had a particularly good bunch of philosophy students that academic year, including Jacques-Laurent Bost, the youngest brother of the novelist, Pierre Bost. 'Little' Bost became Sartre's lifelong friend, and de Beauvoir, who saw him as a graceful incarnation of youth, became his occasional lover.

In order to meet the various demands of his students, his writing, his frequent trips to Rouen and Paris, Sartre started taking pep pills and would carry on doing so, on and off, for years to come. Stimulants certainly fuelled his pen but they prevented him from sleeping. The antidote was sleeping pills which he took for the rest of his life. He slept like a log, lulled by a chemical cosh, seldom dreaming.

The uppers and downers, the workload, the status anxiety, the sense that his youth was far behind him and that he was growing old and fat, all pushed him to the brink of depression. At times he was irritable with his students, though none claimed he was ever bored teaching them.

He put his feelings of depression into his factum on contingency, into his alter ego, Antoine Roquentin, the central character of *Nausea*. Always the factum, adding, cutting, polishing, refining. De Beauvoir felt it was coming on, but she was merciless in her constructive criticism and relentless in her demand for revisions.

Excellent opportunity and further burden, he was given his first commission: to write a philosophy book for a new series to be published by Alcan. He immediately started work on an ambitious book about the psychology of imagination called *L'Image*. His long-standing interest in psychology had been further stimulated by his exhaustive Berlin investigation of Husserl, research he was continuing back in Le Havre alongside all his other commitments.

Not content simply to write a book outlining various theories of the imagination from Descartes onwards – which would have been enough to satisfy the particular requirements of the proposed series – he outlined various theories for the purpose of demolishing each in turn from a Husserlian phenomenological perspective. He then put forward his own phenomenological theory of the imagination based on the notion that mental images are not pictures *in* consciousness but intentional objects *for* consciousness.

Never one to do things by halves, Sartre decided that if he was going to write convincingly about that most elusive of all imaginary phenomena, hallucinations, then he needed to hallucinate, to 'see' something that was absolutely not there. It was a classic case of 'be careful what you wish for' because the opportunity to hallucinate soon arose in early 1935.

Shortly after a Christmas skiing trip with de Beauvoir, an old friend from his ENS days, the psychiatrist, Dr Daniel Lagache, author of the recently published *Verbal Hallucinations and Speech*, invited him to take part in a psychology experiment at Sainte-Anne's hospital, Paris. In a dimly lit room, under controlled conditions, the man who no longer had dreams because of his dependence on sleeping tablets, was injected with the powerful psychoactive drug mescaline.

Sartre does not appear to have had a bad trip in the classic sense of suffering a major and prolonged panic attack, but it was not a good trip and he did not enjoy it. There was the usual stuff: time and space distortion, an umbrella that looked like a vulture, an attack of devil fish. The devil fish were interrupted by a phone call from de Beauvoir enquiring how he was getting on. A call he took! Who but Sartre would take a phone call while tripping?

His visual faculties remained distorted for weeks. 'Houses had leering faces, all eyes and jaws, and he couldn't help looking at every clockface he passed, expecting it to display the features of an owl' (*The Prime of Life*, p. 210). De Beauvoir goes on to say that he knew the objects were in fact just houses and clocks, but he feared that one day he would no longer know. He even told her while they were out walking in some miserable spot by the Seine in Rouen that he was 'on the edge of a chronic hallucinatory psychosis' (*The Prime of Life*, p. 210) and would eventually become insane. He never took an hallucinogenic again. Once was enough.

Never a fan of crustaceans, the sight of them in particular caused him nauseating visual flashbacks for years after his mescaline trip. He never saw ordinary objects in quite the same way again. Although objects eventually ceased to threaten to morph into something less familiar, predictable, functional and mundane, into something crawling, crustaceous and alien, he always felt that they could, that it was within the bounds of logical possibility.

The long-term effects of the mescaline intensified when he was feeling down. Most sinister, because most suggestive of genuine mental illness, was the recurrent feeling, the delusion, that he was being pursued by a giant lobster, always just out of sight. Sartre's infamous, unseen, lurking lobster has become one of the great, darkly comical features of Sartre folklore, of existentialist folklore generally: but what was it exactly?

Anxiety, angst, anguish, dread, apprehension, fear of pain, fear of death, fear of growing old, fear of growing up, a lurking sense of the fundamental absurdity of existence, depression, fear of depression, fear of insanity, a symptom of the uppers and downers as much as the mescaline, the three working together, a symptom of mental and physical over-tiredness and nervous exhaustion, a symptom of too much philosophical reflection or merely a psycho-gastronomic side effect of too much French cheese?

Probably, it was a combination of all these things. Nobody really knows. Sartre did not know. The damned thing was perpetually about to arrive, its antennae and giant claws perpetually about to round the corner or appear over the hill. If he ever tried to look for it, it would hide itself or immediately get around behind him, so its existence was impossible to prove or disprove. Arguably, he just *said* he felt a giant lobster was following him. He did not believe it. It was just his way of expressing how unaccountably and uncomfortably weird he felt in those strange days.

De Beauvoir insisted that his only madness was believing that he was mad. She urged him to get a grip and pull himself together. Looking back, twenty-five years later, she offered this diagnosis:

All that his session at Sainte-Anne's did for Sartre was to furnish him with certain hallucinatory patterns. It was, beyond any doubt, the fatigue and tension engendered by his philosophical research work that brought his fears to the surface again. We afterwards concluded that they were the physical expression of a deep emotional malaise: Sartre could not resign himself to going on to 'the age of reason', to full manhood.

(*The Prime of Life*, p. 211)

What is certain is that crustaceans became a recurrent theme in his writing from 1935 onwards, representing malice, blind will, base nature and naked, absurd, unjustifiable existence. They repeatedly scuttle their way into *Nausea*, one of his earliest publications, but they are still creeping about as late as 1959 in his play *Altona*, in which the paranoid and delusional central character, Franz, believes he is being watched and judged from the future by malignant crab-like creatures.

Ostraconophobia was Sartre's main hang-up, but it was only a part of a broader dislike of flora and fauna generally. He found babies and small children slightly repulsive, was afraid of dogs, preferred exploring buildings to woods, saw trees – when you look at them too closely as Roquentin does in *Nausea* – as the very embodiment of brute, superfluous existence and even once told de Beauvoir that he was allergic to chlorophyll.

> I am afraid of towns. But you mustn't leave them. If you venture too far, you come to the Vegetation Belt. The Vegetation has crawled for mile after mile towards the towns. It is waiting …
> In a town … you rarely come across anything but minerals, the least frightening of all existents.
>
> (*Nausea*, pp. 221–2)

For all the psychological damage it caused, though it certainly fed his writer's imagination, the experiment with the mescaline achieved the purpose Sartre intended. As he tells in *The Imaginary: A Phenomenological Psychology of the Imagination*, he managed to hallucinate three small parallel clouds that appeared to float before him in the hospital room where he was sitting. Sufficient material, or rather non-material, for him to analyse in an extremely clear-headed way that has influenced philosophers and psychologists ever since.

He argues that his hallucinations existed by stealth on the margins of his consciousness: that they disappeared when he turned his full attention on them. That they disappeared when he focused suggested to him that he was in some sense dreaming them. He concludes that hallucinations occur when perception crumbles and a person, having become unreal to himself, begins to dream the world of perception.

In other words, hallucinations occur when the distinction between perceiving and dreaming becomes blurred for a person experiencing a loss of self. The person's loss of self will be due in large part to the most consistently reported feature of hallucinogenic drug experiences, a dislocation of time and space.

The mescaline had seriously shaken Sartre up, opened a door in his mind, in his perceptions, that he could not quite close again. A chill draught cut through his sense of himself. He eventually shut the door by simply pronouncing himself cured and choosing to believe it, by recommitting himself to a faith in reality.

In the meantime, he was prescribed work as a distraction by a doctor who refused to sign him off sick. The same doctor also prescribed belladonna as a relaxant, which in larger doses is another hallucinogenic and a deadly poison. His fears and flashbacks were at their most acute when he was alone, so he spent more and more time in Rouen with de Beauvoir who introduced him to her pupil and friend, Olga Kosakiewicz.

The beautiful, intelligent, proud, tempestuous and capricious Olga was more than enough to keep Sartre company in de Beauvoir's absence. Olga was to mess with his head even more than the mescaline, though the experience was not so entirely unpleasant.

9

La Petite Russe

Olga, 'la petite Russe', was something of an aristocrat, the daughter of a Frenchwoman and a Russian nobleman. She had cried in de Beauvoir's class and de Beauvoir had taken her for a walk to calm her down. De Beauvoir immediately found she could talk to the young woman, eight years her junior, far more freely than she could talk to increasingly reserved and sensible friends of her own age. They began seeing a lot of each other and Sartre, because he was so frequently in Rouen seeking distraction from his depressing flashbacks, soon became involved.

Olga became their shared obsession for the next two years. They were both madly in love with her, infatuated with her beauty and her youthful haughtiness and impetuosity. She seemed to offer them the opportunity to recapture their own lost youth. They could learn from her, emulate her spontaneity, act, as she did, on emotion rather than reason, evade routine, go without food and sleep, dance and party until they dropped. They pursued her, charmed her, discussed her, repeatedly quarrelled over her and even fell into the habit of trying to sort out her messed-up life as though she were their daughter.

Sartre's passion for her intensified to the point of posses-siveness. Besotted with her, he was unhappy unless he had her undivided attention, and he exhausted every trick of his charm and intelligence in an ultimately futile effort to keep the fickle, erratic girl focused solely on him. From 1935 to 1937, as he tried everything in his power to win her, her refusal either to reject or accept him drove him repeatedly from the heights of ecstasy to the pits of despair.

Sartre and de Beauvoir's long-held belief that their 'necessary love' could tolerate and even benefit from the 'contingent love' of their various affairs was seriously challenged by the passions that Olga stirred in both of them. De Beauvoir was not particularly jealous that Sartre was so intensely infatuated with Olga, but his unbecoming behaviour irritated her. She hated to see him embarrass himself over a girl more than a decade younger than he was. She felt somewhat sorry for Olga that Sartre insisted on coming on so strong towards her, but was also often angry with Olga for being so ready to flirt with him. In the absence of the other, de Beauvoir criticized and counselled both about their role in the ménage à trois. The whole business placed de Beauvoir under a lot of strain.

Sartre later claimed that he never knew jealousy except where Olga was concerned and undoubtedly his affair with her was a life-defining episode that haunted his writing for many years.

Several of Sartre's female characters have some of Olga's personality traits. Lulu in his short story, *Intimacy,* for example, and Inez in his play, *In Camera.* The Sartre character most identifiable as Olga, however, is Ivich Serguine in Sartre's series of novels *Roads to Freedom.* In the first volume of the series, *The Age of Reason*, Ivich is pursued by another of Sartre's alter egos, philosophy teacher, Mathieu Delarue.

De Beauvoir based the love triangle at the centre of her first novel, *She Came to Stay*, on the stormy relationship between herself, Sartre and Olga. She even dedicated the novel to Olga. She also writes about the relationship at length in *The Prime of Life*, her great account of that giddy, emotional time. Here, she reveals that it was as much a source of joy to the participants as a source of misery, especially early on. There were many wonderful times when three was not a crowd.

In early 1937, while out drinking with Little Bost, de Beauvoir started to shiver. Two days later she was rushed to hospital with pneumonia. For a time she was seriously ill. De Beauvoir had been working and playing too hard, smoking too much, living in damp accommodation and neglecting her health, and doubtless the tensions of the ménage à trois also made a significant contribution. The 'woman of steel', as Sartre had spitefully called her behind her back shortly before, was only human after all.

Sartre was shocked out of his fruitless and increasingly ridiculous infatuation with Olga. He finally realized he had been taking de Beauvoir for granted. Her illness, the possibility that he might lose her, was a sharp reminder of how much she, above all others, meant to him. He visited her every day in hospital and arranged a comfortable, less damp hotel for her discharge. She was still bedridden at Easter, so he waited on her hand and foot, carrying food from a nearby restaurant and generally making it up to her.

As for Olga, they remained good friends with her, but things cooled to a level more tolerable for all three of them. Having flunked her medical exams and been unable to keep up with Sartre's absurd attempt to train her as a philosophy teacher, Olga found she was happiest as a waitress on the Boulevard Saint-Michel. She had been having a relationship with Little Bost for some time and they eventually married. He was her age. Despite the wake-up call of de Beauvoir's brush with death, Sartre sought to compensate for losing Olga to Bost by flirting with Olga's younger sister, Wanda, whose temperament was similarly unpredictable and engaging.

10

The Mighty Gallimard

During the height of the Olga entanglement, at the end of the 1935–36 academic year, Sartre finally left Le Havre for a job in Laon, one step closer to Paris. He hoped to be transferred to Paris after a year. De Beauvoir would already be working there, having left Rouen for Paris at the same time as he left Le Havre for Laon.

Laon would prove to be more of the usual: Sartre enjoyed the teaching but he disliked most of the staff. He was largely disapproved of because of his resistance to authority in general and his refusal to attend boring meetings in particular. A telling off about a missed meeting is said to have led to a punch-up in the staffroom, our boxer and another guy circling the room.

Prior to Laon and the punch-up, Sartre and de Beauvoir took their summer vacation in Italy, where they heard about the outbreak of the Spanish Civil War. Sartre, in particular, was becoming more interested in politics. The sight of dire poverty in Italy, and later in Greece, did more to draw him to the political left than the sight of swastikas had done in Germany. All that absurd flag waving had only served to turn him off politics altogether. He followed events in Spain closely, his eyes more often staring at a newspaper than the charms of Rome. De Beauvoir complained that he spent much of the summer of 1936 obsessing about Spain, Germany and Olga.

All this time, despite school, depression, the lurking lobster, Germany, Spain and Olga, Sartre continued to write. Nothing ever stopped Sartre from writing. 'My commandments have been sewn into my skin: if I go a day without writing, the scar burns me; and if I write too easily, it also burns me' (*Words*, p. 104).

By the late 1930s he had publishable works lined up like bullets in a machine gun magazine. His first significant publication was *Imagination: A Psychological Critique* in 1936, the first and less original half of *L'Image*. To Sartre's disappointment, Alcan had rejected the groundbreaking second half, which did not see publication until 1940 as his now famous, *The Psychology of Imagination*, aka *The Imaginary*. His tightly written post-Husserlian masterpiece, *The Transcendence of the Ego*, was also published in 1936 as an article and then the following year as a book. It soon entered the canon of key texts in phenomenology.

During the post-mescaline and Olga years he had returned to his childhood habit of writing short stories. The first to appear, though not the first to be written, was *The Wall*, in the July 1937 edition of *La Nouvelle Revue Française*.

Set in the Spanish Civil War, the story explores the different ways in which a group of prisoners confront the prospect of being shot at dawn against an unyielding wall. The story considers such familiar existentialist themes as despair, death, absurdity, meaninglessness and nihilism. Above all, it explores the existential truth that life has no meaning other than the relative meaning given to it by our projects. Believing that his time has run out, the central character, Ibbieta, can have no projects, other than dying with dignity, and as a result all objects and all human endeavours appear to him absurd.

Very simple in style, yet extremely psychologically penetrating, *The Wall*, tapping into widespread concerns about the war in Spain, caused a sensation. It was the work that first brought Sartre to the attention of the public, an attention he would hold tight from then on. Other equally brilliant short stories followed: *Intimacy, The Room, Erostratus* and *The Childhood of a Leader*. These stories were eventually published as a collection dedicated to none other than Olga Kosakiewicz.

But what of the factum on contingency, the masterpiece among masterpieces, the philosophical novel he had poured his heart, soul and mind into for several years? Nizan, already established as a novelist, submitted it to Gallimard on Sartre's behalf. It was rejected by Gallimard in late 1936. Sartre could not understand why. He shed tears of disappointment and frustration, one of the few times that anyone ever saw him cry. It turned out later that there had been a mix up. The work had been rejected as a submission to *La Nouvelle Revue Française*, also published by Gallimard.

Sartre's friends, who had read his manuscript and marvelled at it, shared his disbelief. They were to prove decisive in finally getting the work onto the right desk. Pierre Bost went to see the head of the publishing house, Gaston Gallimard, in person, and Charles Dullin, an old friend of Gallimard, who knew Sartre through Simone Jollivet, put in a favourable word. The mighty Gallimard undertook to read the manuscript himself.

In April 1937, Gaston Gallimard summoned Sartre to his office. Picture a scene that a million budding authors dream of. The great publisher loved everything but the title, *Melancholia* – a title inspired by *Melencolia*, the famous sixteenth-century engraving by Albrecht Dürer. Publishers generally like to change authors' working titles and Gallimard wisely suggested *Nausea*. The book reminded him of the work of Kafka, while his associate, Jean Paulhan, drew comparisons with Dostoevsky. High praise indeed. Subject to certain small revisions, the book would be published the following year. Meanwhile, did Sartre have any short stories for *La Nouvelle Revue Française*? That was when Sartre offered Gallimard *The Wall*.

Among the many letters that Sartre received in response to *The Wall* was the offer of a teaching job in Paris. At last, an end to provincial school teaching, to visiting his beloved Paris by train whenever he could, to that sinking Sunday evening feeling of heading back to the sticks. He and de Beauvoir would finally be working in the same city, close to the majority of their friends, part-time lovers and favourite cafés.

With everything finally coming up roses, with de Beauvoir recovered from pneumonia, they spent the summer of 1937 touring Greece with Bost. Just turned thirty-two, Sartre was invigorated by a new confidence and optimism. The lobster had gone, Olga's spell had broken, he was on the road to fame and glory. To celebrate, he slept the night in an ancient ruin and stole a skull from an ossuary.

11

Sex Before War

Both based in Paris at last, Sartre and de Beauvoir moved into a comfortable hotel near the Montparnasse Cemetery. True to form, they took separate rooms, a move that preserved the vitality of their relationship by preserving its essential freedom. 'Sartre lived on the floor above me; thus we had all the advantages of a shared life, without any of its inconveniences' (*The Prime of Life*, p. 315).

Sartre started work on a book called *La Psyché* which he abandoned after four hundred pages, publishing only a fragment, *Sketch for a Theory of the Emotions*, in 1939. This fragment is important, not only because it offers excellent insights into the nature of emotion, but also because, like *The Imaginary*, it develops concepts and categories that play a central role in Sartre's major philosophical work, *Being and Nothingness*.

In his superb introduction to *Sketch for a Theory of the Emotions*, Sartre contrasts phenomenology with psychology, arguing that phenomenology is superior to psychology because it grasps essences whereas psychology only lists facts that appear as accidental. Psychologists can only say that there is emotion, that it involves certain behaviours in certain situations. They cannot explain why there is emotion, what it signifies or why it is an essential aspect of human consciousness and a necessary feature of human reality.

Sartre goes on to demolish several classic theories of emotion. For example, the peripheric theory which argues that a person feels sad because they weep rather than vice versa. He also critically examines psychoanalysis, arguing, as he does in *Being and Nothingness*, that Freud's distinction between the conscious and the unconscious is nonsensical. Freud considers emotion to be a signifier of whatever lurks in the unconscious, but his radical separation of conscious and unconscious means that the signifier is entirely cut off from what is supposedly signified.

By the time he wrote *Being and Nothingness* Sartre was arguing that there is really no such thing as the unconscious because consciousness must actually *know* what is in the so-called unconscious in order to be able to select certain thoughts for repression. In *Being and Nothingness* he entirely rejects Freud's theory of a compartmentalized mind in favour of his own theory of bad faith, describing as behaviours of self-distraction and self-evasion what Freud describes as self-deception.

Sketching his own theory of emotion, Sartre argues that

although people can always consciously reflect on their emotions, emotion is not primarily a phenomenon of mental reflection. Emotional consciousness, argues Sartre, is first and foremost consciousness *of* the world. Emotions are *intentional*, they are a way of apprehending the world. For every emotion there is the object of that emotion: every emotion is directedness towards its object and exists in relation to its object. To be afraid is to be afraid *of* something, to be angry is to be angry *with* something and so on.

Emotion occurs when the world becomes too difficult for a person to cope with. Finding all ways of acting in the physical world barred by difficulty, a person spontaneously wills that the world be transformed from a world governed by causal processes into a world governed by magic where causal processes no longer apply. Emotion is a spontaneous attitude to a situation that aims to magically transform that situation in such a way that it suddenly no longer presents an insurmountable difficulty or threat to the person concerned.

A person faced with great danger, for example, may faint as a means of removing that danger from his conscious grasp, even though fainting does not normally serve to remove a danger in any real, practical sense. Similarly, a person may angrily curse, hit or throw a tool that is proving difficult to utilize, as though the world had magically become a place where the difficulty presented by a tool could be removed by these 'means'.

For Sartre, all emotions are functional. Emotion is a magical behaviour that functions to miraculously transform a situation when that situation becomes too difficult for a person to deal with practically. In formulating his 'frustration theory' of emotion Sartre must have had his relationship with Olga in mind.

Sartre's career is littered with such substantial but unfinished works as *La Psyché*. He was always full of new ideas and often laboured on several projects at once, not least because he felt his latest theories needed to be expressed in both a philosophical treatise and a work of fiction. He would always start a new project if a new idea engaged his interest, regardless of how many projects he already had on the go. Inevitably, he abandoned many projects, although these abandoned projects always played an important role in the development of his thought and provided valuable raw material for other works.

With regard to their level of completion, Sartre's works can be roughly divided into the following categories:

- Works that are complete in the sense of having been fully polished for publication and rounded off.

- Works that are extensive and polished for publication but incomplete in the sense that he intended to add further volumes but never did. Some of these further volumes were started but for various reasons were never finished.

- Works that are extensive but unfinished in the sense that they are drafts or notebooks not ready for publication or never intended for publication. Several of these manuscripts have been published posthumously providing scholars with valuable new insights into Sartre's thought.

- Works that he abandoned early in their development, either because he realized they were not going to work or because he quickly lost interest in them.

As this biography proceeds you will see which of these categories his various works belong to. Generally, he was suspicious of the notion that any work can really be finished. With a philosophical work in particular there is always more that can be said. Better to leave a work blatantly open-ended as an invitation to others to continue developing its themes.

With *La Psyché* abandoned, Sartre focused on his collection of short stories. He paid particular attention to the longest short story in the book, *The Childhood of a Leader*. This story tells the tale of Lucien Fleurier, his journey to adulthood and his descent into the bad faith of believing he is a necessary being defined by bourgeois rights and values.

The finishing touch to the transformation and solidification of Fleurier's self-image is added when, dissatisfied with his pretty, childish face, he decides to grow a moustache in the hope that others, particularly his social inferiors, will fear and respect him. 'He would have liked to find on his own face the impenetrable look he admired on Lemordant's. But the mirror only reflected a pretty, headstrong little face that was not yet terrible enough. "I'll grow a moustache," he decided' (*The Childhood of a Leader*, p. 144).

Moustaches are a recurrent theme in Sartre's writing. A man cannot see his own moustache, at least to the extent that others see it, so a moustache exists primarily for others and a man with a moustache is a man who has undertaken to exist for others rather than for himself. In so far as it is typical of the bourgeois to strive to *be* his social role, the moustache, for Sartre, became the emblem of the shallow, self-satisfied, respectable, reactionary middle-class gentleman that he despised even more than crustaceans.

> The fine gentleman exists Legion of Honour, exists moustache, that's all; how happy one must be to be nothing more than a Legion of Honour and a moustache and nobody sees the rest, he sees the two pointed ends of moustache on both sides of the nose; I do not think therefore I am a moustache.
>
> (*Nausea*, p. 147)

The Childhood of a Leader and *Nausea* complement each other in that they explore many of the same philosophical themes: contingency, indeterminacy, self-identity and bad faith. Both Fleurier and Roquentin are haunted by issues of self-identity and bewildered by existence generally. Their existential anxieties are largely the same. They differ in terms of their response to their anxieties, each choosing himself as the kind of person the other detests.

Roquentin detests those who, like Fleurier, seek to fool themselves that their existence is necessary, while Fleurier comes to detest those who, like Roquentin – and Sartre – think and question too much and dwell on their contingency and superfluity. Fleurier suppresses his anxieties by striving to *be* something, and eventually becomes a narrow-minded, racist bourgeois steeped in bad faith: a character very much like one of the *salauds* (bourgeois swine or bastards) described in *Nausea* that Roquentin so despises. For his part, Roquentin sees through the deluded posturing of the *salauds* and in opposition to them thoroughly indulges his anxieties.

Nausea was finally published in March 1938 and by May started to receive rave reviews in many Paris-based journals and newspapers. In *Ce Soir*, Nizan praised Sartre as a 'philosophical novelist of the first order' – nothing like getting one's friends to review one's book. Meanwhile, a young Albert Camus, not yet known personally to Sartre, writing in the anti-colonialist newspaper, *Alger républicain*, said Sartre had 'infinite talent' and a 'singular and vigorous mind'.

The basic plot of *Nausea* is simple. In terms of events relatively little happens. This is quite deliberate on Sartre's part.

He is at pains to present a slice of ordinary life and to avoid doing what novels usually do, which is to impose on ordinary life the features of an adventure with clear-cut beginnings that portend clear-cut endings where characters are reconciled to themselves and to each other and above all fulfilled.

Roquentin, in his self-destructive attempt to live free from all comforting misapprehensions, strives to avoid living life as if he were recounting it. Roquentin, and therefore the novel itself, walks a thin, ironical line between telling a story and striving not to tell a story. When Roquentin slips into turning his life into an adventure, into literature, he catches himself and pulls back. 'I have no need to speak in flowery language. I am writing to understand certain circumstances. I must beware of literature' (*Nausea*, p. 85).

Although *Nausea* seeks to have no plot and treats the whole business of plots and literature as deeply suspect, there is nonetheless a succession of events resembling a plot.

Roquentin drifts about Bouville anxiously contemplating the loss of all sense of meaning and purpose in his life and the lies and bad faith by which the *salauds* seek to give their lives meaning, purpose and a sense of necessity. Roquentin is pursued by *the nausea*, a terrifying, overwhelming awareness of the utter contingency and absurdity of existence. Though the novel makes no reference to mind-altering drugs, *the nausea* echoes Sartre's disturbing encounter with mescaline.

Roquentin is writing a biography of Adhémar, the Marquis de Rollebon, but abandons it deciding that he is merely trying to distract himself from his own futile existence by attempting to give Rollebon's existence a significance it did not possess. Writing and reading biographies is absurd and pointless, but then so is everything else.

Roquentin avoids friendships but is nonetheless befriended in the library by a man he calls the Autodidact. The Autodidact is attempting to educate himself in all knowledge *autodidactically* by working his way through the library catalogue from A to Z. He is a humanist and a socialist, a lonely, unattractive man who rapturously declares his love for all humankind and labels Roquentin a misanthrope. Roquentin finds him physically and intellectually repulsive and flees a meal with him in disgust as he begins to suffer a serious attack of *the nausea*. The Autodidact is eventually exposed as a paedophile when he molests a boy in the library.

Despite being a loner Roquentin finds himself looking forward to visiting his former lover, Anny, though he reminds himself that there are no perfect moments. When they meet they discover they have developed similar thoughts on life. Anny says she has outlived herself. Roquentin can offer her no reasons for living. They part company, perhaps forever, realizing there is nothing they can do for one another. Alone again, Roquentin dwells on his limitless freedom and the pointlessness of his superfluous existence in a meaningless universe:

I am free: I haven't a single reason for living left, all the ones I have tried have given way and I can't imagine any more. I am still quite young, I still have enough strength to start again. But what must I start again? Only now do I realise how much, in the midst of my greatest terror and nauseas, I had counted on Anny to save me. My past is dead, Monsieur de Rollebon is dead, Anny came back only to take all hope away from me. I am alone in this white street lined with gardens. Alone and free. But this freedom is rather like death.

(*Nausea*, p. 223)

The novel ends on a relatively optimistic note with Roquentin deciding to leave Bouville and write a novel. He does not think this will distract him from his existence, as he hoped writing the biography of Rollebon would, but he hopes that once it is written he will be able to look back on writing it and that it will at least give some meaning and purpose to his past.

Rivalled only by Camus' *The Stranger*, which it inspired, *Nausea* has achieved cult status as the archetypal existentialist novel. Its central themes of contingency, absurdity, anxiety and alienation have become synonymous with existentialism in the popular consciousness, even if, properly understood, existentialism is a far more optimistic and constructive philosophy than *Nausea* suggests. *Nausea* is a truly philosophical novel in its questioning of the nature of existence and self-identity but it is not a treatise on the philosophy of existentialism. Essentially, it is a superbly crafted, disturbingly incisive, darkly witty exploration of extreme nihilism.

If there was one thing better than receiving praise from an as yet unknown Albert Camus, it was all the attention Sartre's newfound celebrity was attracting from young women. Despite his relative physical ugliness, women had always liked him for his personality, his intelligence, his chat, and his generally easy and familiar manner in their company. Now, at least a few of them were positively throwing themselves at him. Without getting carried away with the attention, and preserving a sense of humour about it, he took full advantage.

He liked to spend hours in bed with women, caressing them all over, getting to know the individual charms and peculiarities of their bodies. He would often take several days to work his way up to first time intercourse with them, partly because several of them were virgins and he balked at the effort of deflowering them. He described himself as a masturbator of women rather than a copulator. Penetration was not where his main pleasure lay.

He had a problem with reciprocity, which eventually led him, in *Being and Nothingness*, to formulate a fascinating theory as to why full sexual reciprocity is impossible and sexual desire inevitably becomes sadomasochistic. His sense that he was physically ugly, which he had mainly inherited from Simone Jollivet, led him to feel that a woman could not really enjoy his body. He felt that during sex it was her beauty that was being enjoyed by both of them.

We know all this because he wrote to de Beauvoir in exhaustive detail about his various affairs, striving to be as articulate as possible in describing the intimate details of his lovemaking. Ever the writer, he needed to transform even his sex life into written words in order to fully experience and enjoy it. His sometimes spiteful intellectualized voyeurism was also a way of involving his necessary love, de Beauvoir, in his contingent loves: a way of confirming that only she was to be treated with complete honesty and openness, and all other women with a slightly amused, slightly ironic, slightly distanced curiosity.

His successes with various women gave him a newfound confidence with Olga's sister, Wanda, with whom he had been flirting without progress for some time. He threatened to end their friendship if she did not become his lover. She acquiesced, but as moody, fickle and fussy as her sister, it was months before she yielded her virginity to him.

As Sartre enjoyed his newfound fame, made love in grubby Parisian hotel rooms, read Heidegger in translation and wrote until his pen smoked in the Café Flore, dark clouds were gathering in the world beyond. By the time he and de Beauvoir returned from a trip to Morocco in the summer of 1938, where they had suffered food poisoning and watched a tattooed woman smoke a cigarette with her vagina, Europe was on the brink of war.

In March 1938, political scheming had led to the bloodless annexation of Austria by Hitler's Nazi Germany. This was the first step in the *Anschluss*, the linkup of ethnic Germans. Hitler had then turned his attentions to the Sudetenland of Western Czechoslovakia, an area inhabited by a majority of ethnic Germans. Hitler made himself their advocate, demanding their liberation.

War seemed inevitable if France and Britain were to honour their alliances with Czechoslovakia, but in the early hours of 30 September 1938, Germany, France, Britain and Italy signed the Munich Agreement authorizing the German annexation of Czechoslovakia's Sudetenland, a move that effectively undermined Czechoslovakia's ability to function as a sovereign state. Czechoslovakia had not even been invited to a conference that saw Europe officially abandon it to Nazi tyranny. The stark truth was that France and Britain were simply not ready to confront German military might.

The reprieve won under the terms of the Munich Agreement represented the high point of *appeasement*, the habit of attempting to appease and pacify Hitler by giving in to his expansionist demands. Despite his personal preoccupations Sartre had pondered appeasement and was against it. De Beauvoir, at that time less interested in current affairs than Sartre, held that war should be prevented at any cost.

The 'peace for our time' secured by appeasing Hitler proved to be nothing but a short-lived and unsatisfactory reprieve. Eleven months after signing the Munich Agreement, Hitler broke it by invading Poland.

The second novel in Sartre's *Roads to Freedom* series, *The Reprieve*, published in 1945, covers the eight days leading up to the Munich Agreement. Adopting the non-linear style of Dos Passos and other writers that Sartre so admired, *The Reprieve* unfolds events through a myriad personal perspectives rather than through an abstract historical account.

Cutting from one scene to another, sometimes in mid-sentence, the novel deliberately and radically dispenses with continuity of place and action – though not continuity of time, which it cleverly maintains – to produce a panoramic, multifaceted view of a Europe teetering on the brink of total war. The novel's fragmented structure can be confusing at first, but the writing is expertly managed and soon serves to produce a coherent and almost omnipresent overview that forges profound connections between diverse events.

Sartre remained fascinated for the rest of his philosophical career by the relationship between the so-called grand sweep of history and the individual actions occurring in diverse places that entirely comprise it. Great political events such as wars, invasions and reprieves are identified as a single unified phenomenon only with the benefit of hindsight. At the time there is nothing beyond the series of individual lives, decisions, triumphs and tragedies. Only the novelist, filmmaker or historian has an overview, and then only after events have occurred.

At the end of the 1930s, as will be seen, history and politics crashed into Sartre's personal life like a tidal wave. No wonder he brought them crashing into his *Roads to Freedom* series: into his writing generally.

Sartre started work on what was to become the first volume of *Roads to Freedom*, *The Age of Reason*, in July 1938. Set in Paris in June 1938, the novel reflects to some extent Sartre's life at the time and his own personal transition from peacetime profligacy and immaturity to eve-of-war responsibility and true manhood.

The Age of Reason tells the story of two days in the life of Sartre's alter ego, philosophy teacher, Mathieu Delarue, as he strives to borrow money to pay for an abortion for his mistress, Marcelle. If Marcelle has the baby, Mathieu's profligate life, free from serious commitments, will be curtailed. Meanwhile, he unsuccessfully pursues the young, capricious, tantalizingly sensual Ivich – based on Olga. He is both infatuated with Ivich and tired of her moody ways: tired of the futility of his ridiculous obsession with her.

Mathieu's brother, Jacques, a bourgeois lawyer, refuses to pay for the abortion but offers him considerably more money if he marries Marcelle and keeps the baby. Jacques argues that

Mathieu's relationship with Marcelle – like Sartre's relationship with de Beauvoir – is like a marriage but without any of the responsibilities. He insists that now Mathieu is in his thirties he has reached, or should have reached, *the age of reason*. The age when a man must stop playing the bohemian and face up to his moral and social responsibilities. The age when it is a man's duty to marry, settle down, conform and sell-out.

Mathieu rejects Jacques' age of reason along with his cash, saying, "'Your age of reason is the age of resignation, and I've no use for it'" (*The Age of Reason*, p. 108). Mathieu intends to define the age of reason differently, as the age when he asserts his freedom by refusing to conform.

By the end of the novel he has lost Marcelle and given up pursuing Ivich. He has only his freedom. Freedom, he has learned, is not actually about avoiding responsibility but about choosing to commit oneself to a course of action without regret. He was not prepared to commit himself to family life as a course of action. Choosing it would have gone against his fundamental choice of himself, his fundamental lifelong project of asserting his freedom.

When Mathieu reappears in *The Reprieve*, he has abandoned philosophy teaching and his profligate, womanizing, bohemian lifestyle in favour of fully committing himself, without regret, to serving in World War II. By the time Sartre finished *The Age of Reason* and *The Reprieve* he had already travelled a similar road to freedom as his hero.

From *The Age of Reason* onwards, from the eve of war onwards, the themes of freedom, fundamental choice, responsibility, action, commitment and refusal to regret, became central both to Sartre's own life and to his uncompromising philosophy of the human condition: central to what was eventually labelled *existentialism*.

Sartre's collection of short stories, *The Wall and Other Stories*, was published in February 1939. With his name so firmly established by *Nausea*, the collection was an immediate hit. Some critics even thought it superior to *Nausea:* others condemned it as obsessively vulgar.

Perhaps with the intention of deliberately offending him, Sartre sent a copy to his hated stepfather, Mancy, who soon returned it with a note indicating the point at which he had stopped reading it. What point I know not, but it could well have been a paragraph at the start of *Intimacy* where Lulu reflects on the tender feelings of intimacy evoked by the sight of her husband's yellow-stained underpants.

In March 1939, Germany occupied Czechoslovakia and in May Sartre attended an anti-fascist conference. With war looming, he and de Beauvoir shelved plans to visit Russia, deciding instead to play it safe and spend the summer at various locations in the south of France. Sartre expected to be called up for active service at any moment. Like his alter ego, Mathieu, he had no intention of shying away from his duty.

In Marseilles, with war now virtually inevitable, fate seemed to play a hand in bringing old friends together. Sartre and de Beauvoir ran into Paul and Henriette Nizan and their two children. The family were due to set sail for Corsica. Later that day, Bost appeared, a handsome, youthful figure in the uniform of an infantryman. He was enjoying a few days' leave. They all sat at the Café Cintra, drinking and chatting about times past and the war to come, before the Nizan family departed. Sartre and de Beauvoir never saw Paul Nizan again.

Back in Paris, many places were closed for the August recess and an uneasy peace prevailed. All their closest friends were away. The city, which now seemed to belong to the past, awaited its dark future. They kept hoping. Even on 31 August they were still hoping. They found such desperate hope deeply unpleasant. 'I was far less calm than I pretended,' writes de Beauvoir. 'I was afraid. Not for my own skin, though: I never for one moment thought of fleeing Paris. It was Sartre I was afraid for' (*The Prime of Life*, p. 378).

On 1 September 1939 Hitler invaded Poland. All French reservists were immediately mobilized. Sartre paid a quick farewell visit to his mother before digging out his kitbag and army boots and heading to the assembly centre. The following morning saw him and de Beauvoir shivering at the Gare de L'Est as he awaited the 7.50 train to Nancy. He tried to reassure her that as a meteorologist he faced no danger.

On 3 September 1939, France and Britain declared war on Germany. Sartre was thirty-four years old. The madness of war had finally reached him. He had finally reached full manhood, a condition of unavoidable responsibility; he had finally reached the age of reason.

12

War of Words

Sartre was posted to a small meteorological unit in Alsace, northeast France, near the front line, the border with Germany. For the next few months his unit would transfer between various small towns around Strasbourg, wherever the artillery division to which it was attached required it to establish wind speed. The French and Germans were at a stand-off. With the Germans busy elsewhere there was to be no significant fighting in that theatre of war until the German spring offensive of 1940.

Sartre found himself in the centre of a phoney war, living, as he had always done, in a succession of seedy hotel rooms. The only demand on his time was to help float a weather balloon once a day. He had no school teaching to do and no Parisian friends and lovers to swirl about with. It was the perfect writer's retreat, especially for a practised café writer who was not disturbed by background noise and commotion.

He was in the eye of a storm. The war all around infused him with dark energy, a profound sense of world history unfolding and his personal destiny with it, a personal destiny *he* was responsible for. He *chose* the war. He firmly decided that he was not in a situation that was merely happening *to* him. He *chose* his past, even his birth. His life had all been leading to that time and place. He must take full possession of his situation without regret.

What mattered was authenticity, realizing to the full his being-in-situation. Unlike a comrade who declared that he was not really a soldier but a civilian in disguise, Sartre would not resort to the bad faith of choosing not to choose, the bad faith of refusing to take responsibility and get real. This response to his situation became a key principle of the philosophy he was soon to write.

Within a few days of his posting, often sitting on one crate and leaning on another, he threw himself into what would become his second published novel, *The Age of Reason*. He did not know how long this golden opportunity to write afforded by the Phoney War would last, so he wrote with great urgency, drafting several pages a day. He mailed these pages to de Beauvoir for safe keeping, fifty at a time.

The novel alone was not enough to fill his time or satisfy his insatiable desire to write, so he began to keep a diary, as a temporary exercise. It could, he thought, be published posthumously, which it was. He described daily events and analysed his comrades: their mundane remarks and their sometimes filthy personal habits. Never a paragon of personal hygiene, Sartre became a slob himself, allowing his beard to grow unchecked.

Above all, the diary became a place for depositing, exploring and refining his philosophical ideas. In the absence of philosophy books to consult he was able to step back from his great learning and appraise it from a distance. He indulged in pure, free flowing reflection on the ideas of Kant, Kierkegaard, Husserl, Heidegger and others, and in so doing sowed the seeds of his own profound philosophy.

When some volumes of his *War Diaries* were later lost, after de Beauvoir lent them to Bost, Sartre was unconcerned. The diary really only mattered as a place to evolve and organize his thoughts. Once they were evolved and organized they were firmly in his great, brainy head. What was to eventually emerge from that head, through the all-important *act* of writing, following the diary-based process of evolution and organization, was his vast philosophical masterpiece, *Being and Nothingness*, one of the most extraordinary, energetic and groundbreaking contributions ever made to the history of ideas.

With the novel, the diary and countless letters to de Beauvoir, Wanda and others, it is said that Sartre wrote a million words between September 1939 and the early summer of 1940. That is about thirteen times more words than there are in this book. He not only wrote all day from six in the morning, but sometimes all night as well. When his light duties allowed, or he could get others to cover for him, he would stay in his hotel room for several days in a row, skipping washes and meals to save time, eating only bread and chocolate, filling page after page like some manic writing machine.

He decided that fatigue was only a choice of himself, so he chose not to be tired. This radical freedom and responsibility thesis became the very core of the philosophy he was living and writing. Almost everything we do we choose to do it and are responsible for having done it.

He apologized to de Beauvoir for not feeling depressed about his situation, for seeing it as a golden opportunity to think and write, for finding the war all rather exciting and invigorating. But he was missing her. He needed to talk to her in order to put it all into perspective. Above all, he wanted to glimpse her beautiful, smiling face as an antidote to the ugly, macho world that surrounded him.

He was not particularly fond of his unsophisticated comrades, ordinary Frenchmen whose main occupation in life seemed to be to sweat, belch and fart, and he wrote in his diary that his situation had cured him of socialism. Sartre became a champion of socialism, but like most educated socialists, he always preferred the more refined company of bourgeois intellectuals to that of the common man, even though, ironically, like Marx before him, he naively held that the future hope of humankind somehow resided with the plebs. As Ronald Hayman says in his outstanding, highly detailed biography of Sartre, *Writing Against*, 'His liking for the people was generalised and theoretical' (*Writing Against*, p. 166).

Sartre was not allowed to tell de Beauvoir where he was, but through a series of coded letters he managed to arrange a rendezvous. She met him in Brumath at the beginning of November. The moment she saw him she strongly advised him to lose the awful beard, and he returned from his morning duties clean-shaven. They found a room they could share for several days where they made love and discussed the latest one hundred pages of *The Age of Reason*.

Immediately after de Beauvoir's return to Paris on 5 November Sartre wrote to her expressing his deep love and describing himself as her 'little husband'. As de Beauvoir well knew, he was still romantically involved with Wanda, albeit entirely by amorous letter, always his biggest turn on.

His unit continued to periodically shift location around Alsace. He continued to shift his punishing writing regime around his changing but generally light duties. The most irksome thing he had to do during that time was operate a switchboard in Morsbronn-les-Bains once every few days. Twelve hours at the switchboard gave him a headache and exhausted him in a way that twelve hours of writing never did.

On 4 February 1940, he was granted eleven days' leave. Changing into civvies the moment he reached Paris, he visited his mother and divided the remainder of his time between de Beauvoir and Wanda. He found Paris strangely quiet: few men around and no nightlife. In mid-February, on the train back to the front, there was frightened talk of a German spring offensive.

He resumed his monastic routine, writing with ever greater urgency to make the most of the time and the opportunity afforded to him by Hitler's decision to draw breath, at least in that theatre of war.

On 12 May 1940, as the Germans invaded Holland and Belgium, he found himself growing a little impatient with final adjustments to *The Age of Reason*. He wanted to get on with his philosophy book. He and the diary had the whole book more or less worked out. He just needed time to get it all down: there was an awful lot to get down.

The Germans took Laon in northern France, close to the Belgian border, a town where he used to teach, and soon he was scribbling to the sound of distant gunfire. Even he began to find it difficult to concentrate and increasingly his writing was interspersed with games of chess, a way of being with his comrades. They tried to reassure one another that the Germans would treat the French better than they had treated the Poles, but some of his comrades were Jewish and were very afraid.

The French Army was in rapid retreat before the might of the German blitzkrieg, Sartre with it. The Germans crossed the Marne River on 12 June and two days later marched into Paris unopposed. An armistice, the qualified surrender of France, was expected any day. By the time Sartre and hundreds of other soldiers reached the area around Padoux in Lorraine, the French Army was in disarray.

In *Iron in the Soul*, the third volume of *Roads to Freedom*, published in 1949, Sartre draws heavily upon the events of that time, describing the despondency and sense of defeat of soldiers shamefully abandoned by several hundred officers who walked away waving a white flag.

Sartre was finally swept up by the German advance on 21 June 1940, his thirty-fifth birthday. He was marched at gunpoint to a police barracks where he and many other men were locked up for several days with little food. This period of hunger and the undignified, animal response of grown men to hunger is also described in detail in *Iron in the Soul*. 'Brunet deliberately put his foot on the scrap of bread, and trod it into the ground. But ten hands laid hold of his leg, forced it away, and scraped up the muddy crumbs' (*Iron in the Soul*, p. 264).

On 22 June, an armistice was agreed, reducing France to a client state of Nazi Germany. Germany would pull the strings of

Marshal Pétain's puppet Vichy government to control the north and west of France, including Paris and the Channel Ports, leaving the remainder, the south, to be governed by the French. Meanwhile, General Charles de Gaulle flew to London and was soon recognized as the leader of the Free French Movement.

Sartre's captivity became a form of camping. He lived in a tent, subjected to meagre, disgusting rations and cold nights. His biggest complaint, however, was the degenerate behaviour of his fellow prisoners, which at times descended to coprophilia. More disgust with the existential reality of ordinary blokes, more material for *Iron in the Soul*.

When his hunger allowed him enough energy, he did what any sane man with sufficient intellect ought to do when surrounded by the concrete realities of abject and inescapable squalor: he allowed himself to become absorbed by the eternal, abstract and elevating truths of philosophy. The diary now abandoned, he started writing *Being and Nothingness*, one of the many great works of refined thought that have emerged from the ruins of war. He was lucky to have paper and pen and within a few weeks had dashed off seventy-six pages.

De Beauvoir's letters reached him in his captivity and he responded with postcards and a few smuggled notes. He was anxious for news of Nizan, Bost, Maheu and Aron. He got caught up in the false hope that he and his comrades would be released before the end of August, but by the middle of August he was on his way to a POW camp at Trier, inside Germany, near the Luxembourg border.

The brutality of the German guards, the mockery of the French defeat by Poles and Czechs, gave Sartre a strong sense of solidarity with the other French prisoners. He had never felt so strongly that he was a Frenchman. He laughed heartily with his fellow prisoners after he received a kick in the backside from a sentry for breaching the nightly curfew. He was lucky it was not a bayonet, and his laughter was largely an expression of relief.

He made less vulgar, more intellectual friends than at any time since his active service began. Some knew his work and arranged for him to give lectures on Heidegger. They also found him a job in the infirmary as an interpreter. When the infirmary job ended he succeeded in becoming one of the camp artists responsible for maintaining prisoner morale.

The artists had their own hut with musical instruments on the wall. The Germans even paid them a small wage for their entertainment services. To keep himself physically fit Sartre took up boxing again. For mental exercise he continued to speed-write *Being and Nothingness*. All in all it was a good set-up, enlivened by the constant threat of a hilarious kick up the arse. There is no doubt that he rather enjoyed himself.

One of the main tasks of the artists was to put on a fortnightly play to entertain the entire camp. Rediscovering theatrical skills from his days at the ENS, Sartre soon became a mainstay of these performances. As the best means of advocating freedom and promoting an anti-authoritarian agenda right under the nose of the Nazis, he decided to write, direct and perform in the camp's Christmas play, *Bariona*. A decision that launched his career as a renowned playwright.

Set at the time of the birth of Christ, the play tells the story of the rebel, Bariona. Distrustful of news of the Messiah as told by the Magi, Bariona leads resistance against the forces of Herod, a puppet of Judea's Roman occupiers. The play's message of resistance was not lost on its huge, captive audience and Sartre and the rest of the cast received rapturous applause. Sartre, who played the role of the black magus, Balthazar, later wrote,

> As I addressed my comrades across the footlights, speaking to them of their state as prisoners, when I suddenly saw them so remarkably silent and attentive, I realised what theatre ought to be: a great, collective, religious phenomenon ... a theatre of myths.

(Sartre on Theatre, p. 39)

Sartre's love for the theatre was firmly established and over the next twenty-five years he was to turn repeatedly to drama as a means of conveying his philosophical and political ideas to a wide audience.

Sartre was, of course, not a man to languish in captivity for any longer than he had to, especially when there was a complete lack of female company. He was shocked but not surprised to discover that Nizan had died a hero's death alongside British troops during the retreat to Dunkirk on 23 May 1940. Sartre felt the need to do more to resist the Nazi terror than merely putting on plays, and by the start of 1941 he began to seriously consider staging an escape.

Escape from the makeshift stalag close to the Luxembourg and French borders was not particularly difficult and several men had managed it, mostly smuggled out with the mail for an extortionate fee. What did it really matter to the Germans, especially those on the ground, if a few Frenchmen got away? Fewer mouths to feed. France was occupied and thoroughly defeated anyway.

It emerged that Sartre might be able to simply bluff his way out if he could convince the Germans to declare him a civilian on the grounds that he was unfit for military service. The camp forgers produced a document declaring that the near blindness in his right eye caused problems of orientation. It is widely held that Sartre was released on medical grounds, and this may well have been the case – it was the story he put about when he returned to Paris and the one that de Beauvoir more or less endorses in *The Prime of Life* (pp. 478–9) – but another account has it that in March 1941 a more straightforward opportunity to escape presented itself.

Among Sartre's prison friends was the priest, Marius Perrin. Sartre taught Perrin Heidegger and offered to teach him how to fake the symptoms of epilepsy as a means of gaining his release. Perrin declined the offer, choosing to remain in captivity. He survived the war and in 1980 published a book, *Avec Sartre au Stalag XIID*, in which he gives a dramatic account of Sartre's escape that may be true despite being pure Hollywood.

According to Perrin, a practised pilferer, Braco, offered Sartre a genuine, undated note he had procured, granting permission to a German farmer to take two prisoners away as labourers. Making the most of his acting skills and his by now competent German, Sartre brazenly walked out of the camp disguised as a wealthy farmer carrying a briefcase. Two prisoners, who also escaped, trudged behind.

Sartre's escape from the stalag at Trier remains controversial. The PCF later insisted that his escape was staged, and some Sartre commentators are inclined to agree. It is interesting that the Nazis never recaptured him in Paris, which they could easily have done, but then again, he was hardly high on their list of priorities. For mundane reasons the authorities in Paris probably never received word that he had escaped, and if anyone started asking awkward questions he had the excuse of his very obvious squint.

It is alleged that the Nazis released him because he agreed to work for them as an informant and propagandist. There is, however, no evidence that he became a collaborator after he returned to Paris and plenty of evidence to the contrary. This does not mean that his escape was not staged, but if it was facilitated by the Germans, it was most likely for broader reasons.

Early in the war, when the Nazis were still confident of outright victory, they were keen to show the French people that they were not oppressors – except, of course, where Jews were concerned. Allowing French intellectuals to function freely was a means by which Francophile Nazis in love with French culture deluded themselves that they were urbane and civilized. The Nazis believed that allowing well-known French intellectuals such as Sartre to operate showed how reasonable and permissive they were towards a French population that they hoped to govern largely by consent.

If Sartre's escape was staged then he was at least complicit in willingly making a small contribution to Nazi propaganda. If his escape was staged he could have insisted that, if they wanted him on the outside for their propaganda purposes, they would have to officially release him. Same propaganda end for them but no complicity for him. Sartre could talk the hind legs of a donkey, even in German by that time, so perhaps he managed to fool whoever allowed him to go, if indeed anyone did, that he would collaborate after he returned to Paris.

There are too many ifs here, too much speculation arising from an accusation for which there is no solid evidence. It is unlikely that the exact truth will ever be established, but surely what matters as regards his reputation is that he did not collaborate after returning to Paris.

13

Occupation

Sartre was reunited with de Beauvoir in a Paris café at the end of March 1941. They had been living very different lives and it took a little time for them to adjust to one another. He was naively disapproving of the realities of occupation, shocked that de Beauvoir had bought black market tea and signed a form stating that she was not Jewish. He moved into her hotel, a separate room of course, and a new low in terms of domestic squalor.

He resumed his old teaching job. Despite the upheavals of war, rumour had reached his students that their new philosophy teacher was friendly and laid back. They were to be disappointed by his standoffishness. He was formal and efficient in a smart suit and tie. Determined to keep a low profile, he dictated dry summaries at the end of each lesson and told them nothing about his war adventures. The occupying authorities were dangerous. To draw attention to himself by being an unconventional, opinionated teacher and a sartorial rebel would have been nothing but reckless, futile bravado.

For the start of the new school year in September 1941 Sartre switched to a part-time teaching post at the Lycée Condorcet. According to Professor Ingrid Galster, writing in the spring 2000 issue of *Commentaire*, Sartre was able to take up this post because his predecessor, Henri Dreyfus-Le Foyer, was dismissed for being Jewish.

Responding to Galster's serious charge in the summer 2000 issue of *Les Temps modernes*, the famous journal founded by Sartre and de Beauvoir, Jacques Lecarme, Professor of Literature at the Sorbonne, pointed out that Dreyfus-Le Foyer was in fact succeeded by Ferdinand Alquié who was then succeeded by Sartre. This was not a prestigious university post where one tends to know whose chair one is taking over. It was just another of Sartre's many school teaching jobs and he is unlikely to have known whom he was replacing, let alone who had held the job before his predecessor.

Sartre of course knew that Jews were being dismissed from their teaching posts. So why did he not speak out? He could have protested – to do so would perhaps have been in keeping with the philosophy he was developing, but the Nazis would almost certainly have deported or executed him for his defiance. Sadly, under the extreme circumstances that prevailed, an open protest would have changed nothing. It would have been a futile, suicidal exercise in drawing further attention to an atrocity that everyone knew all too well was happening anyway. Like millions of people caught up in the Nazi occupation and disempowered by it, Sartre's behaviour was expedient and pragmatic rather than admirably moral; at best a choice to live to fight another day.

Those who constantly seek to characterize Sartre and de Beauvoir's World War II survival pragmatism as collaboration, complicity and anti-Semitism seem to hold the absurd belief that their voices were so influential that they had only to speak out on whatever issue for the Third Reich to immediately mend its ways. The pen *is* mightier than the sword, but over time and in subtle ways. Those who chose to confront the Nazis head on were better off using a bomb than a ball-point. Sartre could have taken up the bomb directly but he chose not to, a choice he perhaps later regretted. Had he done so he would probably not have survived the war and you would not be reading this biography.

There was little organized resistance in Paris at that time. To most Parisians resistance seemed useless in face of the apparent inevitability of an outright German victory. Best to reach an accommodation with their new Nazi masters without actually collaborating with them. A difficult balancing act. Some, of course, did actively collaborate. More than a few positively approved.

The PCF, the group most ideologically opposed to Nazism, had so far rendered itself unable to resist through its naive allegiance to the Hitler-Stalin Non-Aggression Pact of 1939. This absurdity finally ended when Germany invaded the Soviet Union on 22 June 1941, the day after Sartre's thirty-sixth birthday.

As a POW Sartre had hatched a plan to form his own resistance group, 'Socialism and Freedom'. He began to recruit members from among his friends and former students, who, as we know, were often one and the same. Their first meeting took place in de Beauvoir's hotel room. The philosopher and former infantry officer, Maurice Merleau-Ponty, was present, as was Bost, recovering from a war wound. Someone suggested that they start assassinating prominent collaborators. Instead, they opted for the standard, far less risky response of bourgeois, intellectual activists: a major leafleting campaign.

Sartre wrote a one-hundred-page manifesto outlining the group's socialist vision for a post-war France. The document was flushed down a toilet when nerves overcame the woman tasked with smuggling it into the free zone.

In the summer of 1941 Sartre and de Beauvoir were smuggled into the free zone themselves, where they combined a cycling holiday with seeking to recruit prominent writers to their cause. They approached André Gide and André Malraux but neither were interested. Gide was too old to care and Malraux, who fed a hungry Sartre chicken Maryland, said he was depending on American planes and Russian tanks to secure victory over the Nazis. In Malraux's defence it must be said that he fought bravely for the Allies towards the end of the war.

During this quixotic expedition, Sartre's bicycle sustained a puncture that neither he nor de Beauvoir knew how to repair. Typical intellectuals. They were seeking to fix the world but they did not know how to fix a puncture. Sartre enjoyed cycling, it was easier than walking, but he would sometimes go so slowly that he fell off. His credible excuse was that he was thinking of other things.

It is easy to mock Sartre's ineffectual resistance movement, but any resistance was risky. Producing and distributing resistance literature was punishable by deportation or worse. It is a miracle that nobody in Sartre's group was arrested given the risks they took moving pamphlets and copying machines around Paris.

Morale sank as members of 'Socialism and Freedom' began defecting to other groups. The capitalist Gaullists on the right and the communists on the left were both far larger and far better organized. There was really no place for Sartre's third political way. Given that his group was achieving next to nothing in real terms it was simply not worth the risk of continuing and in the autumn of 1941 Sartre and Merleau-Ponty officially dissolved it.

Resistance generally was beginning to gather pace however. Relations between the French and Germans deteriorated rapidly in the latter half of 1941 as assassinations were met with reprisals. In October, ninety-eight Frenchmen were shot to avenge the deaths of two German officers. In early December, the USA finally entered the war following the Japanese attack on Pearl Harbor. As an outright German victory began to seem less inevitable, resistance began to seem more worthwhile. Not least, people had to consider where they might be left standing if the Germans lost. The pressure was on to do one's bit to resist, lest one be labelled a collaborator at the end of it all.

With his well-meaning but ineffectual resistance movement disbanded, Sartre decided to repeat what he had done with *Bariona* and put over a thinly veiled message of resistance by writing another play: *The Flies*.

During the winter of 1941–2 the harsh realities of war and occupation bit ever deeper. Without tourists to sustain them, many bars and cafés closed, while petrol rationing kept most cars off the streets. Public spaces were militarized with barbed wire, trenches and pillboxes and the Germans requisitioned many hotels and cinemas. Little wine was coming in from the free zone and there was a strictly enforced midnight curfew. Jews in particular lived in increasing fear of oppression and deportation.

People kept disappearing after being taken in for questioning. Sartre later commented that it was as if the population of the city was being slowly emptied through hidden holes. Parisians who asked too many questions about the disappeared soon disappeared themselves. The one advantage to living in central Paris was that the Allies did not bomb it, although there were countless air raid warnings which Parisians largely ignored.

All this was endured on an achingly empty stomach. Tasty luxury foods were virtually non-existent, meat was scarce and even vegetables were in short supply. Prices soared until finally, Sartre, de Beauvoir and their little family of Olga, Wanda, Bost and one or two others, could no longer afford to eat out.

For the first time in her life, de Beauvoir resigned herself to cooking. She found a hotel room with a small kitchen attached and borrowed pots and pans from her sister. Though no domestic goddess, de Beauvoir, always more practical than Sartre, soon became proficient in cooking meals for 'the family' from whatever basics she could find in the sparsely stocked shops and markets.

She found it harder to work on an empty stomach than Sartre. He needed only a little food to survive, although to write he desperately needed tobacco. He resorted to scavenging in the gutter for cigarette ends to smoke in his pipe.

He spent a large part of the days when he was not teaching, writing in the Café Flore or the Café Coupole. All forms of heating fuel had become increasingly scarce and expensive, so cafés now had the added advantage of being places to keep warm. It was of mutual benefit for regular customers to burn their coal ration at their favourite café, and this is precisely what Sartre did. Probably one of the most genuinely socialist things he ever did.

Although Sartre and de Beauvoir chose to stay in Paris, it was a relief to escape the city occasionally to the provinces. They spent Christmas 1941, part of the following Easter and a whole month of the following summer relaxing, recuperating and reading at La Pouëze, near Angers, with their wealthy, eccentric friend, Madame Morel, who treated them to meat and eggs. Sartre first met Madame Morel when, as a student himself, he had helped tutor her son. He had soon become a favourite at the regular soirées she held in her grand apartment on the Boulevard Raspail.

As the Occupation ground on and food rationing grew ever more severe, Madame Morel proved a lifesaver to Sartre's inner circle by sending regular food parcels. Though some of the food had often gone off by the time it reached Paris, it was nonetheless gratefully received and as much of it eaten as possible.

Before visiting Madame Morel at Easter they visited Rouen and Le Havre, not least to see the damage wrought by Allied bombing. Many of Sartre's old dockside haunts in Le Havre had been blown away. They found it more exciting than scary to listen to the BBC news while Allied bombs exploded nearby. Surely the tide had to turn against the Germans soon.

This feeling was finally confirmed in November 1942 when

the Allies defeated German and Italian forces at the second battle of El Alamein in North Africa – an event that Winston Churchill brilliantly described as 'the end of the beginning'. The beginning of the end of the Third Reich came just a few months later in February 1943 when the Soviet Red Army crushed the German Sixth Army at the Battle of Stalingrad.

The month Sartre and de Beauvoir spent at La Pouëze in the summer of 1942 was a kind of convalescence following a difficult cycling trip to the south of France. It began well with Bost accompanying them. Bost's presence suited Sartre as it meant de Beauvoir had someone to go off walking and climbing with while he lingered in the town or village where they were staying to work simultaneously on *The Flies*, *The Reprieve* and *Being and Nothingness*.

As the holiday progressed, however, it became increasingly difficult to find food and shelter and they often had to sleep rough having eaten nothing. After Bost left them to visit friends in Lyon they travelled on, hardly having the strength to pedal their bicycles. De Beauvoir lost sixteen pounds and broke out in spots while Sartre collapsed from hunger and spent several days in bed. They only just made it to Madame Morel's in one piece, but worse things were happening on the Russian front.

In September 1942, back in Paris once more, Sartre favourably reviewed Camus' now cult, existentialist novel, *The Outsider*, which had been published in June. It would be a few months yet before their first meeting.

In November, in response to Allied successes in North Africa, the French free zone ceased to be free as the Germans rushed to occupy it in an attempt to defend the Mediterranean coast. The freezing cold Parisian winter that followed was even harder than the previous one. Power cuts increased while the limited supply of candles and coal diminished still further.

It was a good idea to get to the Café Flore just after it opened at 8 am to bag the warmest seats. Sartre wrote and smoked in one corner while Picasso drank ersatz coffee in another. As the perilous but dreary Occupation wore on and Paris gradually starved, the only solace was literature and art interspersed with news of the all too slow demise of the Wehrmacht.

Sartre had decided to hide *The Age of Reason* in a locked drawer until after the war. With its talk of abortion and homosexuality it would not pass the censor. As de Beauvoir later wrote in *The Prime of Life*, 'No publisher would have dared to bring out so "scandalous" a novel' (*The Prime of Life*, p. 514). He had made good progress with its sequel, *The Reprieve*. The two were destined to be published together in September 1945.

Back in the spring of 1943, Sartre's main concern, apart from finishing his philosophical magnum opus, was to have his play staged. As with *Nausea*, the actor, theatre manager and director Charles Dullin came to the rescue and rehearsals began. It was at the dress rehearsal of *The Flies* at the Théâtre de la Cité that Sartre first met Camus, when Camus introduced himself in the foyer. He struck Sartre as attractive, well-built and athletic. He was. But he was also suffering from tuberculosis.

The Flies opened on 3 June 1943. It started off well but audiences soon dwindled and it ran for only forty performances, some of them in October following the summer recess. Reviewers were fearful of commenting on the play's political content and those reviews that were written were not ecstatic. The play was much better received after the war by audiences in the USA and elsewhere.

The Flies, set in the ancient Greek city of Argos, is based on the Greek legend of Orestes. Argos, infested with flies, represents occupied Paris. Initially calling himself Philebus, Orestes returns to Argos having been sent away as a child when Aegisthus murdered his father, King Agamemnon, and married his mother, Clytemnestra. The fat bluebottles that infest the town epitomize the sin and corruption of the people of Argos and the collective remorse they suffer for failing to defend Agamemnon or avenge his murder. Orestes' sister, Electra, tells him that confession is the favourite pastime of Argos and that the endless guilt and repentance of its people is like a pestilence.

Acting against the will of Zeus, Orestes eventually kills Aegisthus and Clytemnestra. He refuses to feel any remorse for his deed and takes full responsibility for it. Rather than take the throne as the rightful king, Orestes leaves Argos, taking the plague of flies with him.

The Flies explores the key existentialist themes of freedom and responsibility through the radical conversion of Philebus the peace-loving intellectual into Orestes the warrior. Orestes resists bad faith and achieves authenticity by bravely rising to the demands of his circumstances and fully realizing his being-in-situation.

Orestes is free to choose not to choose in the situation in which he finds himself and to walk away from Argos and its troubles, but instead he chooses to act positively, to avenge his father's death and to live with the consequences of killing his mother. Unlike his unfortunate sister Electra, who falls into the bad faith of regretting her past deeds and praying for absolution, Orestes triumphs over both God and guilt becoming a true existentialist hero. He asserts his free will against the will of God revealing the limitlessness of human freedom. He takes full responsibility for his past deeds accepting that he is the sum total of all his actions. In so doing he overcomes regret: the desire to repent and the desire to be forgiven.

Sartre often developed his current ideas through both a work of fiction and a work of fact. The interplay between them always inspired him. *The Flies* and *Being and Nothingness* were written at the same time and explore many of the same themes. They even appeared in the same month, June 1943, the month in which Sartre reached his thirty-eighth birthday.

For Sartre, *Being and Nothingness: An Essay on Phenomenological Ontology* – the bible of existentialism – was the extraordinary distillation of everything his monumental intellect had read, written, cogitated, experienced and discussed for more than twenty years, but at the time there were no fanfares.

There was a war on and his vast 650-page work was, and still is, more or less unreadable to people lacking some philosophical training. Like other great works of philosophy – Hume's *Treatise*, Kant's *Critique* – it was going to have to catch on slowly as serious thinkers and academics eventually got around to reading it, absorbing it, utilizing it, commenting on it and recommending it to others. Today it is part of the canon of Western philosophy and is the work that will assure Sartre's place in the long and magnificent history of that subject.

Most of the analysis of Sartre's existentialism conducted by philosophers around the world has centred and continues to centre upon *Being and Nothingness*. Even those who for whatever reason do not like the epithet 'bible of existentialism' accept that *Being and Nothingness* is one of the cornerstones of the existentialist school of thought.

In its grand proportions and ambitions, in its structural and linguistic density and complexity, the work aspires to take its place alongside other epic, challenging, heavyweight texts of continental philosophy, such as Heidegger's *Being and Time*, Schopenhauer's *World as Will and Representation* and Hegel's *Phenomenology of Spirit*. Works that in their different ways also offer a comprehensive, integrated, holistic account of the essential features of the human condition.

Sartre's abiding question or concern in *Being and Nothingness* is more or less the same as that of his three major influences, Hegel, Husserl and Heidegger: what must be the nature of a being that has and is a relationship to the world: that is an awareness of the world and acts upon the world?

Employing the dialectical style and method of his philosophical influences as an effective means of revealing the fundamental, internal relations existing between apparently distinct phenomena, Sartre argues that the only kind of being that can exist as a relation to the world is a being that is, in itself, nothing: a being that is a negation, non-being or nothingness.

It is certainly the complex dynamics of the relationship between being and non-being, or more accurately *being-in-itself* and *being-for-itself* as Sartre calls them, that forms the core of *Being and Nothingness*. To understand these complex terms it helps to think of them, at least initially, as *the world* and *consciousness* respectively. The work develops wide-ranging descriptions of both the relationship between consciousness and the world, and the relationship between one consciousness and another, descriptions that highlight countless implications and ramifications that extend to all aspects of a person's being in the world – perception, temporality, embodiment, action, desire, freedom, anxiety, responsibility, bad faith, being-for-others, mortality and so on.

It is the sheer saturation of *Being and Nothingness* with examples, illustrations, associations, insights, suggestions and pointers that most strongly reveals Sartre's genius and makes his philosophy – his philosophical psychology – so interesting to study, criticize and develop.

Precisely because Sartre strives at every turn to highlight the diverse implications of his complex thought, the arguments in *Being and Nothingness* are somewhat convoluted and the progress of the work rather meandering. Sartre undertakes to leave no stone unturned, and to get through *Being and Nothingness*, or even significant parts of it, the reader must commit time and effort to taking a rambling but fascinating journey with Sartre as he maps out a vast and complex territory. The committed reader will eventually recognize that the book is relentless, even ruthless, in its pursuit of an overall thesis, building up into an exhaustive, unified, brutally honest and largely coherent theory of human reality.

From its exploration of the basic nature and relationship of being and non-being the book moves on to explain that consciousness *is* non-being as it is manifested at the level of what we experience. Consciousness is variously and painstakingly described as that which exists as a relationship to being rather than as a thing in itself, as a *lack* of being that strives in vain to achieve identity with itself by overcoming that lack, and as essentially intentional, temporal, embodied and free.

Sartre's thesis that people are radically free derives directly from his philosophy of mind. Each person, he argues, is a *futurizing intention*, a temporal flight from his present nothingness towards a future coincidence with himself that is never achieved. It is in that open future that defines him and at which he aims that a person is free. As essentially free, people cannot not be free. They have to continually choose who they are and what they do: and every attempt to evade this responsibility by choosing not to choose constitutes bad faith.

A major theme of the book is how consciousness, freedom and bad faith function in, and are conditioned by, relations with other people. Sartre describes the fundamental nature of being-for-others before offering an intriguingly penetrating analysis of concrete relations with others. He brilliantly describes love, hate, sexual desire, masochism, sadism and indifference, explaining what is essential to them, how they arise out of the very nature of our being in the world, and how they are intimately related to one another.

Meanwhile, as he proceeds with his main agenda of analysing these concrete relations, he offers a wealth of thought-provoking insights into the nature and significance of various Other-related phenomena such as nudity, obscenity, grace and humiliation.

The extraordinary ability to identify and describe the essential nature and connectedness of all aspects of the human condition that Sartre demonstrates throughout *Being and Nothingness* is remarkable and inspiring. Although, inevitably, there is a lot in the work that demands criticism and clarification, it is nonetheless a work of piercing insight and breathtaking intellectual creativity.

De Beauvoir had already been cycling alone for three weeks when Sartre travelled by train to central France to meet her. He nearly lost the only copy of *The Reprieve* in a storm when his bicycle blew over outside a hotel and the manuscript fell out of his saddlebag. He had to retrieve it from the gutter, dry the pages and restore certain passages that were badly smudged.

Sartre acquired a reputation for being careless with his manuscripts: but how careful could he really be? He always wrote while travelling and continually making copies for safekeeping would have been impractical. He would certainly have benefited greatly from the ease of back-up offered by modern technology. Doubtless he would also have written a regular blog on his iPad for good measure.

In the late summer of 1943, Sartre and de Beauvoir made their way once more to the comfort of Madame Morel's at La Pouëze where they heard the news that Italy had surrendered. Meanwhile the Red Army was regaining swathes of lost territory.

Back in Paris, Sartre was bitten once again by the theatre bug and decided to write another play. It took him just two weeks of frantic effort to draft *In Camera*, probably his best play and certainly his most famous. He transformed his acquaintance with Camus into a friendship by inviting him to direct the play and take the lead male role of Garcin. Camus had formed his own theatre group as a student in Algiers. Camus accepted the offer and rehearsals began, though he later withdrew. The job of director finally went to Raymond Rouleau and the role of Garcin to Michel Vitold.

Sartre was attracted to the company of people younger than himself and to rough-hewn, straight-talking, working-class intellectuals. Camus fitted the bill on all counts, being eight years younger than Sartre and a child of the Algiers slums. Before their relatively short-lived friendship foundered on the rocks of political differences and Camus, in Sartre's opinion, became vain, the two had great fun together.

The former Normalien mummy's boy and the former tough street urchin jokingly exchanged obscene stories in an effort to shock de Beauvoir, Camus' wife, Francine, and the actress Maria Casarès, who had an affair with Camus and became most famous as Death in the film, *Orphée*. On a more serious note, Sartre began writing for Camus' underground resistance magazine, *Combat*.

Sartre was soon to find an even more yobbish intellectual younger friend in the guise of the ex-convict, poet and dramatist,

Jean Genet, a discovery of the writer and filmmaker, Jean Cocteau, most famous for his novel, *Les Enfants Terribles*, and his movie, *Orphée*. Descriptions of the social world through which Sartre and de Beauvoir now moved certainly read like a Who's Who of French literature, art and cinema.

Actually, Sartre was not such a great friend of Genet – Genet was not the kind of guy you could invite to a polite social gathering. They were simply drawn to one another on the grounds that Sartre liked to study interesting characters like Genet, while Genet, as Sartre later recalled, was interested only in Genet and loved to talk about himself.

Sartre eventually published *Saint Genet, Actor and Martyr* in 1952, the second of his three published biographies of French writers. The first was *Baudelaire*, an exhaustive psychological study and character assassination of the great French poet, a work Sartre began in 1944 and published in 1946.

The world of Parisian theatre was intimate with that of French cinema and Sartre's associates arranged for him to be placed on a small retainer to write film scripts for Pathé. If he could get a script accepted he might finally be able to give up his teaching job. In late 1943, he laboured to finish *The Chips Are Down*, a rather melodramatic story about two people who become lovers in the afterlife. Unfortunately, certainly as far as Sartre's bank balance was concerned, the script was rejected, though it was finally made into a film in 1947.

Meanwhile, de Beauvoir's bank balance also took a hit when her collaborationist headmistress sacked her for corrupting a student with her radical ideas. Unperturbed, the ever-resourceful de Beauvoir soon found a job in radio and certainly had the means to go skiing at the start of 1944.

It is fascinating that although Sartre and de Beauvoir were now notable figures on the Parisian intellectual scene and on the brink of a wide and lasting fame – de Beauvoir had published her first novel, *She Came to Stay*, in 1943 – they were both poor and often hungry. The explanation seems to be that Sartre's various royalties were simply not that high at the time, largely because the war was preventing him from reaching a wider audience. He was only big in Paris. Also, as anti-bourgeois, they never invested their money and were inclined to splash it around whenever they had any, not least on helping to support their little family of friends and lovers.

Despite the ever-growing hardships of occupation, Nazis with increasingly itchy trigger fingers and the Allied bombing of its outskirts, the start of 1944 ushered in an atmosphere of celebration in Paris. The Allies were already penetrating what Churchill called 'the under-belly of the Axis' and the liberation of Paris and the rest of France was only a matter of time.

There was to be a non-Nazi future after all. An Anglo-French-American future, as well as a Russian future. Sartre celebrated by playing the buffoon at a series of drunken parties held in the large apartments of wealthy Parisians who, despite the war, loved to patronize the intellectual and artistic elite of the city. In those days, anyone who was anyone had a play to offer. At one party, Sartre performed in a play directed by Camus, and written and attended by Picasso.

Easter saw Sartre and de Beauvoir in La Pouëze once again, enjoying some much-needed rest and recuperation. They returned to Paris to find that the RAF had bombed the railway stations. The Allied advance made life ever more difficult and dangerous, and ever more exciting.

In Camera opened at the Théâtre du Vieux-Colombier on 27 May 1944. Unlike *The Flies*, *In Camera* falls short of being an implicit commentary on the political situation of the time, but in focusing on captivity and conflict generally it certainly explores themes that had a particular relevance to Parisian audiences living under Nazi occupation.

Simple in structure – one act, one scene – the play is Sartre's vision of hell. Three unpleasant characters – Garcin, Inez and Estelle – find themselves trapped in a room for evermore. They seek to justify the life they have lived and the deeds they have done as each suffers their being-for-others. To some extent relations between the three reflect the stormy Sartre, de Beauvoir, Olga ménage à trois of the mid-1930s.

The characters torture each other with personal criticisms and with the knowledge they soon acquire of each other's faults.

Being dead, they cannot change who they are and so cannot *transcend* the judgement of the Other. Garcin, for example, cannot persuade the others to persuade him that he is not a coward. Sartre had become fascinated with the question, particularly relevant during wartime, of how one decides whether or not one is a coward.

Towards the end of the play Garcin sums up its central message: 'There's no need for red-hot pokers. Hell is other people!' (*In Camera*, p. 223). This most famous of all Sartrean maxims reflects the pessimistic view expressed in *Being and Nothingness* and elsewhere that the basis of all human relationships is conflict.

The conflict off stage was reaching a climax. On 6 June 1944 – D-Day – the massive Allied invasion of France began on the beaches of Normandy. By 11 August the Americans had reached Chartres, only fifty miles from Paris. Not wanting to miss the liberation of Paris, Sartre and de Beauvoir rushed back from Neuilly-sous-Clermont. Following the advice of Camus, they had been in hiding there for three weeks after names of contributors to *Combat* were confessed to the authorities.

Narrowly avoiding the German retreat by taking side roads to Chantilly they caught a train to Paris. The train was strafed by the RAF causing them to dive for cover in a nearby ditch. Several people at the front of the train were killed. Despite fearing another attack they resumed their journey. Back in Paris they met Camus in the Flore. Interestingly, even though he was editor of *Combat*, he had not been in hiding, at least to the same extent they had. Perhaps this is not a criticism of them, but rather a criticism of Camus' lack of caution.

With the American Third Army approaching the doorstep, it was decided that Paris would liberate itself, lest history have it that Paris was liberated by the Americans. The liberation began on the 19 August 1944 and lasted until the 25 August when the German garrison finally surrendered. Certainly, the French Resistance, the French Forces of the Interior and the Free French Army of Liberation played a role in toppling the garrison, but these efforts would have been totally ineffectual without US military might to back them up and US military equipment to enable them. The French, the Parisians, did what they could when they could.

Camus had tasked Sartre to write articles for *Combat* on the liberation of Paris. He walked the streets observing events, running the risk of getting caught in the sporadic crossfire as French communist and non-communist liberators fought humiliated, fearful, vengeful German soldiers who were in part attempting to retreat and in part standing their ground.

Danger, confusion, excitement. Tricolours raised here, swastikas still flying there. Even as Allied forces began rolling into the city, German snipers picked off members of the cheering crowd. The crowd went on cheering, waving flags, hugging soldiers, dispensing rough justice to anyone judged to be more of a collaborator than the next man or woman.

Though the war in Europe would last another eight months, the grinding four-year occupation of Paris was finally over. Like all Parisians who lived through that time, Sartre had done well to survive. Through ingenuity and hard work he had also managed to thrive.

Was Sartre a collaborator? No. There is no evidence that he was a traitor or did anything to directly support the enemy occupying his country. He was certainly not a Nazi sympathizer. He cunningly avoided direct confrontation with a powerful and merciless occupying force and, like the vast majority of Parisians, appears only to have reached an accommodation with the authorities where it would have been very dangerous, even suicidal, not to do so.

Could he have done more to resist? Certainly. He could have taken greater risks, as some rash or valiant souls chose to do. He could have been even more outspoken than he dared to be, and very likely he would have been almost immediately deported or executed. He certainly took some serious risks in doing what he did. He was not the bravest, but neither was he a coward. As the cliché goes, he did his bit and lived to tell the tale. He chose to survive a fierce, murderous enemy over a considerable period of time. What would you have done? Existentialism does not imply martyrdom.

14

Political Animal

Soon after the liberation of Paris, Sartre began work on *Reflections on the Jewish Question* or *Anti-Semite and Jew*. The work was published as a book in 1946 after being excerpted in an early issue of *Les Temps modernes*. The book was inspired by Sartre's desire to address the taboo subject of French complicity in the Nazi oppression of Jews as the widely unwelcome return to France of Jews deported by the Nazis began.

Sartre argues that it is the anti-Semite who *makes* the Jew. There is no Jewish problem, only the problem of anti-Semitism. Sartre has been criticized for implying that Jewishness is nothing more than a reaction to anti-Semitism. Jewish intellectuals in particular argue that this negative definition of Jewishness signifies a lack of understanding of Jewish history and culture. Many Jews who are not Marxist revolutionaries or in pursuit of complete assimilation, object to Sartre's claim that Jewish culture, history and religion will end when social revolution makes being Jewish irrelevant.

Undoubtedly, Sartre wrote *Anti-Semite and Jew* partly because he felt guilty that he had not done more to help Jews during the Occupation. It has been argued that *all* the intense political activism that characterized the post-war Sartre was motivated by the feeling that he should have done more during the war. His political activism was, according to the philosopher, Vladimir Jankélévitch, 'a kind of unhealthy compensation, a remorse, a quest for the danger he did not want to run during the war' (quoted in Hayman, *Writing Against*, p. 182).

This is perhaps a little unfair, as Sartre certainly also had a genuine desire to use his growing influence to prevent a resurgence of fascism. He believed the best way to do this was to promote radical socialism. So began Sartre's long and difficult relationship with the PCF. They wanted to fully recruit him to their cause but he insisted upon being a freethinking 'fellow traveller'. They both naively believed that the USSR was the great hope for bringing about a worldwide socialist utopia.

Les Temps modernes, Sartre and de Beauvoir's political and literary journal named after a film by Chaplin, began life in September 1944 when its editorial committee was formed. Apart from Sartre and de Beauvoir, the committee included Merleau-Ponty, Michel Leiris, Aron, who had been in London since 1940, and Sartre's editor at Gallimard, Jean Paulhan. Being a freethinker himself and not wanting Sartre as his boss, Camus refused to join, as did Malraux.

Various disagreements regarding the precise political identity and direction of the journal, but above all a shortage of paper, meant that the first issue did not appear for nearly a year. The journal became highly influential in post-war French politics and literature, and still sells about 3,000 copies per bimonthly issue.

In late 1944 Sartre had an audience with Ernest Hemingway. The nearly great French writer was ushered into a hotel room to find the already great American writer prostrate on his bed with flu. The big man bear-hugged Sartre and called him 'a general' and they proceeded to drink a great deal of whisky. Sartre lasted until 3 am: de Beauvoir lasted all night.

Hemingway was a living piece of a country Sartre was keen to visit. He had been in love with American literature and cinema for years and needed no persuading when Camus asked him to visit the USA as a representative of *Combat*.

Sartre needed a break from dreary, war-weary Paris, perhaps from de Beauvoir too. He could have taken her with him to the USA but he did not, and he took the opportunity to have relationships with other women while he was there. Certainly, from this time onwards, their relationship began to cool, at least on his side. They would always be best friends, their intellectual and spiritual bond was unbreakable, but they were no longer in each other's pocket. Perhaps it was just a matter of maturity. Perhaps they were now more in love with their own success than with each other.

Certainly, for de Beauvoir, the cooling of her relations with Sartre meant that she directed far more of her energy towards her work. Her 1943 novel, *She Came to Stay*, was a great success, but it was all she had published of any significance by her mid-thirties. She soon made up for lost time and by the end of the 1940s had published a play, a couple more novels and her philosophical, feminist masterpiece, *The Second Sex*.

Sartre was among a small group of French journalists who took off for New York on 12 January 1945 in an uncomfortable, unpressurized, military turboprop. He enjoyed neither the journey nor the company of the other journalists but he was excited to be visiting a country that had always loomed large in his imagination. He was to spend four life-changing months there.

In many respects Sartre had a romantic view of the USA inspired by the American comic books, detective stories, novels and movies he had devoured as he grew up. For Sartre, at that time, the USA was a land of adventure where anything might happen. Its architecture, art and music represented the future. It had always provided the perfect antidote to the middle-class stuffiness of his childhood: it would now provide a welcome relief from the misery and austerity of war-torn France.

Sartre could not fail to appreciate the boldness and optimism of the USA and of New York in particular with its skyscrapers and bright neon lights. Like all far-left European intellectuals, however, he became increasingly critical of many aspects of the USA. Above all, he came to despise its interventionist, neo-colonialist, post-war foreign policy. In the mid-1940s, however, he was most indignant about the shameful and undemocratic way in which black Americans were treated by the white majority.

As his notes on the USA made during the long flight reflect, Sartre had already given the country a lot of serious thought, particularly the contemporary American literature of John Dos Passos and William Faulkner. In the 1930s, he had recommended these writers to his students, lectured on their themes and techniques and praised them in articles of literary criticism.

In *Being and Nothingness* (pp. 427–8), during his analysis of sadism, Sartre quotes at length from Faulkner's *Light in August*, a novel in which an Afro-American, Joe Christmas, is hunted down and castrated by the 'good citizens' of Jefferson, Mississippi. Faulkner's novel, with its focus on the theme of racial hatred in the USA, greatly influenced Sartre's 1946 play, *The Respectful Prostitute*, also set in the Deep South.

Through his reading, Sartre was well aware of the evils of racial segregation and inequality in the USA prior to encountering it for himself. Encountering it – witnessing two black soldiers refused a table in a dining car, for example – motivated him to become one of the first intellectuals outside of the USA to join the struggle against it.

On 16 June 1945, *Le Figaro* published Sartre's article, 'What I Learned About the Black Problem', in which he writes, 'In this country, so justly proud of its democratic institutions, one man out of ten is deprived of his political rights; in this land of freedom and equality there live thirteen million untouchables.' For Sartre, it was particularly galling that widespread, institutionalized racism should fester at the heart of a country that in other respects had so much to commend it and had done so much to further the ideals of human liberty and opportunity.

With his play, *The Respectful Prostitute*, he continued to add his voice to the voices of those who recognized that the existence of officially sanctioned racial oppression in the so-called land of the free was an indefensible, intolerable and ultimately unsustainable contradiction.

Sartre found America, or more specifically New York, disorientating at first. It was difficult to walk anywhere and there were no café-lined boulevards as in Paris. Every place on the vast grid of numbered streets seemed like every other place and the skyscrapers were so large as to be inhuman. He had barely found his feet in New York before he and the other journalists were flown by their hosts from one American city to another to view and report on architecture and infrastructure. Sartre found this boring. He wanted to find the real America, the America of people.

His key to the real America came in the form of the intelligent, attractive, de Beauvoir lookalike, Dolorés Vanetti. She worked at the Office of War Information and he flirted with her during a visit there. Fluent in English and French – a formidable woman who had been an actress in Paris – she became his personal interpreter and guide and they soon began a serious relationship.

Dolorés was not Wanda or Olga, there primarily to be toyed with and analysed by himself and de Beauvoir. Dolorés threatened de Beauvoir's supremacy, the only one of Sartre's many women ever to do so. For a time she became Sartre's number one confidante. His letters to de Beauvoir became less frequent and intimate. She was hurt, but their 'understanding' meant she had no right to seek to curtail his precious freedom or tell him he was acting like a shit.

He was equally disloyal to Camus, and sent all his best articles to *Le Figaro*. Unlike Camus' leftist *Combat*, *Le Figaro* was broadly conservative, but what it lacked in socialism it made up for in a vastly superior circulation. Sartre was not obsessed with self-promotion but like most highly successful people he was certainly not indifferent to it either. He always had one eye on the prize and he only had one good eye. Sartre's articles to *Le Figaro* from and about America, and the various responses they provoked, certainly served to place him in the spotlight at a time when the differing war fortunes of America and France made them intensely interested in one another.

On 10 March, Sartre met President Franklin D. Roosevelt and commented in *Le Figaro* on his charm and good looks: 'at once delicate and hard'. Within weeks the only American president to serve four terms was dead.

A few days after Sartre had left for America a more personal death had occurred. He was finally rid of Mancy. His stepfather was hardly the villain Sartre's childhood jealousy had painted him out to be. Indeed, Sartre had softened a little towards him during the war. They found common ground in their hatred of collaborators and occasionally Sartre even helped him wash his car. Returning to Paris in May, Sartre was finally able to resume his cherished role as mummy's boy without interference.

While he had been living it up in the USA, the war in Europe had been raging towards a close. Hitler committed suicide on 30 April 1945 and Victory in Europe was declared on 8 May. By mid-summer France was safe enough for Sartre to take his mother on holiday.

Between the Americans' first and second atomic bombings of Japan that ended the war in Asia on 14 August 1945, Sartre met up with de Beauvoir at La Pouëze. Although the bombings avoided a protracted war with a fanatical aggressor that would not otherwise have surrendered, Sartre was outraged by the

American action. It was a good subject for a play, perhaps, but instead he chose to write one about the French Resistance.

Men without Shadows concerns a group of resistance fighters who have been captured by forces loyal to the Vichy government. They await their fate: to be tortured then killed. They fear pain and death but their primary concern is to avoid exposing themselves as cowards. If they scream and beg for mercy their torturers will triumph. If they keep silent they will win a moral victory. They view the situation more as a battle of wills on a personal level than anything to do with the cause for which they are fighting.

Comparable to Sartre's 1939 short story, *The Wall*, *Men without Shadows* explores the complex psychology of torturers and tortured, executioners and condemned, and the struggle for transcendence that exists between them. It is not enough for the torturer to inflict pain or even death: he gains ascendancy over his victim only if his victim cries out, pleads for mercy or discloses information. If the tortured person endures his suffering and remains silent he has refused to be a victim, he has won the power struggle with his torturer and gained ascendancy over him.

The play also explores the situation of a person for whom others suffer torture. One character's lack of suffering excludes him from the group and makes him feel inferior. He experiences such intense guilt over his lack of suffering that he desires to be tortured himself. His own torture would remove his guilt and sense of inferiority and reunite him with those who have suffered for him. Arguably, this is Sartre once again revealing his own guilt that he did not do as much during the Occupation, did not suffer as much, as others did.

A recurrent theme in the play is the fear people have of dying without a witness and being utterly forgotten. The characters try to console themselves that they will live on in the memory of others and continue to have a being-for-others. The prisoners' fear that they will not be missed after they die gives the play its title. They fear being men without shadows, anonymous corpses that died for nothing with only their killers knowing how or when they died.

Returning to Paris at the end of the summer, Sartre and de Beauvoir discovered that they were the talk of the town. Existentialism, as the philosopher, Gabriel Marcel, had called it as early as 1943, was now famous. Earlier, they had tried to resist the label, Sartre saying that he did not know what existentialism was and de Beauvoir that her ideas 'reflected the truth rather than some entrenched doctrinal position' (*The Prime of Life*, p. 548). Resistance was useless. The label had stuck. Better to surf the wave. But why was existentialism suddenly making such big waves?

Existentialism offered the perfect antidote to the French post-war malaise. It counselled people to confront the shame and bad faith of their actions or inactions during the Occupation, to take full responsibility for them, but above all to move on from them. Rather than simply regret the mistakes of the past a person must learn from their mistakes with the aim of becoming a better, more authentic person in future.

Humankind, the little guru of existentialism preached, is a *futurizing intention*. The destiny of each of us is in our own hands. We make ourselves through our choices. We are even free to choose what is happening to us, to take it on board rather than bemoan it, to realize to the full our being-in-situation.

Sartre's time had come, the 'existence philosophy' of which he was the major exponent, with its perfect blend of realism and optimism, was perfectly tailored to the needs of the time. Existentialism did not so much capture the spirit of the time, as give the time the positive spirit it craved. Even if he could not have seen just how apt his philosophy would become, Sartre appeared as a visionary, as the prophetic leader of a group of thinkers who would take France, the whole world, into a new age where the central values would be freedom and responsibility.

Other groups were staking their claims on the future too, particularly the communists. In their view, the now spectacular failure of the far right surely meant that the future belonged to the far left. They saw existentialism as a threat to their ambitions of domination. Sartre was an upstart, an individualist, a maverick socialist who refused to join the party and toe the line.

Sartre, for his part, began to form the view that Marxism and existentialism were compatible with each other, even essential to one another if a future based on both individual liberty and social equality was to be realized. Marxists who did not understand this, not only did not understand existentialism, they did not understand Marxism.

His thinking along these lines, his constant spats with Marxist activists, many of whom, unlike him, were second-rate philosophers, eventually led him to write *Critique of Dialectical Reason*, a titanic work that makes even *Being and Nothingness* look like a pamphlet in comparison. In the *Critique*, he undertakes to synthesize existentialism and Marxism: *true* Marxism that allows room for genuine freedom, as opposed to *false* Marxism that entirely subjugates humankind to historical processes.

The Age of Reason and *The Reprieve* were finally published together in September 1945, taking existentialism to those parts that *Being and Nothingness* was too complicated to reach. The following month Sartremania seemed to reach new heights when, on the evening of 29 October, he delivered his now fabled lecture 'Existentialism is a Humanism' at the Salle des Centraux, Paris. Legend has it that there was shocked fainting in the audience when he first referred to existentialism as a humanism, a philosophy that endorses atheism and so on, but the swooning was probably due only to the dense crowd, the heat and the stale air.

The lecture was published the following year as *Existentialism and Humanism*. Unfortunately, Sartre's desire to shock and entertain his bourgeois audience at the height of his celebrity led him to distort and oversimplify some of his views and it is generally accepted that the work is somewhat unrepresentative. Sartre came to regret its publication and even rejected some of its conclusions in later writings.

Despite its faults, however, *Existentialism and Humanism* remains Sartre's most popular philosophical work. Its brevity and accessibility, its brusque and provocative style, make it an undeniably useful introduction, not only to existentialism, but also to Sartre himself as a challenging, iconoclastic philosopher. The work creates an exciting and thought-provoking first impression that often inspires people to explore the far more detailed and accurate explanation of existential phenomenology contained in Sartre's far less brief and accessible work, *Being and Nothingness*.

The third successful issue of *Les Temps modernes* was published towards the end of 1945, providing Sartre and his comrades with yet another platform from which to preach their ever more political philosophy and dispute with their increasingly hostile political opponents. Sartre was by now so pervasive a presence in Paris that there was no need for him to be there in person, so away he went again to the USA.

15

Differences

Sartre set sail for America on 12 December, on a military cargo ship that would take eighteen days to cross the Atlantic. He would not return for four months and considered not returning at all. His days as a mere schoolteacher were well and truly over. His love for de Beauvoir was not over and never would be, but his current passion was Dolorés. He felt there was nothing in particular to keep him in dreary old France and much to draw him to glamorous America.

It is hard not to feel sorry for de Beauvoir, abandoned on the eve of the Christmas holidays after all they had been through. Their shared world-view meant she was not allowed to feel sorry for herself, however, even if she was hurting. She threw herself into her work and drew solace from her own growing celebrity and the fact that Sartre was not the only interesting man in the world.

Sartre divided his time between Dolorés and the university lecture circuit. He spoke at New York, Harvard, Yale and

Princeton and then at various universities in Canada. The Canadian lectures were better paid than the American lectures but he was still often short of cash. One thing he was not short of was admirers. It was dining out with them and Dolorés and generally enjoying his fame that took all his money. His financial troubles were considerably eased when he began to receive handsome advances on productions of *In Camera* – 300,000 francs for the Broadway production alone.

In writing terms it was probably the most unproductive third of a year since his early infancy. He seemed happy to slouch around with Dolorés for a while, taking a well-earned break. He came close to marrying her and taking up a job at Columbia University. It seems to have been the language barrier above all else that drove him home. They agreed to spend at least a couple of months a year together and before the end of April 1946 he was back in France.

As honest or tactless as ever, he told de Beauvoir how much Dolorés meant to him. De Beauvoir tells in *Force of Circumstance*, the third volume of her autobiography, how she could not help asking him who was more important. His answer was evasive but de Beauvoir accepted it: Dolorés was enormously important to him but de Beauvoir was the one he was with. Existentialists realize no one has a genuine right to expect more from another person than this, and everyone should resist demanding more.

He went down with mumps and had to have his face coated with black ointment. Despite his appearance and discomfort he still received visitors to his bedside. He recovered just in time for lucrative lecture tours of Switzerland and Italy where media attacks upon the supposed corrupting influence of existentialism guaranteed him large audiences.

Although the committee of *Les Temps modernes* agreed that the journal should be left wing, opposed to the Gaullist right and so on, they could not agree about much else. Should it be more or less socialist, more or less aligned with the communists, was it correctly interpreting Marx, did it too often excuse Stalinism and argue that the end goal of socialism justifies the means of revolutionary violence?

Tired of the disagreements and increasingly uncomfortable with what he saw as the journal's naive adherence to Marxist ideology, Aron resigned from the editorial committee of *Les Temps modernes* in June 1946. He later wrote a book, *The Opium of the Intellectuals*, a title that plays on Marx's famous maxim about religion being the opium of the people. The book brilliantly argues that in post-war France Marxism became the religion of many intellectuals, including Sartre: an opium that blinded them to the benefits of capitalism and democracy and led them to defend Marxist oppression.

Sartre's relationship with Aron rapidly deteriorated long before the publication of Aron's book. The more left wing

Sartre became the more intolerant he became of views that did not accord with his own, especially if they were views that offered any defence whatsoever of the Western capitalist system. Political differences were eventually to destroy several of Sartre's key friendships. He managed to fall out with acquaintances over politics on an almost daily basis.

Part of the problem was *Les Temps modernes* itself. Like Facebook and Twitter today, it provided all-too convenient a channel to a wide audience. Sartre would get into a heated debate with someone in a café about how many communists can dance on the head of a pin. Then, in the very next issue of *Les Temps modernes*, he would publish a withering retort that irreparably damaged his friendship with that person, not least because a written rebuke, being set down in enduring black and white, always causes more offence than a spoken one.

The all-too convenient conduit of *Les Temps modernes* also tempted him to publish material that was not as well considered or written as it might have been. He was taking less time to stand back and reflect at length in order to produce work of lasting value, work equal to his best, work worthy of a great writer and philosopher.

He developed the questionable theory that it is a bourgeois pretension to craft one's prose – this from the author of *Nausea*, a stylistic masterpiece. Prose should be functional, sufficiently lucid to get the message across. To some extent, this theory provided him with an excuse to bang out too many angry, poorly structured, repetitious political polemics.

In his defence, it must be said that in the years immediately after the war he felt a sense of urgency as far as politics was concerned. The fight was on for nothing less than the political future of the post-war world. The situation was shifting and changing on a daily basis and he had, above all else, to be current. Unfortunately, his desire to be *happening* and *engaged* all too often reduced him from a philosopher and psychologist of the first order to a blustering critic of current affairs who was prepared to get into petty, destructive scraps with unworthy opponents.

Arguably, the best material he wrote during the late forties was not published until after he died, most notably, his *Notebooks for an Ethics*, largely written during 1947 and 1948. Here we see him doing some proper philosophy as he seeks to construct the existentialist ethics promised at the end of *Being and Nothingness*.

An existentially ethical world would be one where a history driven by human freedom has realized an end to the exploitation and oppression that results when one free being does not respect and affirm another. He is repeatedly tempted towards a broadly Kantian position, towards a Kantian kingdom of ends where everyone treats everyone with respect as an end in themselves and never uses them as a mere means. Yet he resists aligning himself with Kant on the grounds that an existentialist ethics cannot be based on an abstract, inflexible, a priori moral principle such as Kant's categorical imperative.

So, in advocating something similar to Kant's kingdom of ends, Sartre's ethics are somewhat Kantian. However, in wanting to make his ethics a matter of authentic responses to concrete situations, responses that depend on the authentic assessment of situations rather than upon adherence to a universal moral principle, Sartre is not a Kantian deontologist but arguably the advocate of a form of virtue ethics. Like the virtue ethics of Aristotle, Sartre's ethics is not about following abstract moral rules but about achieving one's full potential and flourishing as a free human being alongside other free human beings.

Alas, he was too busy politicking, travelling, womanizing and generally enjoying his celebrity to craft the quality moral philosophy outlined in his notebooks into a 'completed', publishable treatise. His ethics notes did, however, become a valuable resource for much of the best work he produced later on.

In the summer of 1946 he needed a new play to form a money-spinning double bill with *Men without Shadows*, so he wrote *The Respectful Prostitute*, a play about racism in America.

The play is well structured but all the characters are stereotypes. A prostitute, Lizzie, who at first does the right thing and protects a black man wrongly accused of trying to rape her, is persuaded by a smooth-talking, white senator to betray the black man in order to protect the senator's white nephew, Fred. Fred has killed the black man's black friend in a racially motivated attack, and is lying that he did it only to stop the two black men from raping Lizzie. Lizzie signs a statement supporting Fred's version of events. The play ends with another black man being lynched for the rape that did not take place and with Lizzie becoming Fred's mistress.

The Respectful Prostitute clearly highlights the violence and injustice of racism in the USA prior to the emergence of the Civil Rights Movement. It shows how racism in the USA is rooted in an ideology of white supremacy that appeals to patriotism and a distorted version of history, and how it is promoted by corruption and nepotism at the highest levels of authority. Sartre was seeking to expose what he saw as a great hypocrisy. The USA had defeated Nazism abroad in the name of liberty and democracy, yet it tolerated racial prejudice, inequality and violence on its own streets.

Lizzie represents the ordinary person caught up in this or any other unfavourable political situation. She is well meaning with an initially clear sense of justice but she is too easily influenced by the rhetoric of those with power and wealth. She ultimately fails to stand up for justice by yielding to the demands and expectations of her social superiors. She falls into bad faith, aspiring to relinquish responsibility for herself in order to become a plaything of the ruling class.

In Sartre's view, her acquiescence makes her a collaborator, as responsible in her own banal way for the racial injustices that surround her as those who actually commit the crimes. Sartre's message is revolutionary: injustice will continue until ordinary people like Lizzie find the intelligence and courage to positively affirm their freedom by resisting corrupt authority.

Around the middle of 1946 Sartre moved into the small flat his mother had purchased at 42 Rue Bonaparte. He had the biggest and best room for his study and bedroom, Anne-Marie and the housekeeper had the rest. He needed a retreat from his fame, and moving in with his mother provided that. He was forty-one years old. Lodging with his dear old mum, playing piano duets with her while the housekeeper provided regular meals, was his way of starting to settle down, just a little.

He began collecting books and soon built up a large library. Apart from a few sticks of furniture, his pipe, his pen and the suit he wore every day and replaced once a year, these books were just about the only things he ever owned.

He even took on a secretary, Jean Cau. Cau called at the flat every morning to perform a variety of duties that included answering the phone, running errands and managing Sartre's finances. His main task was to keep Sartre's appointment book, to protect his boss's precious writing time from unwanted visitors and engagements. Cau left at lunchtime to be replaced by de Beauvoir who would write in Sartre's room all afternoon. She too needed a retreat from pestering fans and friends wanting to argue about politics.

In October 1946 Sartre became a friend, or at least a drinking partner, of the Hungarian-born writer and journalist, Arthur Koestler. Koestler had become disillusioned with Stalinism as early as 1938, publishing the anti-authoritarian novel, *Darkness at Noon* in 1940, and he liked to mock Sartre and Camus' naive communist sympathies. Despite their political differences, Sartre and Camus were attracted to him on a personal level because he was the kind of hard-drinking, intellectual ruffian type that appealed to them.

During one night of heavy drinking with Sartre, de Beauvoir and Camus, Koestler, who had a reputation for violence, hit his wife, Mamaine, in the eye with a crust of bread. Sinking into a drunken depression, de Beauvoir suggested they all commit suicide by throwing themselves into the Seine from a bridge. Arriving home after dawn, Sartre had to dose himself with the stimulant, Orthedrine, in order to prepare and deliver a lecture at the Sorbonne.

Sartre, Camus and de Beauvoir fell out with Koestler after about a year over politics and his propensity for violence. One of the final straws came when Koestler threw a glass at Sartre for flirting with Mamaine. He then punched Camus for trying to calm him down. Camus drunkenly drove Sartre and de Beauvoir away from the scene in his car, weeping that his friendship with Koestler was over.

In November 1946, de Beauvoir conducted a lecture tour of Holland. Sartre met up with her there and they visited an art gallery to view the Rembrandts. De Beauvoir was starting to play Sartre at his own game. At the start of 1947 she would leave for her own lecture tour of the USA and start an intense affair with the American novelist, Nelson Algren. Sartre simply took the opportunity to invite Dolorés over to Paris. De Beauvoir met her lookalike in America before Dolorés left for France. De Beauvoir insisted afterwards that she found Dolorés thoroughly charming.

By the end of 1946 arguments over politics were starting to blow friendships and alliances apart. Camus, who had been politically engaged longer than Sartre, had started to question left-wing assumptions about the use of revolutionary violence. Camus was to grow increasingly disillusioned with communism generally as Sartre grew increasingly left wing and radical.

In December, at a party thrown by the writer, Boris Vian, and his wife, Michelle, Camus accused Merleau-Ponty of seeking to justify the Moscow Trials of 1936–8, a series of brutal purges in which Stalin used the police to wipe out opposing elements within the Soviet Communist Party and gain absolute power. When Sartre joined the bitter row in defence of Merleau-Ponty, Camus stormed out, refusing to return despite Sartre and Bost's best efforts to coax him back in from the street. Camus and Sartre's friendship still had some mileage left but it too would eventually have an equally bitter although far more public ending.

Sartre's growing interest in politics and political engagement, combined with his long-standing interest in literature, led him to write *What is Literature?*, a work that appeared in *Les Temps modernes* between February and July 1947 and the following year as a book.

The work analyses from a philosophical and political perspective the nature and purpose of writing and reading and the relationship between writer and reader. It is a political manifesto in which Sartre identifies literature as a form of social and political action, but it should also be seen as Sartre's most significant contribution to the philosophy of aesthetics. The work offers various insights into some of the fundamental questions of aesthetics: What is art? How do visual art, music, poetry and prose compare and contrast? What is the relationship between a work of art and its audience?

The art form Sartre is primarily concerned with in *What is Literature?* is prose, which he argues is radically distinct from poetry. A poet is interested in words themselves. A poem is an end in itself, language being the object of poetry rather than its instrument. Prose, on the other hand, is essentially utilitarian: it *makes use of* words. For the prose writer words should be transparent instruments unnoticed in themselves, the surpassed means by which the writer conveys his message and hits his target. It is important, he argues, for a writer to write well and with style, but the beauty of his writing should be imperceptible, a hidden force that serves the message of his writing rather than being its goal.

What, in Sartre's view, constitutes literature and sets it apart from other forms of writing, such as non-political, non-philosophical poetry or mere storytelling, is the *intention* of the writer, his *commitment* to tackling current issues and raising relevant questions. Literature, in order to be literature, must reveal and challenge aspects of the contemporary world. It must heighten the social, political, historical and philosophical awareness of both writer and reader.

Sartre is not saying poetry cannot be literature. Some poetry is literature, but it is its broadly defined political and philosophical message that makes it literature rather than its poetic form and language. Arguably, Sartre separates *message* and *form of message* too radically in *What Is Literature?* As a result, he characterizes literature too narrowly as an exclusively politico-philosophical phenomenon.

For Sartre, the relationship between writer and reader is of central importance. Without the generosity of the reader the writer cannot exist. His books do not exist as works of art that convey certain ideas unless the reader freely consents to make his books, his ideas, real by reading them. 'Reading is creation' (*What is Literature?*, p. 43).

The effect of literature on the reader should be liberating. Literature is nothing if it is not a liberating force. 'However dark may be the colours in which one paints the world, one paints it only so that free men may feel their freedom as they face it' (*What is Literature?*, p. 47).

The view of literature Sartre puts forward in *What is Literature?* is very sympathetic to Marxist theory. Nonetheless, he maintains that a writer, in his quest to liberate himself and others, should not be a slave to political ideology to the extent that he becomes a mere mouthpiece of party dogma.

By mid-1947, Sartre was under attack from all sides. Communists hated him for not being communist enough, for accusing them of dogmatism and so on, while non-communists and anti-communists hated him for being a communist sympathizer. Meanwhile, Christians and other narrow-minded, conventional moralists were condemning his existentialism as pessimistic, atheistic, self-centred, morally corrupting nihilism.

Sartre still had the constitution of a concrete elephant and generally he thrived on the controversy surrounding him. He took Oscar Wilde's view that the only thing worse than being talked about is not being talked about. Confident that he could counter all his critics in due course, he retreated to his notebooks to ponder the philosophical questions that most needed answering before he took his critics on: What is the relationship between ethics and politics? Exactly how are Marxism and existentialism compatible?

Although he was no longer a schoolteacher he kept the habit of lengthy summer holidays. In July 1947, he visited London with de Beauvoir to watch a production of *Men without Shadows* and *The Respectful Prostitute*. In August they headed north, visiting Denmark, Sweden and Finland. A few weeks later de Beauvoir returned to America and her lover, Nelson Algren.

At the start of October Sartre began taking part in a series of radio shows, *La Tribune des Temps modernes*, arranged by Alphonse Bonnafé, an old friend from his Le Havre days. The shows included contributions from Sartre and his colleagues at the journal. The theme, of course, was politics. The very first show caused outrage in the right-wing press when Bonnafé compared de Gaulle to Hitler and Sartre mocked his physique. Unlike Sartre, de Gaulle was very tall.

Sartre was challenged to a radio debate by two well-known Gaullists, who insulted him in the studio before the debate even began. Aron, who was also present, found the insults embarrassing and said nothing. He was no Gaullist but neither did he agree that de Gaulle was comparable to Hitler. Sartre took his silence as a betrayal.

Aron was one of Sartre's oldest and wisest friends but they had been on a collision course since Aron resigned from the editorial committee of *Les Temps modernes* the previous year. Hearing that Sartre felt betrayed, Aron called at his flat to smooth things over. Sartre was superficially friendly, saying that they must meet for lunch soon, but it was not to be. From the legendary apricot cocktails meeting of 1933 to this. It was all very sad. On their quest to find a politics to heal the world Sartre and his friends could not even stay on good terms with one another.

16

Crushing Camus and Genet

De Beauvoir was back from the USA by Christmas and, as ever, she and Sartre retreated to the provinces, to the tranquillity and comfort of Madame Morel's house at La Pouëze. He spent his 'holiday' writing the play, *Dirty Hands*.

The play examines the then topical subject of personal ethics within a fevered political situation. Whereas *The Respectful Prostitute* explores the intrusion of the political into the personal, *Dirty Hands* explores the intrusion of the personal into the political.

A young man, Hugo Barine, is sent to assassinate Hoederer, a leading figure in the communist party to which they both belong. A faction within the party wants Hoederer dead before he compromises and forms a coalition government. Hoederer is not an idealist but a pragmatist prepared to dirty his hands in pursuit of political goals that benefit the people.

Hugo is in bad faith for believing that his own motives in wanting to kill Hoederer are political. In truth, he desires to become a killer so that his wife Jessica, his father and members of the party will stop disrespecting him. Ironically, only Hoederer shows Hugo any respect, but Hugo kills him anyway in a fit of jealousy after Jessica – a part written for Wanda – becomes infatuated with him. Two years later the party U-turns, adopts Hoederer's policy and restores his reputation. They kill Hugo, who has undergone a radical conversion to authenticity, for refusing to help them cover up the fact that they sent him to kill Hoederer.

The most philosophically significant aspect of *Dirty Hands* is the psychological study it offers of Hugo Barine. It is, however, best known as an expression of Sartre's supposed disillusionment with communism. In fact, Sartre did not reject communism in *Dirty Hands*. He is not attacking communist ideals and aspirations as such but *all* political dogmatism that refuses to engage in reality or to compromise. The play is certainly a response to the dogmatism and arrogance of certain members of the PCF that Sartre had clashed with.

As the Cold War intensified, *Dirty Hands* was often used as an instrument of anti-communist propaganda. Sartre grew so tired of this exploitation of his play by the political right that, uncharacteristically, he paid heavy damages to have performances of it in Vienna stopped while he was attending a Marxist conference there in December 1952. As he later wrote in the newspaper *Le Monde*, on 25 September 1954, 'I do not disavow *Dirty Hands*, I only regret the way it was used. My play became a political battlefield, an instrument of political propaganda.' Largely because it has been exploited in a manner that it is hard to believe Sartre did not foresee when he wrote it, *Dirty Hands* has proved to be his most enduringly controversial play and his best-selling play in France.

In February 1948, Sartre became involved in party politics himself by helping to found the Rassemblement démocratique révolutionnaire (RDR) with David Rousset. Like his failed resistance movement, 'Socialism and Freedom', the RDR sought a middle way between the undemocratic structures of the PCF and various right-wing groups. The aim was to be both socialist and democratic. Although the meetings of the RDR were attended by thousands of people keen to hear its high-profile speakers, its actual membership remained low.

The PCF accused the RDR of being a right-wing plot and Sartre of being an agent of the USA. He was, in fact, the most anti-American and pro-Russian leading figure in the RDR, his deepest fear being that American post-war financial support would undermine European political and cultural autonomy. His enduring pro-Russian stance would be severely challenged the following year when irrefutable evidence began to emerge of the existence of Soviet forced labour camps and the terrible conditions within them.

Apart from his work for the RDR, Sartre was, as ever, wearing his fingers to the bone writing several pieces at once. Apart from his notebooks on ethics, which eventually reached 360,000 words, and a biography of the poet, Stéphane Mallarmé, which de Beauvoir claims he lost after writing several hundred pages, he was finally working on the promised third volume of *Roads to Freedom*, *Iron in the Soul*, which was completed and published the following year.

In *Iron in the Soul*, a novel that draws heavily upon his experiences as a POW, his alter ego, Mathieu, finally finds freedom and authenticity through the decisive, irreversible act of killing German soldiers rather than surrendering to them. 'He fired. He was cleansed. He was all-powerful. He was free' (*Iron in the Soul*, p. 225). In short, Sartre has Mathieu do what he himself had lacked the courage to do. We are invited to assume that Mathieu is killed when the church tower from which he is firing is seen to collapse, but rather incongruously he shows up again in Sartre's abandoned fourth volume, *The Last Chance*.

Sartre took a spring holiday with de Beauvoir in the south of France before she set off once again to the USA to continue her passionate affair with Nelson Algren. As Paris endured the heatwave of May 1948, Sartre took the opportunity afforded by de Beauvoir's absence to have a brief affair with a young American reporter who was covering the visit of Princess Elizabeth. He shared every intimate detail of the amusing little affair with de Beauvoir when she returned from America and in August they set off for Algeria where they slept in separate rooms.

Later in the year, as Sartre redoubled his efforts on behalf of the RDR, he showed himself to be less opportunistic where money was concerned than where women were concerned. An unauthorized Broadway adaptation of *Dirty Hands*, entitled *Red Gloves*, had taken $280,000 in advanced bookings. He had only to allow the production to proceed to receive a large slice of the action, but he chose instead to veto it.

Although he was utterly un-materialistic, he found money useful. It financed holidays, entertainment and hangers-on. Nonetheless, it was vital that he preserve his artistic integrity and his socialist credentials. There was already a shallow fashion for 'existentialism' that involved little more than wearing black, being moody and striking curious poses with Gitanes or Gauloises cigarettes – Sartre actually smoked Boyards Caporal. The last thing he wanted to do was invite a flood of bastardized versions of his plays – optimistic versions of *In Camera* where the characters escape that awful room.

His artistic integrity was assured in October 1948 when the Catholic Church, offended by his dangerous, atheistic, existentialist ideas, placed his entire works, including those he had not yet written, on the Vatican Index of Prohibited Books (*Index Librorum Prohibitorum*). It was a great honour, placing him on a list of many of the finest minds in history – Descartes, Voltaire, Hume, Kant, etc.

In January 1949, Victor Kravchenko, a Russian official who had defected to the West, sued the communist-backed journal, *Les Lettres françaises*, for claiming that his revelations about the existence of forced labour camps, or gulags, in the USSR were nothing more than American propaganda. Although the revelations undoubtedly served right-wing propaganda purposes, the trial made clear to all but the most blinkered communists that the gulags did indeed exist.

Sartre accepted that the gulags existed but as a diehard socialist he stubbornly held onto the view that the Soviet communist model was nonetheless preferable to the American capitalist model, as it offered more genuine hope for the future of humankind. Once again, the miserable excuse offered by the far left, which Sartre still expressed sympathy with, was that the ultimate goal of a socialist utopia justified all means of obtaining it, even if those means were comparable to the worst excesses of the Nazis.

In his unpublished notebooks, however, Sartre was questioning Trotsky's thesis that certain political ends justify violent means. He explored the idea that the use of violence is not always immoral but that its use always taints the end achieved and ultimately destroys it. Publicly, he was in a difficult position. If he unequivocally condemned the gulags and thereby the Soviet government, he would play into the hands of right-wing, pro-American capitalists. Recall that the PCF had already accused the RDR of being a right-wing plot, and him of being a US agent. Meanwhile, the Hungarian Marxist, György Lukács, in his 1949 book, *Existentialism or Marxism?*, accused existentialism, with its emphasis on individualism and personal freedom, of being a defence of capitalism.

Sartre spent the summer of 1949 with Dolorés in America's back yard, visiting Central America and the Caribbean. In Havana, he had his second audience with Hemingway. According to Hemingway's wife, who had hoped for a legendary discussion of existentialism, the two big beasts spoke like businessmen, cautiously keeping one another at a distance. Sartre was in a bad mood for most of the trip. His relationship with Dolorés was deteriorating and she found him withdrawn and irritable.

Their long affair finally ended the following year with Dolorés later accusing Sartre's circle of an implacable hostility towards her. As said, Dolorés threatened de Beauvoir's supremacy. During the autumn of 1949 Sartre began an affair with Michelle Vian, whose marriage to the writer, Boris Vian, was crumbling and ended in 1951. Michelle was an easy-going blonde who remained close to Sartre for the rest of his life. As Hazel Rowley notes in *Tête-à-Tête: The Lives and Loves of Simone de Beauvoir & Jean-Paul Sartre*, Michelle became pregnant by Sartre three times, but as she already had two children by Boris, and Sartre did not like children, she chose to have abortions (*Tête-à-Tête*, pp. 200, 256). Unlike Dolorés, Michelle knew her place in the hierarchy of Sartre's harem and did not threaten de Beauvoir's supremacy.

At La Pouëze in August he wrote for twelve hours a day every day, working on his ethics notes and his later lost biography of Mallarmé. He was soon to abandon the notebooks but he transposed much of the material into his vast psychoanalytic biography of Jean Genet. He had already published *Baudelaire* and his interest in biography was continuing to grow. He was fascinated with what it took to capture in writing the essence of an individual consciousness. Sartre's biographies of great French writers are unconventional. There is little actual, accurate biographical detail and a great deal of assumption, but they are wonderful repositories of some of his best post-war philosophical ideas and fascinating exercises in existential psychoanalysis.

On 12 October, Sartre resigned from the RDR believing that he could no longer achieve anything with it. The organization folded soon afterwards. He did it no favours by resigning, but with its stubbornly small membership it was doomed to fail anyway. He agreed with Merleau-Ponty that his time was better spent exerting political influence via *Les Temps modernes*.

Controversy over the Soviet labour camps flared up again in January 1950 after Rousset of the defunct RDR remonstrated against them in *Le Figaro littéraire*. Sartre and Merleau-Ponty denounced the labour camps in the January issue of *Les Temps modernes*, or at least reluctantly expressed regret that they existed, but otherwise defended the Soviet system. They offered the usual apologias, mainly along the lines that the end justifies the means. They argued that Soviet labour camps were not as bad as German concentration camps because they were a movement towards a classless society. They also argued that Russian workers did not find the camps intolerable because they assumed they contained various anti-social types, lunatics and men of ill will.

Sartre and Merleau-Ponty were guilty of trotting out the worst kind of dogmatic, ultra-Marxist, hyper-Stalinist claptrap. Their position was and remains shocking and contemptible, excusable only on the grounds of its breathtaking naivety. Admittedly, their position has to be seen in its historical context, but then again, many people of a more sensible left-wing persuasion, Aron and Camus for example, saw their position as utterly crass at the time.

To his credit, Merleau-Ponty, who first turned Sartre on to Marxism, became critical of Stalinism long before Sartre did. By 1952, Merleau-Ponty was ready to accept Gide's conclusion, formed as early as 1936, that Soviet communism was profoundly totalitarian and oppressive and effectively no different to fascism.

For his part, for many years to come, Sartre moved further and further to the left. He adopted the mantra that it was impossible to take an anti-communist view without being against the proletariat. As the best of his contemporaries matured and became more democratic, realistic and moderate, Sartre got into a race with himself to be as communist as possible: an ultra-communist, the chief communist.

What lay behind his ultra-communism, arguably, was the deep hatred of the bourgeoisie that he had carried with him since childhood. To the extent that he was a bourgeois himself, an educated, middle-class pen-pusher with many bourgeois tastes and refinements – he did not deny it – his hatred of the bourgeoisie was a kind of self-loathing.

What Sartre wanted to be was a man of action like Hoederer or Mathieu. What he became was a political activist of the 'major leafleting campaign' variety, brow beating the Western world with his endless public condemnations of this and that because he was too cautious, too sensible, too much a decent middle-class boy at heart, despite his advocacy of revolutionary violence, to take up arms or plant bombs. His mother would never have approved.

Sartre and de Beauvoir visited Africa during the spring of 1950 and crossed the Sahara. They were supposed to meet up with left-wing rebel groups there but failed to make contact. Sartre went down with a fever in Mali and spent the last two weeks of the trip recovering in Morocco. Meanwhile, in Paris, where he had abandoned her, Michelle was making a difficult recovery from the first of her three abortions. Sartre sought to placate her by sending orchids and tender letters.

Returning to Paris in June he found Dolorés waiting for him. He generously offered to rent her a flat, provide her with an income and put her on his rota alongside Wanda and Michelle. Insulted, she broke with him for good and returned to America.

On the 25 June, the Korean War began. There was a genuine fear that the situation would escalate and the USSR would invade France. The invasion of South Korea had clearly been encouraged by the USSR, revealing Stalin to be as much of an imperialist as the Western leaders that *Les Temps modernes* was so fond of condemning. Merleau-Ponty decided that the journal should keep quiet about politics for a while and Sartre acquiesced.

As 1951 began, Sartre started work on his reputedly favourite play, *Lucifer and the Lord*. Set in Medieval Germany, largely at a siege of Worms, this long and complex play explores all the existentialist and Marxist themes that had accumulated in Sartre's philosophy. As in *Dirty Hands*, there is the intricate interplay of the personal, social and political that increasingly fascinated him; an interplay further analysed in his biography of Jean Genet published the following year.

Goetz, the initially evil and violent central character of the play, like Barine and Genet, wants to assert his personal identity in face of the Other. Whereas, for Barine, the Other is other people, for Goetz, at least until he ceases to believe in him, the Other is primarily God. In this and certain other respects Goetz resembles Sartre's idea of Genet.

The biography and the play were written concurrently and some of the character traits identified in the biography are sampled in the play. Sartre tells us, for example, how the young Genet, an orphaned charity case, had no right to the things he was given. 'They were quite free not to give him what he was not free not to accept' (*Saint Genet*, p. 9). Everything was a gift for which Genet had to be grateful. Nothing was really his own. Hence, he stole to have a 'possessive relationship with things' (*Saint Genet*, p. 12). Ironically, only stolen things felt as though they belonged to him. They were genuine appropriations rather than charitable gifts and he enjoyed his power of ownership over them.

Goetz reveals the same key character trait as Genet when he argues that he hates to be granted anything. Goetz prefers to take what he wants, to steal it, from land to sex. 'Nothing belongs to me except what I take' (*Lucifer and the Lord*, Act 1, Scene 3, p. 74).

It emerges that Goetz also chooses to be evil in order to exercise his freedom and assert his will over the will of God. He believes that if he is sufficiently evil he will *force* God to damn him, thus revealing a limit to God's power.

The play takes an unexpected turn when Goetz is persuaded that there is nothing special about doing evil because everyone is doing it, whereas nobody has ever done only good. Goetz likes the idea of being the only person to do only good. He undergoes a radical conversion from evil, undertaking to live righteously. He lifts the siege of Worms without bloodshed and returns to his own lands. To the dismay of the neighbouring barons, he gives his lands away to his peasants. Peasants on the neighbouring lands revolt demanding the same and a war begins that costs more lives than a massacre at Worms would have done.

Darkly comical, the play generates an atmosphere of fear and hysteria as it traverses a broad range of existential and theological issues, raising questions and dilemmas about morality, love, hate, reason, superstition, salvation, damnation and the silence of God. Various Marxist themes run through the play, with Sartre, like Marx, attributing the greater part of human suffering to religious superstition and social inequality.

Sartre found writing the play and assisting with its extravagant production very demanding. His relationship with the director and the cast became strained beyond the bounds of civility. Pierre Brasseur, who played Goetz, angered by the length and complexity of the play and Sartre's imperious refusal to make cuts, sent him insulting notes: 'I'm fed up with you, Sartre, you're a cunt. I'm fed up to the teeth. I shit on your play with my piles' (quoted in Hayman, *Writing Against*, p. 268).

Despite the difficulties with its production, the play proved to be as successful as it was controversial and it ran at the Théâtre Antoine without interruption from 7 June 1951 until March of the following year.

With the play up and running, Sartre and de Beauvoir took their summer holiday. Norway, Iceland, Scotland, ending with two weeks in London. Returning to Paris, he met with contributors to *Les Temps modernes*. The journal had broken its silence on politics, moving much closer to the views of the PCF in the process. The PCF were grateful for the publicity and for a while Sartre was in their good books.

In October 1951, Camus published a book-length essay, *The Rebel*, in which he attacked the communists for slavishly supporting the USSR, for their indifference to individuals and for their conviction that the end goal of socialism justifies violent means. He even dared to criticize Hegel and Marx for encouraging the situation with their respective philosophies of history.

The book received praise from the mainstream and right-wing press but Camus awaited the verdict of *Les Temps modernes*. He waited for over six months, until May of the following year. Nobody at the journal liked the book, but nobody would volunteer to take Camus on and review it. Sartre eventually appointed his young protégé, Francis Jeanson, to the task. The fact that Sartre did not review the book himself was to be only the first thing that offended Camus.

Sitting at a café with Camus in April 1952, an embarrassed Sartre kept silent as Camus complained about hostile reviewers. Next time Sartre saw Camus he warned him that the review would not be good. Seeing that Camus was upset by the news, Sartre, always as civil towards people face to face as he was harsh towards them in writing, offered Camus the right to reply.

Even though Sartre had Jeanson tone his review down, it was unreservedly hostile, accusing Camus of indulging in naive moralizing and pseudo-philosophy. According to his lover, Maria Casarès, Camus was so depressed by the review that he lost all appetite for life. Why on earth was Camus so upset? Surely it was a no-brainer that everyone at the journal would hate his book. Perhaps he did not realize just how far to the left *Les Temps modernes* had shifted. Perhaps his vanity led him to hope that he could inspire a wholesale political conversion.

All writers receive bad reviews. It goes with the territory. If you stick your neck out you can expect to get it chopped off. The prudent thing for a writer to do is bite his lip and keep silent. If his work has any merit others will defend it. However valid a writer's response to his critics, people will only remember that he was bothered, offended. Never let them know you are bothered. Camus hesitated about replying but in the end he gave way to his hurt, to what Cohen-Solal describes as his 'lachrymose narcissism' (*Jean-Paul Sartre: A Life*, p. 332).

Driven by narcissism or not, Camus' reply, dated 30 June 1952, perfectly took the measure of the *Les Temps modernes* project. He addressed Sartre as 'Monsieur le Directeur'. Then, intending his remarks to apply to everyone at the journal, he referred to Jeanson as a 'bourgeois Marxist' who was in revolt against everything but the PCF. He wrote that he was tired of seeing himself and other old militants chastised by critics 'who have always tackled history from their armchairs'.

Sartre was incensed, above all by Camus' contemptible touchiness. His response to Camus appeared in *Les Temps modernes* in August while he was on holiday in Italy with de Beauvoir. He went for the jugular, arguing that Camus' 'dreary conceit' and 'vulnerability' had turned a political and philosophical disagreement into a matter of his 'wounded vanity'. With his first sentence, Sartre all but invited Camus to end their friendship: 'My dear Camus: Our friendship was not easy, but I will miss it. If you end it today, that doubtless means that it had to end.' And again later on: 'Who would have said, much less thought, that everything would finish between us in a petty author's quarrel?'

Clearly, a lot more poison had accumulated in the Camus-Sartre relationship than had been put there by this petty business over *The Rebel*. It simply served to bring things to a head, presenting Sartre with an irresistible opportunity to tell Camus exactly what he thought of him, to distance himself once and for all from an upstart pretender to the kingship of existentialism who had written some good stuff, as Sartre acknowledged, but who was barely capable of reading *Being and Nothingness*, let alone writing it.

In telling Camus that he should have kept his vanity out of the disagreement, the ENS über-scholar pulled philosophical rank: 'And suppose you are wrong? Suppose your book simply attested to your ignorance of philosophy? Suppose it consisted of hastily assembled and second-hand knowledge? … I don't dare advise you to consult *Being and Nothingness*. Reading it would seem needlessly arduous to you: you detest the difficulties of thought.' It was cruel stuff from a master polemicist and it is easy to feel sorry for Camus, but Camus had asked for it, which was really Sartre's main point. They were never actually the closest of friends, people who believe that they were have an overly romantic view of those times, but, as the saying goes, they never spoke again.

There is, of course, nothing the public love more than a public quarrel, and the Sartre-Camus bust-up, one of the great intellectual bust-ups of all time – whole books have been written about it – sent sales of *Les Temps modernes* so high that even reprints sold out. This most serious and Marxist of political, philosophical and literary journals was selling soap opera by the tonne and raking in the profits.

His smouldering good looks, his footballing prowess, his violent and untimely death, his genius as a novelist, have all contributed to the modern-day cult of Camus: to making him the most attractive and popular of the existentialists. But is he the greatest? It is a stupid question: it is not a competition. But people will still ask, as they ask with de Beauvoir and Sartre, who is the greatest, Sartre or Camus?

Sartre's own more subtle vanity gives us the answer perhaps: Camus did not write *Being and Nothingness* and Sartre did. And if Sartre's insinuations are to be believed, Camus never read it either. Is *The Stranger* superior to *Nausea*? I do not think so, but you may have been persuaded otherwise. Camus is not the greatest of the existentialists – he rejected the label anyway – but if it is any consolation, and it would certainly have been a consolation to him, he is certainly the coolest. Too cool for school, in Sartre's far from humble opinion.

During his bust-up with Camus, Sartre finally published his biography of Genet, *Saint Genet, Actor and Martyr*. Sartre offended Camus with his criticism while crushing Genet with his praise, or at least with his all too close attentions. The biography is a brilliant demonstration of the methods of existential psycho-analysis, the search for a person's original and fundamental choice of himself, but it is an analysis performed on a Genet largely of Sartre's own invention. Sartre had not questioned Genet about the actual biographical details of his life in any systematic way.

Genet was presented with a work of magical realism: a vast

and exotic caricature of himself that he hardly recognized, an ornate monument that buried him alive. He attempted to throw the typescript into the fire after reading it and complained that Sartre had turned him into a statue. How was a statue to find something new to say, to move on as an artist? Sartre's relationship with Genet deteriorated almost as rapidly as his relationship with Camus, and Genet soon abandoned literature, at least in part as a result of Sartre's premature tombstone.

17

Blood Pressure Rising

While in Italy with de Beauvoir in the summer of 1952 Sartre wrote the second part of his long essay, *The Communists and Peace*. Like the first part, it appeared in *Les Temps modernes*. Both parts and further parts later appeared as a book. The work argues that the Communist Party is the only hope of the proletariat. Workers raise themselves above a sub-human state only by uniting with their fellow workers and rebelling against their oppression. The Communist Party is not separate from the proletariat, an organization in its own right: it is entirely the union and directed action of the proletariat.

After delivering a lecture at Freiburg University in late 1952, Sartre had an audience with Heidegger. Like Sartre's meetings with Hemingway, the meeting with Heidegger is legendary for having taken place, not for anything that happened during it. Despite Heidegger's towering importance as a philosopher and his huge influence on Sartre, second only to that of Husserl, the meeting lasted just half an hour, insufficient time for the two philosophical giants to get to grips with deep issues relating to the current state of phenomenological ontology. There was time only to exchange pleasantries. Sartre had a train to catch.

Why did Sartre not make more of this meeting? There was no other living man for whose philosophical ideas Sartre had more respect. Perhaps he did not want to associate too closely on a personal level with a former member of the German National Socialist Party. In which case, why did he meet with him at all? Probably, the meeting was added to Sartre's Freiberg schedule by whoever organized it, and Sartre went along just to be polite. However much Sartre respected Heidegger as a philosopher, he had become a big beast himself and was not prepared to sit at anyone's knee. As Hayman notes, 'He could tolerate only dead masters' (*Writing Against*, p. 284).

Arriving at his reserved railway carriage Sartre discovered that the old Nazi had been so kind as to have it filled with roses. Sartre tossed the flowers out of the window as the train left the station.

The Communists and Peace set Sartre on a collision course with Merleau-Ponty. The problem was not primarily the content of the work, but the fact that Sartre did not consult him about it as editor-in-chief at *Les Temps modernes* until the work was at the proof stage. Merleau-Ponty had always been meticulous in running his contributions past Sartre well before they were in proof.

Merleau-Ponty began to feel that he was being increasingly circumvented by Sartre and the young communist zealots surrounding him. Since he had helped to create *Les Temps modernes* in 1944, Merleau-Ponty had worked tirelessly to control the direction of the journal, but the decisive move towards orthodox, hard-line communism that Sartre insisted on was increasingly reducing him to an overruled figurehead.

For a time, Merleau-Ponty kept quiet, avoiding confrontation, which meant that he did not engage the support of other senior figures at the journal who were equally unhappy about the way things were going.

He began to arrive late to meetings and say nothing in them – always a bad sign. In truth, though he continued to value Marx as a philosopher, he was beginning to lose faith in Marxism as a movement. He had certainly lost faith in the Soviet system, despite his vigorous defence of it in the past, and was becoming increasingly disillusioned with communism and communists generally. His interests were turning away from left-wing politics and armchair activism towards linguistics and structuralism.

In May 1953 Sartre overruled Merleau-Ponty for the last time. Following a heated exchange over the phone, during which each accused the other of abusing his power, Merleau-Ponty resigned. Already a colleague of the structural anthropologist and ethnologist, Claude Lévi-Strauss, at the Collège de France, Merleau-Ponty was soon made a professor of philosophy there: its youngest ever. He held the post until his untimely death in 1961 at the age of 53.

Recognizing the huge importance of Merleau-Ponty's major philosophical work, *Phenomenology of Perception*, published in 1945, a leading figure of twentieth-century French philosophy, Paul Ricoeur, insisted that Merleau-Ponty – not Sartre – was the greatest of the French phenomenologists.

Sartre was in Venice with Michelle in June 1953 when he heard that the USA had executed two scientists, Julius and Ethel Rosenberg, for passing information about nuclear weapons to the USSR. Sartre stayed in his hotel room venting his anger in an article for *Libération*. He had a right to be angry: not least because the evidence against the Rosenbergs was questionable. He raged against the paranoia and 'new fascism' of the USA.

Sartre's general willingness to speak out against the USA and condemn it as the most evil country in the world contrasted sharply with his deafening silences about atrocities and executions in the USSR. His lack of even-handedness was publicly criticized by the writer, François Mauriac, winner of the 1952 Nobel Prize for Literature.

A month later in Rome Sartre wrote *Kean, or Disorder and Genius*, a play adapted from the 1836 romantic melodrama, *Kean*, by Alexandre Dumas. The play was not only Sartre's least political work during the Cold War period, but the least political of all his plays. 'To the devil with politics!' (*Kean*, Act 2, p. 34). It is probably the most cheerful thing – the only cheerful thing – that Sartre ever wrote, though the lightness of touch is more attributable to Dumas than to Sartre.

Sartre's play largely preserves the farcical plot and witty, comical tones of Dumas' original. The play opened on 14 November at the Théâtre Sarah-Bernhardt and was a great success. As ever, Wanda, who played the beautiful young heiress and actress, Anna Danby, was grateful for the work.

For Sartre, as for Dumas, the play is primarily a study of the character of the great English, Shakespearean actor, Edmund Kean, a womanizing alcoholic whose intense and turbulent personality spilled over into his brilliant performances of Shakespeare's tragic heroes. Kean does not know who he really is, just as the young Sartre did not know who he really was until his decision to write defined him as a writer.

Kean suspects that he is nothing more than the parts he plays, that even when he is not acting on stage he is playing the part of Edmund Kean the great actor. 'I am nothing, my child. I play at being what I am' (*Kean*, Act 2, p. 51). Kean plays the part of Hamlet or Kean just as the Prince of Wales plays the part of the Prince of Wales. Sartre's view that people can only ever play at being what they are, a view emphasized repeatedly in *Kean*, was first put forward in *Being And Nothingness*.

Kean re-visits the purely existentialist, pre-Marxist concerns of the early Sartre, exploring once again issues of personal identity, bad faith and authenticity as it highlights the relentless, free, angst-ridden transcendence of being-for-itself. But it is more than a mere recapitulation, a harking-back. It significantly advances Sartre's grand biographical-psychoanalytical project, his sustained attempt to provide a comprehensive answer to his most abiding philosophical question: 'What is it to be a person?' This project had already produced *Baudelaire*, *Saint Genet* and the lost *Mallarmé*, and would go on to produce *Words* and his vast biography of Gustave Flaubert, *The Family Idiot*.

No sooner did Sartre return to Paris from Rome than he left again, this time for the Netherlands and Germany, where he and de Beauvoir visited the remains of his old POW camp. It was his third holiday in a row, but Sartre's holidays were always working holidays where sightseeing was fitted in around his demanding writing schedule. It seemed that Paris was so full of politics and self-generated controversy, so full of distractions, that he needed to be away from it to work.

In 1953 he started work on his autobiography, *Words*. His original idea was, of course, to write a huge tome in at least two volumes, but the end product was to be as short and concise as it was rich in philosophical and psychological insights. *Words* would not be published for eleven years. In that time, as he had done with *Nausea*, he painstakingly polished it to perfection.

Such attention to detail is unique in the writings of the angry, restless, impatient, post-war Sartre and flies in the face of his theory that it is a bourgeois pretension to craft one's prose. *Words*, like *Nausea*, is a masterpiece, arguably Sartre's only post-war masterpiece, a tantalizing glimpse of what he might have written had he valued quality over quantity.

But who are any of us to criticize the man who wrote *Nausea*, *Being and Nothingness*, *In Camera* and *Words*? Everything else is a bonus. Sartre owes us nothing. And in defence of the *quantity*, even if much of it is not as well written and edited as it could have been, it is nonetheless so rich in profound insights that it continues to this day to open up many new territories of intellectual enquiry. Even working as hard and as fast as he did, Sartre's life was barely long enough for him to reveal the extraordinary breadth of his thought.

At the beginning of 1954 Sartre was busy denouncing proposals for a European Defence Community (EDC). Under pressure from the USA, a treaty had already been signed between France, Italy, West Germany and the Benelux countries approving a pan-European military force as a bulwark against the Soviet bloc. Sartre was opposed to the EDC because it bound France to the capitalist USA and set it in opposition to his beloved USSR.

Fearing the rearmament of Germany and the erosion of French sovereignty, the French Parliament eventually rejected the plan in August 1954. Also, the death of Stalin in March 1953 and the end of the Korean War a few months later reduced demand for the EDC by reducing fears of a Soviet invasion of Western Europe. The role of the proposed EDC was to some extent taken on by NATO.

Sartre condemned the proposed EDC at a conference of East and West writers in Belgium in February. At the conference he met the famous German Marxist poet and playwright, Bertolt Brecht, who was there to condemn American nuclear weapons testing in the Pacific. The upshot of the conference, apart from formal condemnations of various Western as opposed to Eastern political shenanigans, was a formal proposal to have a similar but bigger writers' conference at a later date. Sartre also received an invitation from a group of Russian writers to visit the USSR in May.

In April 1954, eighty-eight pages of *Les Temps modernes* were given over to the third part of *The Communists and Peace*, in which Sartre explored the history of the French working-class movement from the French Revolution onwards and the nature and development of proletarian collective consciousness. He carried out extensive research for the essay, even reading books on nineteenth-century agriculture.

Overwork fuelled by amphetamines and other stimulants, late nights, lack of sleep, sleeping tablets, smoking, drinking, rich food, courting controversy and a lack of regular physical exercise were all combining to give Sartre high blood pressure. As ever he was working too hard and playing too hard, living like an overexcited student in his early twenties determined to make the most of his crazy student life. It was no way for a man in his late forties to behave: then again, perhaps it was.

Sartre's existentialism supports the view that as death is a non-event that one does not even experience for oneself, it is the life in one's years that count, not the years in one's life. His doctors recommended rest but Sartre had no concept of rest, so instead he set out for Moscow at the end of May, addressing a Berlin meeting of the Peace Movement on the way.

His Russian hosts gave him no time to explore the country for himself, no time to meet the proletariat on his own terms. He was subjected to an exhausting itinerary. Formal visits to factories, universities and palaces of culture. A train journey to Leningrad and a flight to Uzbekistan. Banquets with copious amounts of wine. Countless vodka toasts. All rounded off with an evening at the ballet. He ended up spending ten days in a Moscow hospital suffering from hypertension and alcohol poisoning.

Sartre felt his trip to Russia had been a *diplomatic* success. It was good to forge positive links with communists in the heartland of communism. He did not, however, particularly enjoy the trip, where he was constantly the hostage of hosts obliged to act in accordance with the strict requirements of the authorities.

Returning to Paris on 24 June 1954, he gave predictably glowing reports about Russia to the press: the people enjoyed complete freedom of speech, the individual and the collective were in complete harmony, there was ceaseless social progress and so on.

He submitted these reports, full of pro-communist platitudes and generalities, largely to save face before a French press keen to know what France's arch-communist had made of Russia. Two decades later he admitted that they were largely written by his secretary, Jean Cau, and that in truth he was not filled with enthusiasm by what he saw and had many reservations:

> After my first visit to the USSR in 1954, I lied. Actually, 'lied' might be too strong a word: I wrote an article – which Cau finished because I was ill – where I said a number of friendly things about the USSR which I did not believe. I did it partly because I considered that it is not polite to pour shit on your hosts as soon as you are back home, and partly because I didn't really know where I stood in relation to both the USSR and my own ideas.
>
> (*Situations*, Vol. 10, p. 220)

He was simply not prepared to give his enemies and his detractors the satisfaction of so obvious an 'I told you so' moment. Not least, in 1954, his Marxist view that the USSR offered the best hope of realizing a worldwide socialist utopia was too deeply held *philosophically* to be undermined by a single, short visit, ten days of which were spent in hospital.

As he had done the previous summer, he travelled to Italy with Michelle. He was still exhausted from his Russian adventures and found it difficult even to write. After several positive meetings with the Italian Communist Party – he always found Italian communists easier to get on with than the PCF – he returned to Paris only to set out again immediately with de Beauvoir on a tour of Germany and Austria. At the start of the tour he could do little more than sit slumped in his hotel room, utterly exhausted and unable to work. As the trip progressed, however, he recovered his characteristic strength and resumed his long-standing practice of writing and sightseeing.

In February 1955, having recently taken on the vice-Chairmanship of the Franco-Soviet Association, he made a speech at their commemoration of the Victory of Stalingrad. He flattered the Soviets by emphasizing the decisive contribution the Battle of Stalingrad had made to the defeat of the Nazis. Meanwhile, he downplayed the contribution made by American and British forces. Sartre had become nothing if not predictable in his anti-Western sentiments and his hackneyed socialist determination to portray the USA as the Great Satan.

In his hatred of the USA Sartre was typically socialist, in his ingratitude towards those who had saved France from the Nazis he almost seemed to share in the wounded pride of a nation ashamed that it was unable to liberate itself. In his view, if the Americans had made some small contribution to the liberation of France it was only for their own selfish, imperialist purposes.

18

The Ghost of Stalin

In early 1955, alongside tinkering with his own autobiography, Sartre started yet another biography of a French writer. This time the subject was Flaubert. Over the coming years the project would mushroom into his longest work, *The Family Idiot*, one of the most ambitious attempts ever made by one person to systematically understand another.

'The Flaubert', as he nicknamed it, eventually became an almost all-consuming project, but in early 1955 Sartre still felt the need to dash off another play. With a play in mind, he travelled by car to Marseilles with de Beauvoir and her new lover, Claude Lanzmann. Over seventeen years de Beauvoir's junior, Lanzmann, a film director, writer and journalist, became chief editor of *Les Temps modernes*, a post he still held when this book was written.

The play Sartre wrote while on his working holiday in the south of France was *Nekrassov, A Farce in Eight Scenes*, a not particularly subtle though at times genuinely amusing satire. Peopled with caricatures, the play lampoons the methods and machinations of the French, right-wing, pro-capitalist press during the Cold War. Sartre saw France as suffering from the same anti-communist paranoia as the USA, an atmosphere in no small part whipped up by the media.

The play is to some extent a comment on the anti-communist McCarthy witch-hunts that had recently taken place in the USA, although Senator Joseph McCarthy is mentioned only once. 'Here, read this telegram. It's from McCarthy, offering me an engagement as a permanent witness' (*Nekrassov*, Scene 5, p. 222).

The central Marxist message of the play is that throughout the Western world the popular press is owned and controlled by capitalists for the purpose of preserving and promoting capitalism. Inciting fear of communism, or any other non-capitalist ideology, helps to sell newspapers and to create a sense of collective identity and purpose in face of a common enemy.

The masses are persuaded that they are better off and better protected under their system of government than are people who live under alternative systems. One character points out that to the workers of Billancourt fabricated stories in the right-wing press about the terrible conditions in Russia mean: 'Leave capitalism alone, or you will relapse into barbarism. The bourgeois world has its defects but it is the best of all possible worlds. Whatever your poverty, try to make the best of it, for you can be sure you'll never see anything better, and thank heaven that you weren't born in the Soviet Union' (*Nekrassov*, Scene 5, p. 232).

For Sartre, as for Marx, it is simply a part of the *ideology* of the popular press that its primary function is to tell the truth. In reality, its primary function, apart from maximizing circulation, is to preserve the political and economic order that most benefits the kind of wealthy, powerful people who own newspapers. Exaggeration and lies further this end at least as much as telling the truth.

Stripped of the ideology it perpetuates, that truth telling and reasoned argument are sacrosanct, the popular press is revealed as shaping the opinions of the masses through its relentless appeal to their fear, hatred, lust, envy and conceit. The popular press enables the ruling class to shape and define the social and political values of the masses to such an extent that the masses become incapable of distinguishing truth from lies, reality from appearance.

The play, which premiered on the 8 June 1955 at the Théâtre Antoine, outraged the French press, and was slated by all but the most left-wing newspapers. Many journalists felt betrayed by Sartre, a journalist himself. They felt the philosopher-playwright was talking down to them, questioning their competence and above all their integrity. Hostile reviews did nothing for the popularity of the play and it was pulled after just sixty performances. Once again there had been a role for Wanda.

Michel Vitold, who played the swindler, Georges de Valéra, in *Nekrassov*, had played Garcin in the original production of *In Camera* in 1944 and again in 1946. Following the demise of *Nekrassov*, Vitold decided to revive *In Camera* for a third time. To play Estelle he chose Evelyne Rey, the stunningly attractive sister of de Beauvoir's lover, Claude Lanzmann.

Sartre, now fifty, became one of Evelyne's lovers. According to the writer and singer Shusha Guppy, who was part of their social circle, Sartre was always very grateful for whatever sex Evelyne, twenty-five years his junior, was prepared to have with him.

In the same month that *Nekrassov* premiered, Merleau-Ponty published a book, *Adventures of the Dialectic*, a critique of Marxism with a whole chapter dedicated to attacking what he called Sartre's 'ultra-Bolshevism'. De Beauvoir made Sartre's initial response for him in her essay, 'Merleau-Ponty et le Pseudo-Sartrisme'. She argued that the Sartre Merleau-Ponty was criticizing, not only in *Adventures of the Dialectic* but also in his earlier work, *Phenomenology of Perception*, was a Sartre of his own invention: a pseudo-Sartre.

Despite their differences, Sartre had great respect for Merleau-Ponty as a thinker. He took Merleau-Ponty's key criticisms on board and eventually responded to him and others in his closely related works, *Search for a Method* and *Critique of Dialectical Reason*, first published in 1957 and 1960 respectively.

At the end of June 1955, as he celebrated turning fifty, Sartre travelled to Helsinki for a conference of the Peace Movement. Advised that the Soviets wanted better relations with the West, Sartre spoke of the need for cooperation between the USA and the USSR. At the conference the idea was floated that Sartre and de Beauvoir visit China.

Sartre and de Beauvoir arrived in China on 6 September and spent eight weeks touring the country under the protection of government minders who made sure there was no informal contact with the people. The Chinese had no real idea who they were and Sartre was taken to be a biographer of the Russian poet and champion of the peasantry, Nikolay Nekrasov. Their most historical moment came when they took tea with the Chinese leader, Mao Zedong. Sartre was disappointed that there was no substantial conversation.

Sartre and de Beauvoir praised efforts made by the Chinese communist regime to eradicate inflation, poverty and anarchy, making no mention of the millions who had died in the rural and urban purges of 1946 onwards. They were not quite so naive as to believe China was all sweetness and light but all negatives were excused on the usual grounds that the end justifies the means. Communism was clearly taking China towards a bright future. Mao was soon to order China's 'Great Leap Forward', a great leap backwards economically and socially that cost between twenty and forty million lives.

Meanwhile, France had growing problems of her own. The Algerian War of Independence had been going on for a year when Sartre and de Beauvoir returned from China. A small white minority of French Algerians ruled over a huge majority of Arabs who had little economic power and few legal rights. Led by the Front de libération nationale (FLN) the Arabs had risen up against their colonial oppressors.

The conflict, which lasted until the early sixties, was both a civil war and a war with France. It shook both countries to the core. Algeria finally gained independence from France in 1962 after a referendum showed that over 90 per cent of the French electorate were in favour of letting Algeria go. The referendum was required as Algeria was politically and legally an integral part of France.

Sartre and *Les Temps modernes* had criticized French colonialism in Africa before the Algerian War began. At the end of 1955 and the start of 1956, Sartre spoke at protest meetings in Paris where he condemned France for its nineteenth-century style imperialism and expressed his wholehearted support for Algerian independence. As the decade progressed, these sentiments were increasingly echoed in the pages of *Les Temps modernes*. It was not long before Sartre and *Les Temps modernes* were also condemning Anglo-French imperialism in Egypt as the Suez Crisis began. So much to condemn, so much ink to condemn it with.

Camus, meanwhile, damaged his reputation as a radical and fell further out of favour with Sartre by dithering over Algeria. A French Algerian himself, Camus criticized but refused to condemn French rule there, holding out unrealistic hopes of a peaceful compromise between French Algerians, Arabs and Berbers. Naive though his desire for reconciliation was, it helped to win him the 1957 Nobel Prize for Literature. The Nobel Committee praised him as a writer whose 'clear-sighted earnestness illuminates the problems of the human conscience in our times'.

In March 1956, the attentions of several women including the beautiful Evelyne Rey not being enough for him, Sartre began an affair with a nineteen-year-old Jewish Algerian, Arlette Elkaïm, after she sought his advice on her philosophy dissertation. Despite or because of the huge age gap the relationship endured.

They became great friends, travelling widely, and in 1965 Sartre adopted her. He needed, as he said, someone to push him in his wheelchair when he was old. After he died in 1980 Arlette Elkaïm-Sartre inherited his estate, managed the posthumous publication of various works and generally sought to over-protectively control his legacy.

At the end of March, Sartre attended a conference in Venice aimed at enhancing relations between Eastern and Western intellectuals. Perhaps in an effort to enhance relations between

Western and Western intellectuals, Merleau-Ponty was given the seat next to him. Arriving late, Merleau-Ponty touched Sartre on the shoulder and smiled. Sartre smiled back. Several years of acrimony were not suddenly forgotten, but it was a reconciliation of sorts. They spent some time together outside the conference hall, though always in the company of others, their interactions friendly but awkward.

Within the hall, the two philosophical heavyweights treated the audience to several erudite exchanges. With his biography of Flaubert in mind, Sartre argued for an integration of Marxist and psychoanalytical perspectives for the purpose of better understanding the individual. Merleau-Ponty retorted by reminding Sartre of Sartre's view that psychoanalysis is a bourgeois ideology. Sartre agreed that it is but that it could be transformed from a bourgeois ideology if integrated with Marxism according to a method he himself was developing.

Before heading off on a very long summer holiday in two cars with de Beauvoir, Lanzmann and Michelle, Sartre finished writing a screenplay version of Arthur Miller's play, *The Crucible*. True to form, Sartre added a strong theme of class-conflict to Miller's story of the Salem witch trials, an allegory of McCarthyism. Sartre received 6,000 francs for his troubles, which doubtless helped pay for the holiday.

After visiting Venice and Belgrade, the four drove down into northern Greece. De Beauvoir and Lanzmann then headed off to Athens while Sartre and Michelle drove all the way to Rome. Sartre was not the greatest philosopher who ever lived but he was surely by far the best travelled. De Beauvoir and Lanzmann joined them in Rome before Lanzmann headed back to Paris. Sartre, de Beauvoir and Michelle then lingered in Rome until late October.

Following his return to Paris, Sartre finally spoke out against the USSR in early November 1956. Since Stalin's death there had been a progressive thaw in East-West relations under the rule of his successor, Nikita Khrushchev. To the amazement of the whole world, Khrushchev, speaking at the Twentieth Congress of the Soviet Communist Party in February 1956, denounced the dictatorship of Stalin and condemned his 'bloody crimes'. The USSR began signing various trade deals and in April Khrushchev even made a ten-day visit to Britain. The PCF were, to say the least, cautious about what they saw as a faction within the Soviet Communist Party cosying up to the capitalist West.

The removal of Stalin's iron grip and Khrushchev's perceived softness led to uprisings in several of the 'satellite' countries occupied by the USSR since the end of World War II. In the summer of 1956, there were serious disturbances in Poland and in October the Hungarians revolted against their Soviet-backed leaders. Soviet forces invaded Budapest on 4 November and within days brutally crushed the Hungarian Revolution. East-West relations rapidly refroze.

Noting that Hungary had been a member of the Axis powers during World War II and had participated in the invasion of the USSR, the PCF described the Hungarian Revolution as a foreign-backed fascist coup and applauded its defeat. Outraged by this insulting characterization of a popular uprising, Sartre gave an interview to *L'Express* in which he criticized the position of the PCF and reviled the brutal Soviet intervention as 'a crime'.

Although Sartre mainly blamed Khrushchev for mismanaging the regime he had inherited from Stalin, he predictably directed some of his venom towards the USA for interfering with the development of communism in the satellite countries of the USSR. Sartre was distancing himself from the USSR and finally ending his stormy relationship with the PCF, but he was not condemning communism. He made a point of expressing his continued support for communist ideals and for honest communists everywhere before resigning from the Franco-Soviet Association.

Sartre's newfound freedom and honesty was reflected in the pages of *Les Temps modernes*, which for five years had given its unqualified support to the PCF. Rather than write yet another instalment of *The Communists and Peace*, he wrote a powerful article, 'The Ghost of Stalin', in which he finally confronted truths he had long evaded in an effort to comprehend the causes and consequences of the Hungarian uprising. The Red Army, he argued, was not oppressive, but Khrushchev's Kremlin had made it look oppressive.

19

Corydrane Creations

Where Sartre's political activism was concerned, 1957 saw a shift in emphasis from communism to anti-colonialism. Having finally lost patience with the USSR and the PCF, he looked increasingly to the south, to French atrocities in Algeria, accusing the French people of denial and complicity. When he looked to the east it was to support the satellite countries of the USSR, particularly Poland. He was on good terms with Polish intellectuals in Paris and in January 1957 he travelled to Poland to watch the Polish premiere of *The Flies*.

During a decade of pondering and promoting Marxism, he had come to the conclusion that it needed to be updated if not radically revised. He, of course, was just the man to do it. In becoming far less the communist activist, he became far more the Marxist intellectual, throwing himself into the most ambitious project of his philosophical career.

Marxism, he insisted, was the dominant philosophy of the

age, but in its present form it was focused on the collective, on 'humankind', and had little to say about the individual people who comprised the collective. Marxism required radical modification in order to be able to absorb philosophies of the individual such as existentialism and psychoanalysis; indeed, the *existential psychoanalysis* Sartre had already developed in *Saint Genet* and elsewhere. He had suggested as much to Merleau-Ponty at the Venice conference in the spring of 1956.

In *Search for a Method*, which appeared in *Les Temps modernes* in the autumn of 1957 and again in 1960 as the book-length preface to *Critique of Dialectical Reason*, Sartre details the 'regressive-progressive' method of reasoning by which an existentialist-Marxism may seek to understand individual people, history and the *relationship* between individual people and history.

The regressive phase of the method involves an analytical/psychoanalytical investigation of a person, while the progressive phase involves synthesizing the results of this analytical/psychoanalytical investigation with the results of a sociological investigation into the economic, political, historical and cultural contexts of a person. The regressive-progressive method aims at understanding a person as an existential whole, as a *totality*, as a thinking, feeling being who exists in relation to a range of interconnecting contexts which they are shaped by and which they in turn shape.

Search for a Method set the agenda for the two vast works that were to follow it: *Critique of Dialectical Reason*, in which the ambitious revision of Marxism is actually undertaken, and *The Family Idiot*, in which the 'regressive-progressive' method is applied to the life of Flaubert in an effort to *totalize* him, to comprehend him as a totality, as a contextualized, existential whole.

Sartre spent the summer of 1957 in Rome and Capri with Michelle, all the while continuing to develop his grand post-Marxist theory. Generally, he was socializing less and less. Absorbed by pure philosophy as he had not been since he wrote *Being and Nothingness*, only the Algerian struggle for independence was allowed to impose significantly on his time.

At the end of 1957 he testified at the trial of Ben Sadok, who had assassinated a former high official of the Algerian assembly. He argued that Sadok had not committed an act of terrorism but a political murder. Partly thanks to Sartre's intervention, Sadok was sentenced to life imprisonment rather than death. Sartre was, however, annoyed with himself afterwards for having given the jury the impression that he, Sartre, disapproved of terrorism.

In February 1958, Henri Alleg published *La Question*, a graphic account of the use of torture in Algeria by the French authorities. There was growing support for Algerian independence among ordinary French people and Alleg's book became a bestseller. Sartre reviewed the book in *L'Express* magazine in March, deliberately dwelling on the grim details and roundly condemning the French Government for their weakness in failing to uphold human rights and justice in Algeria.

The French Government revealed the extent of their growing desperation over the Algerian crisis when they prevented the publication of Sartre's review by having the police seize all the copies of the magazine. An attempt was made to publish the review as a pamphlet but that was seized too. The publicity generated by the seizures benefited the pro-independence movement far more than the publication of the review would have done. *Les Temps modernes*, as outspoken as ever, had already been seized the previous year in both France and Algeria. In Algeria in 1956, it was suppressed no fewer than four times.

Sartre was determined to modify and fuse the two mighty worldviews of Marxism and existentialism in his *Critique of Dialectical Reason* or die trying. It was a mammoth undertaking even by his standards and he knew it. He was already in his early fifties and not in the best of health. He lacked the time and the energy required for such a time-consuming and exhausting project.

The solution was Corydrane tablets, a mixture of aspirin and amphetamine. Legal and widely available in the 1950s, these pep pills were declared toxic in the early 1970s and withdrawn from sale. The recommended dose was a couple of tablets a day. Sartre crunched them constantly as though they were sweets or nuts, sometimes taking ten or even twenty at a time.

The aspirin took care of any aches and pains that might interrupt his concentration, while the amphetamine further increased his considerable work rate and stretched time as he perceived it. Speeding out of his mind, deeply intoxicated yet hyper-lucid, he had no sense of having to form his ideas before he wrote them down. He was already in possession of them and it was just a matter of transferring them to paper as fast as he was physically able. The speed at which he could write – and he could write extremely fast – was the only limiting factor. The act of writing itself became synonymous with thinking about and analysing what was already in his head in unanalysed form. 'Writing consisted of analysing my ideas; and a tube of Corydrane meant: "these ideas will be analysed in the next two days"' (*Conversations with Jean-Paul Sartre* in, de Beauvoir, *Adieux: A Farewell to Sartre*, p. 319).

Alongside Corydrane, he also took advantage of a tube of Orthedrine a day, the feel-good, creativity drug he had favoured for years. Meanwhile, the forty, smelly, unfiltered, high-tar Boyards cigarettes he consumed every twenty-four hours were supplemented by several pipes of the strongest black tobacco. His pep pill and nicotine intake was copiously lubricated with coffee, wine, whisky and vodka. It all served to fuel the engine and drive him ever on. He wrote almost as fast as the average reader reads, ink-strewn pages piling up around him and falling to the floor to be picked up later, much later, when he had half a second to spare.

When he finally stopped writing he was so severely over-stimulated he was unable to keep his body still. His arms flailed about and he paced so much on de Beauvoir's carpet that he wore a hole in it. He was a speed freak. Speed renders the tongue hyperactive, even when one is not talking, and at one point he wore all the skin off the tip of his. A nightly, near overdose of sleeping tablets was the only possible way for him to come down from all the uppers and grab a few hours of rest.

What a marvellous, monstrous, fascinatingly hideous spectacle he must have made. A small, ugly bundle of intellectual and physical energy, likely to self-destruct at any moment, manically pushing himself beyond all reasonable limits of mental and bodily endurance in order to feel ever more intensely what he called 'the speed of my soul' (*Words*, p. 154). He was a hungry ghost striving to fill the void within himself by internalizing the entire world. For him this meant trying to capture and explain the entire world, the entire human condition, in an all-embracing script.

It is a miracle that he did not kill himself, that he did not force his blood pressure into giving him a fatal stroke. But the fact is he did not kill himself. Perhaps he was just too motivated to die, moving too fast for death to catch him. Perhaps the Holy Ghost really had commissioned a long-term work from him and was giving him time to complete it. He trusted to the longevity of the Schweitzers, ignoring the fact that he was now considerably older than his father had been when he died, and continued to run his big engine at full throttle whenever possible.

It was not always possible. At times he would fall into a trance halfway through a meal or a conversation, then suddenly snap out of it again. At the opposite extreme, he would suffer brief periods of intense agitation bordering upon frenzy, then suddenly regain his composure. Strong as he was, he suffered dizzy spells and was periodically ill with chronic hypertension or congestion, or both. His doctors prescribed rest: he self-prescribed more Corydrane. When he was really ill he would cut down on everything, proud of his will power and common sense, but as soon as he felt slightly better he would immediately pump himself up to the max once more.

In this manner, in this state, he made rapid progress with the *Critique* as 1958 advanced towards the summer.

On 31 May, he met the legendary Hollywood film director, John Huston, who asked him to write a screenplay about Freud. Addicted to writing – the drugs really served to facilitate that addiction – he readily agreed, despite already being snowed under with work. His enthusiasm was helped by the fact that Huston happily advanced him $25,000. As we know, he always liked to work on two or more projects at once, and he was pushing himself so hard generally that the screenplay hardly seemed to add to his workload. Besides, he was already in the business of appraising psychoanalysis as one of the key ingredients of the *Critique*.

Michelle translated a biography of Freud for him and he sped reread Freud's, *The Interpretation of Dreams*. He thoroughly enjoyed recreating the richness of Freud's Viennese world. He had long intended to write a work about Freud. The detailed, carefully crafted screenplay he finally produced is yet another of his psychoanalytic biographies: a thorough psychoanalytic investigation of the founder of psychoanalysis himself. The work is now available as a book, *The Freud Scenario*.

Sartre identified with Freud personally. They were both anti-bourgeois, both intent upon subverting bourgeois values, both workaholic druggies. The screenplay-biography was easy work compared to writing the *Critique*, though what he produced would prove to be far too long and intellectually heavy for Hollywood. At the end of the year he sent Huston a prolix synopsis that even included camera and costume directions.

Sartre spent mid-June to mid-September 1958 in Italy, first with de Beauvoir and then with Michelle. Rome had become by far his favourite 'holiday' retreat. He tried to keep up his creative momentum by starting another play, *The Condemned of Altona*, but found progress difficult. He was trying to take a break from the Corydrane but without it he felt tired and uninspired, as though half asleep. He lapsed and took the drug but found, as ever, that speeding did not help the kind of *creative* writing required to produce a play.

Battling against the mid-summer heat of Rome, stuck in his hotel room with the air-conditioning running full blast in the hope that cold air might induce some level of concentration, he managed to outline *Altona* and write the first part. Despite the opening night being set for October, however, he was unable to complete it. He shifted back to studying Freud, which he found easier and more enjoyable.

Returning to Paris on 16 September, exhausted and feverish, he wrote the first of three articles attacking de Gaulle that he had agreed to submit to *L'Express* ahead of the 5 October referendum on the new French constitution. A marathon twenty-eight-hour stint, in which he detailed the reasons for the failure of the Fourth Republic, was followed soon after by a twelve-hour stint that made him appear as though he had gone deaf and blind. Yet somehow he still managed to attend an anti-Gaullist meeting and make a speech. It emerged on the 20 October that he had a liver infection.

Despite Sartre's campaigning efforts, de Gaulle was greatly strengthened when the referendum vote supported his new constitution – the French Fifth Republic – by a huge margin. Sartre, for his part, needed to recognize that he was greatly weakened by illness and was likely to die if he did not take evasive action soon.

He carried on self-prescribing Corydrane and other stimulants for his dizziness and continual headaches until a senior doctor diagnosed heart fatigue and urged him to rest. He cut down on the assorted rocket fuel but carried on working. He looked dreadful, struggled to walk and talk, his handwriting became illegible and he even forgot how to spell.

De Beauvoir risked his wrath by urging him to catnap. Sometimes he would flatly refuse. At other times he would reluctantly agree to take a five-minute break and then sleep for several hours. De Beauvoir arranged to have the production of *Altona* postponed until the following year. As the daddy of a philosophy that preaches self-responsibility and the avoidance of excuses, Sartre hated failing to meet a deadline or a commitment, but he was plainly in no fit state to complete *Altona*. De Beauvoir expected a tantrum when she told him production of the play had been rescheduled. He worried her by responding uncharacteristically with nothing more than an apathetic smile.

In mid-December, he sent his screenplay synopsis to Huston then immediately returned to the *Critique*, completing part one, *Theory of Practical Ensembles*, sometime in 1959. He delivered the manuscript to Gallimard personally, handing Robert Gallimard, nephew of Gaston, a fat package in the foyer. He seemed relieved to be rid of it.

Sartre's former protégé, Francis Jeanson, whose review had sparked the row with Camus in 1952, had become the editor of *Vérités pour*, an underground magazine that supported Algerian rebels. Sartre wanted to help the independence movement in any way he could so he allowed Evelyne Rey to effect a rapprochement with Jeanson. Jeanson, who remained an unreconstructed Stalinist, had fallen out with Sartre in 1956 over his criticism of the Soviet intervention in Hungary. In June 1959, Jeanson's magazine published an interview with Sartre in which he argued that supporting the Algerian rebels was now at one with stemming a rising tide of fascism in France.

Soon after launching this attack on the French right wing he set off once again for Rome with de Beauvoir where he worked on *Altona*. He finally finished the play in Venice, in August, in the company of Arlette. The play went into rehearsal as soon as he returned to Paris.

There were the usual wrangles over Sartre's refusal to make cuts, and the usual roles for Wanda and Evelyne, who otherwise found it difficult to find work. His plays were always as much about supporting his harem and his hangers-on as they were about making profound philosophical and political points. It would be too crude to say that young women threw themselves at Sartre largely because he boosted their flagging careers and helped them out financially, but gratitude was certainly an ingredient in the love that at least some of them held for him.

So, to some extent, Sartre wrote plays in order to be surrounded by the kind of excellent young women who are prepared to be attracted to intelligent, powerful, charismatic, older men. Who can blame him for that? Like all 'rock stars' he had willing groupies.

It has been suggested that Sartre was in the habit of taking advantage of women who were especially vulnerable. Certainly, several of Sartre's women were impressionable and emotionally needy, if not emotionally unstable, and were largely attracted to him because particularly desirous of a clever, powerful, protective and indulgent father figure. Others, however, were exceptionally strong and stable characters, and in his relationships with Olga and Simone Jollivet, for example, he was the needy one, possibly even the vulnerable one.

Although he undoubtedly gained various advantages from his relationships with them, some of Sartre's 'vulnerable women' were nonetheless undoubtedly empowered as people through their relationship with him. Others gained no lasting benefit from it. He did not, it seems, help to destroy any who were not already inexorably inclined towards destroying themselves. Arguably, in allowing himself to form relationships with the susceptible women who displayed a romantic attraction towards him, he always tried, within reason, to help them emotionally, financially and professionally. He could only do so much for them, of course, not least because in the end his own destiny was always his chief concern.

Altona finally opened at the Théâtre de la Renaissance on 23 September 1959 and was an immediate hit with the public. The critics liked it too, describing it as Sartre's 'comeback', his return to form.

Unlike his two previous plays, *Kean* and *Nekrassov*, *Altona* is far from being a bit of relatively light relief. Ponderous, grim and claustrophobic, like all of Sartre's best plays, it explores many of the same weighty Marxist themes as the *Critique*.

Altona is set in post-war Germany in the mansion of Gerlach, a wealthy shipping tycoon who made a fortune building warships for the Nazis and knowingly selling them land for a concentration camp, and another fortune helping to rebuild Germany after the war. Sartre uses the play to put forward the Marxist view that the wealthiest capitalists benefit regardless of who holds political power. Nazis or the USA, it is business as usual.

Gerlach is dying of throat cancer. His wealth cannot save him. His dying wish is to speak to his estranged son, Franz, who has locked himself away for fourteen years in the upper rooms of the mansion. Franz' needs are taken care of by his sister, Leni, with whom he is having an incestuous relationship. As the play develops the story emerges of how Franz and his father became estranged and why Franz is a recluse.

The philosophical focus of the play is German collective guilt, or the lack of it, in face of the Nazi atrocities. Divorced from the outside world in his private rooms, hiding from daylight and the passage of time, Franz sees himself as being on trial before all eternity – before malignant crab-like creatures – for his own war crimes and those of his nation. He identifies one of his crimes as the crime of omission, a failure to act against the Nazis. He resisted them when he helped a rabbi but cooperated with them afterwards.

Like his father, like the majority of the German people, Franz submitted to the Nazis. He could have resisted them regardless of the consequences but in bad faith he acted as though he had to go along with them. Making an excuse of his weakness and his desire for self-preservation he simply despised the Nazis while acting on their behalf.

Sartre's aim in *Altona* is not to attack the German people in particular. He sees the Nazi atrocities, particularly the Holocaust, as shaming all humankind. As a Marxist, Sartre identifies capitalism as the fundamental evil, characterizing Nazism as just one more manifestation of capitalism.

Nazism required capitalism in order to arm itself. In return, Nazism provided capitalism with new markets and new opportunities for growth. The Nazis fell but the capitalists, whose interests the Nazis served, marched on. Germany soon recovered its economic prosperity and the USA committed atrocities worthy of the Nazis – Hiroshima for example. *Loser Wins*, the alternative title of the play, refers to the economic success that Germany enjoyed soon after 'losing' World War II.

Sartre may have been as high as a kite for much of the late fifties but it did nothing to lighten him up artistically.

20

The Philosopher and the Film Director

As soon as *Altona* was up and running Sartre left for Ireland with Arlette. John Huston had a mansion at Saint Clerans in County Kildare where he had lived since 1952 as a tax exile, obsessed with his stable of horses. The purpose of the visit was to finalize the Freud screenplay. That never happened, although a little progress was made thanks to Arlette's translation skills. People took the young woman to be his secretary, which in a sense she was.

Huston's mansion was enormous, like a hotel, with an assortment of houseguests that he largely ignored as he swept about the place, a restless king barking orders at his staff. Sartre found Huston childishly conceited, standoffish, preoccupied, easily distracted, empty. The language barrier and the cultural divide prevented the two of them from establishing any rapport.

Hollywood glamour versus Parisian shabby chic, mogul versus guru. They could only view one another from a distance with an appalled fascination: two monarchs of two very different realms, each hermetically sealed inside his great fame and formidable reputation.

Sartre sought to ridicule Huston in his letters to de Beauvoir. He described how Huston galloped his horse each afternoon on the green Irish prairie followed by a prancing donkey. Huston was equally insulting about Sartre in his autobiography *An Open Book*:

> Sartre was a little barrel of a man, and as ugly as a human being can be. His face was both bloated and pitted, his teeth were yellow and he was wall-eyed. He wore a gray suit, black shoes, white shirt, tie and vest. His appearance never changed. He'd come down in the morning in this suit, and he would still be wearing it the last thing at night.
>
> (*An Open Book*, p. 295)

Given what we know of Sartre's drug abuse, his chain-smoking, his indifference to his appearance and his disinterest in his own body, other than as the hard-pressed vehicle of his mind, Huston's description is surely devastatingly accurate.

Sartre's attitude to life and his own body was shockingly revealed to Huston when he, Sartre, developed toothache. Instead of travelling all the way to Dublin, or even Hollywood, for the finest cosmetic dentistry, as Huston would have done, Sartre simply had the tooth pulled out by the first local dentist he could find. He then carried on as though nothing had happened, indifferent to the latest gap in his terrible teeth. 'He took the first guy he found and had his tooth pulled. One tooth more or less was of no consequence to Sartre. The physical universe did not exist for him. Only the mind mattered. On the other hand, he kept popping all sorts of pills' (*An Open Book*, p. 296).

Sartre was not, however, indifferent to Huston's lack of manners. He told de Beauvoir that when people were sitting around chatting, Huston would often walk out without even waiting for whoever was speaking to finish their sentence. From Huston's perspective, it was always Sartre who was speaking:

You'd wait for him to catch his breath, but he wouldn't. The words came out in an absolute torrent. Sartre spoke no English, and because of the rapidity of his speech, I could barely follow even his basic thought processes. I am sure that much of what he said was brilliant … Sometimes I'd leave the room in desperation – on the verge of exhaustion from trying to follow what he was saying; the drone of his voice followed me until I was out of earshot and, when I'd return, he wouldn't even have noticed that I'd been gone.

(*An Open Book*, p. 296)

Sartre saw himself as gallantly straining to keep the conversation going after the host's abrupt disappearances.

The variance in the stubborn perspectives of great men judging one another through mundane events is as amusing as it is revealing about both of them. Sartre could have got a play out of it, along the lines of *In Camera*, and Huston a movie, along the lines of *The Misfits*. And it is of course priceless material for any biographer looking to affectionately mock Sartre and reveal just how much of a delightfully grotesque figure he had become by the end of the 1950s: Socratic in his wisdom, loquacity, obstinacy, physical ugliness and high pain threshold. A gadfly like Socrates, a flea in everyone's ear. Wiser than Socrates for never marrying. More prolific than Socrates, who wrote nothing.

Huston grumbled that Sartre had written a screenplay for a five- to seven-hour movie. Seeking to cut it when he returned to Paris, Sartre managed to make it even longer. The film that finally emerged in 1962, *The Secret Passion*, starring Montgomery Clift and Susannah York, incorporated some of Sartre's material into a screenplay about Freud written by Charles Kaufman in 1947. Sartre could have at least earned himself a credit for additional material but his disagreements with Huston led him to withdraw his name from the project before its completion.

21

Explosive Situation

The swinging sixties began with the death of an enduring cultural icon. De Beauvoir took a call from Lanzmann telling her Camus had been killed in a car crash at Villeblevin, sixty-eight miles from Paris, while returning from a Yuletide break in the south of France. He was just forty-six years old. The crash, which occurred on the 4 January 1960, fractured Camus' skull and broke his neck, killing him instantly. His publisher, Michel Gallimard, another nephew of Gaston, died six days later of his injuries. Michel's wife and daughter survived. Although Sartre and de Beauvoir had fallen out with Camus and moved on from him, they discussed him nostalgically all evening in the company of Bost.

Sartre paid homage to Camus on the 7 January in *France-Observateur*. Camus, he declared, was a great moralist who would 'go on being one of the main forces in our cultural realm'. Sartre could not ignore their bitter public quarrel so he played it down and romanticized it with moving, illogical rhetoric: 'We had quarrelled, he and I, but a quarrel is nothing, even if you never see each other again. It's simply another way of living together, without losing sight of each other in this narrow little world which is given to us.'

The following month, Sartre and de Beauvoir headed to Cuba to show their support for the revolution. Fidel Castro and his allies had finally seized power from President Batista the previous year after an armed struggle that began in 1953. Batista had become increasingly corrupt and dictatorial, allowing the Cuban economy and the Cuban people to be exploited by organized crime and large US companies. Charismatic and politically savvy, Castro created an enduring one-party socialist state that in many respects did much to improve the lives of ordinary Cubans and free them from US neo-colonialism.

There is a marvellous set of monochrome photographs of Sartre and de Beauvoir sitting with Castro and Ernesto 'Che' Guevara in an office. Sartre is wearing his iconic suit: Castro and Guevara are wearing their iconic military fatigues. The group is discussing the revolution while the three men puff large Cuban cigars. In one shot, from which Castro is absent, Guevara leans forward in his huge boots and beret to light Sartre's cigar.

Sartre and de Beauvoir first met Che Guevara in his office at the Cuban National Bank. Knowing that revolutions are won with guns but sustained with sound finance, he was teaching himself economics.

Castro himself gave them a tour of the island. They made the great leader wait ten minutes when he arrived punctually at their hotel to pick them up. Sartre was impressed by how much ordinary Cubans loved Castro and how willing the father of the revolution was to mix with them and strive to meet their every need. Sartre formed the view that one of the main problems with the USSR was that its leaders were out of touch with the people. His reports on the Cuban Revolution to the French press were as glowing as Castro anxiously hoped they would be. Castro urged Sartre not to use the word 'socialism'.

While in Cuba Sartre wrote a preface to a new edition of Nizan's 1931 novella, *Aden Arabie*. He acknowledged that Nizan had seen the light politically long before he had himself and that, despite having been dead for twenty years, Nizan was truly contemporary in his condemnation of colonialism. Sartre's evocation of Nizan's youthful, rebellious spirit helped to inspire the student-led protests of 1968.

Sartre returned to Paris in mid-March, a few weeks ahead of the publication of part one of his *Critique of Dialectical Reason*. Despite his worldwide fame and his popularity with large sections of the French public, the release of the major philosophical work of the later Sartre aroused little interest. It was just too big and too complicated for anyone except trained specialists in both Marxism and existentialism to understand. Those who ploughed through it found it contained passages of brilliant insight but was poorly structured and confusingly inconsistent in its use of key terms.

The book is drug-fuelled and rambling but not an incoherent rant. Although the general consensus is that it is far from being the masterpiece *Being and Nothingness* is, at any Sartre conference you will find a small minority of eccentrics proclaiming it to be Sartre's greatest work of all. Sartre's monster is out there on library shelves for anyone with sufficient time and education to tackle, and over the years it has undoubtedly exercised a steady influence on post-Marxist thought.

In *Critique of Dialectical Reason* Sartre argues that the notion of human freedom lies at the very heart of Marx's materialist theory of history, but that Marx did not sufficiently clarify it. Existentialism, as a theory of human freedom, is uniquely equipped to clarify it. Existentialism, therefore, belongs at the heart of Marxism as an essential element of Marxism.

The historical dialectic, the development of matter through man and man through matter that results from human activity and productivity, cannot be explained, as some Marxists of Sartre's time supposed, in terms of blind, mechanical processes that do not involve human consciousness and freedom. Sartre accuses some of his Marxist contemporaries of proposing a simplistic 'dialectic without men' (*Search for a Method*, p. xiii).

Man is made by history, but it is also man that *makes* history by responding practically to his present historically derived situation. Through his activity man projects himself beyond his present situation towards his future situation, towards future possibilities that will be realized when a future state of matter is produced.

When Marx argues that men make their history upon the basis of prior conditions, he does not mean, as some Marxists take him to mean, that men are mechanisms conditioned by circumstances to act in certain determined ways. Rather, men make their history by *choosing* their *response* to their conditions. Man is the product of his own productive activity but he is never just a product among products because he is the only product capable of realizing he is a product. Sartre argues that Marxism is not only a theory of history that requires a notion of human consciousness and therefore freedom, Marxism *is* history itself become conscious of itself.

Marx famously urges people to strive for their political freedom. This presupposes that people are at least psychologically free in the Sartrean sense. Political freedom can have no meaning to beings entirely subject to deterministic laws, and it would be impossible for such beings to genuinely strive for political freedom.

In his *Critique*, Sartre recognizes, far more than he does in *Being and Nothingness*, that a person, indeed a whole social class, can be without freedom in any real practical sense as a result of political and economic oppression. A person's existential freedom remains inalienable: he cannot not choose, but his freedom does not amount to much if his only choice is, for example, to endure drudgery and exploitation in a factory for a subsistence wage or to die.

This view develops rather than departs from views expressed in *Being and Nothingness*, in so far as Sartre recognizes in *Being and Nothingness* that the most serious threat to a person's freedom is the freedom of the Other. Just as one person can transcend another and reduce him to an object, so one social class can, through economic and social exploitation, transcend another social class and reduce its members to objects. In this way the Sartre of the *Critique* develops his existentialist theory of being-for-others into a Marxist theory of man's alienation by man.

No doubt fired up by his positive experiences in Cuba, Sartre began part two of the *Critique*, *The Intelligibility of History*, soon after his return, writing most of it by the late summer of 1960. Moved by his Cuban insight that one of the main problems with the USSR was the distance between leaders and led, he dedicated much of part two to considering why the Bolshevik Revolution of 1917 led to Stalinism.

Part two, longer even than part one, reached no conclusion and in that sense remained unfinished. As ever, Sartre promised even more ambitious works to tie off all the loose ends: future works that he ran out of time and energy to write and that would doubtless have created yet more loose ends of their own. All works of philosophy, 'finished' or 'unfinished', leave loose ends. Such is the nature of the subject. Part two was published posthumously in 1985.

Sartre was much in demand from left-wing movements around the world. His celebrity guaranteed them publicity. In May 1960, he continued his role as France's anti-ambassador by visiting Yugoslavia as a guest of the Writers' Union. He lectured in Belgrade where two of his plays were being performed, and had an audience with the reasonably benevolent communist dictator, Marshal Tito.

In August he was off again, this time to Brazil with de Beauvoir, where he spent three months touring the country.

Before leaving he signed the 'Manifesto of the 121', an open letter published on 6 September in the magazine, *Vérité-Liberté*. The Manifesto declared support for the Algerian independence movement, criticized the French Government and condemned the French Army for using torture. It also, in so many words, called for insubordination by those French troops in Algeria who no longer believed in the cause for which they were fighting.

Many right wingers considered the document treasonable and some of its signatories were imprisoned. Other publications that sought to publish the Manifesto were either seized or censored. To highlight the stifling of free speech, *Les Temps modernes* published two blank pages where the Manifesto should have been.

The Manifesto's most famous signatory was thousands of miles from the fallout. In Rio, Copacabana, Bahia, São Paulo, Brasília. Lecturing, meeting left-wing intellectuals, visiting the poor and attending voodoo ceremonies. He was depressed, had shingles and did not like the food. In true Sartre style, however, he soldiered on. Towards the end of the trip de Beauvoir was hospitalized by what may have been typhoid.

While Sartre was in Brazil, Jeanson, who had fled abroad, was tried in his absence for running the Jeanson Network, an organization that aided the Algerian militants of the banned FLN. Jeanson was found guilty of high treason and sentenced to ten years' imprisonment. His lawyers begged Sartre to return to Paris to speak in his defence, offering to pay for his flights. Sartre refused on the grounds that he was ill. He sent a telegram of support instead and allowed Marcel Péju, who worked for *Les Temps modernes*, to forge a letter in his name. Sartre could have dictated the contents of the letter over the phone but instead he allowed Péju to concoct the letter himself.

Lacking Sartre's subtlety, Péju went too far, comparing the Jeanson Network to the French Resistance. He had Sartre say he would have worked for the Jeanson Network without hesitation had Jeanson asked him. Coming on top of the 'Manifesto of the

121', this letter placed Sartre in serious trouble with the French authorities. He expected to be charged with treason and aiding terrorism when he returned to Paris. Also, the Organisation de l'armée secrète (OAS), a right-wing terrorist group opposed to Algerian independence and the FLN, placed him on their assassination list. In his absence Sartre had managed to become the number one hate figure of the French right. War veterans marched through the streets of Paris in their thousands chanting 'kill Sartre'.

He and de Beauvoir returned to Europe via Spain in November 1960. They decided it would be less conspicuous to drive into France than fly. By the time they reached the French border, however, they had decided that they wanted to get themselves arrested after all. The border police informed Paris that they were back in the country. They headed to Paris hoping to be charged when they arrived, but the authorities procrastinated.

The endless delay was ordered from the top. De Gaulle was too clever, and perhaps too fearful, to give France's most famous intellectual and dissident his day in court. The political situation was so volatile in France at that time that a Sartre court case could have precipitated a revolution. It would certainly have led to further unrest. De Gaulle famously declared, 'You do not imprison Voltaire', conveniently forgetting that Voltaire had been imprisoned in the Bastille.

De Gaulle was also clever enough to realize that France could not win in Algeria. He set in train the political process that eventually led to Algerian independence in 1962, all the while fearful of powerful reactionary forces that wanted to keep Algeria French. De Gaulle survived several attempts by the OAS to assassinate him, as did Sartre.

The closer Algerian independence came, the more hostile the OAS became. Paris was infested with OAS and FLN activists planting plastic explosives in the cars and homes of their respective enemies, or simply tossing them indiscriminately into crowds. Plagued by threatening phone calls throughout the winter, Sartre and de Beauvoir escaped Paris in April 1961 and, with Bost for company, headed for Antibes in the south of France.

They were still in Antibes when they received news that Merleau-Ponty had died unexpectedly of a heart attack on 4 May. Sartre honoured his most able contemporary critic with a memorial edition of *Les Temps modernes* in October. Sartre wrote his contribution in Rome during the summer. He struggled uncharacteristically to find words to summarize Merleau-Ponty and their complex intellectual relationship. He felt the need to discuss his thoughts with Merleau-Ponty before he set them down, all too aware that he could not, all too aware that he had allowed Merleau-Ponty to slip away with so much left unsaid.

Returning from Antibes, they found Paris in even greater turmoil than when they left it: civil unrest, bombs, assassinations. In June, Sartre placed his mother in a hotel on the Boulevard

Raspail and abandoned his flat for de Beauvoir's. It was a wise move. On 19 July, just as he and de Beauvoir were about to set off for Rome, he received news that a small bomb had exploded in the entrance hall at 42 Rue Bonaparte, causing limited damage.

Relieved to be away from their Parisian troubles, Sartre and de Beauvoir took it relatively easy in Italy. Sartre's main task that summer was to write his difficult piece on Merleau-Ponty. He also met and spoke at length with the philosopher and anti-colonialist, Frantz Fanon.

He agreed to write the preface to Fanon's classic work, *The Wretched of the Earth*, in which Fanon conducts a psychological analysis of the dehumanizing effects of imperialism upon both colonizers and colonized as well as advocating the use of violence by oppressed peoples in their struggle for freedom and independence. The book was published with Sartre's preface towards the end of 1961, shortly before Fanon died of leukaemia on 6 December.

For Sartre and de Beauvoir, Paris became even less hospitable than it had been during World War II. In the war against colonialism Sartre was *personally* in the firing line in a way that he had not been as a conscript, POW or escapee. It was too risky for Sartre to return to Rue Bonaparte and, understandably afraid of the OAS, no hotel manager would give him a room. Eventually, his secretary Claude Faux, who had replaced Cau in 1957, rented Sartre and de Beauvoir a flat in his own name.

Although Sartre and de Beauvoir lived in the flat in fear of their lives, it did not stop them continuing to stick their necks out. Sartre helped form the League for Anti-Fascist Movements and repeatedly condemned those opposed to Algerian independence as fascists and racists. On 18 November 1961, Sartre and de Beauvoir, walking behind a banner saying 'Peace in Algeria', joined an 8,000-strong demonstration organized by young communists against fascism and racism. The police charged the crowd, beating them with large batons.

On 7 January 1962, 42 Rue Bonaparte was bombed again. This time the bomb went off in the flat above Sartre's, destroying both apartments. The blast was big enough to blow Sartre's front door off and demolish a cupboard where he stored many of his unpublished manuscripts.

There is some suggestion that the cupboard may have been largely emptied by opportunistic collectors before the blast. What is certain is that after the blast a lot of documents were not to be found. It was the least of Sartre's problems. He clearly had the unpublished material that mattered to him safely stashed elsewhere: part two of the *Critique*, his biography of Flaubert, his much-revised draft of *Words*.

Sartre cared little for most of his unpublished manuscripts. For example, when given the opportunity to buy back from a bookseller the two volumes of his *War Diaries* that Bost had lost he refused to pay for his own work. He could have tried to claim the diaries for free, as his property, but he did not bother.

A young writer who observed Sartre's Rue Bonaparte study in March 1961, not long before he abandoned it, described it as having been overrun by literature. Books had long since overspilled the groaning shelves, to be piled up on every available surface including the floor. Every piece of furniture, every corner, was obscured by gravity-defying stacks of scribbled-on paper, loose pages of typescript, notebooks, folders and files. Boyards cigarette packets, pipes, matches, overflowing ashtrays, wine bottles and empty pill boxes littered the scene.

From that gloriously cluttered and chaotic cockpit a remarkable mind with remarkable stamina had waged a long and titanic war of words: ideas and arguments his only weapons, though weapons dangerous enough for people to want to kill him. His study looked like a bomb had hit it even before one actually did. The mess was a by-product of his colossal mental energy and his substance abuse. It took the energy of a bomb to tidy the place up.

He was given police protection, but having officers standing outside all day only served to reveal his location. The officers went off duty at night when the OAS bombers were most active. He and de Beauvoir moved again, trying to find anonymity in a large block of flats down by the Seine. A demonstration in February was once again attacked by the police. This time people were killed, including a teenage boy whose funeral became a mass demonstration and a Paris-wide strike. Over half a million people converged on the cemetery.

A minority of reactionaries, most with vested interests, wanted Algeria to remain French, but the vast majority of the French population was more than ready to let it go. The pressure applied by Sartre and many others had played a significant role in changing public opinion. The pro-independence campaign had opened people's eyes to the evils and injustices of colonialism, not only in Algeria but also around the world. In March, Sartre lectured about Algeria in Brussels to an audience of 6,000 – the same month that French forces and the FLN agreed a ceasefire.

Despite the ceasefire there was an increase in violence surrounding the independence referenda that took place on 7 April in France and 1 July in Algeria. De Gaulle declared Algeria independent on 3 July but the Algerians claimed the 5 July as their independence day: the 132nd anniversary of France's entry into Algeria. Within a year of the April referendum one and a half million people had fled persecution in Algeria for France and elsewhere, including almost the entire European and Jewish populations.

22

Nobel Words

Sartre had not visited Russia for eight years when he decided to accept an invitation from the Union of Soviet Writers. He and de Beauvoir arrived there on the 1 June 1962. The country was more relaxed, with visibly higher living standards. They toured the big cities enjoying the best of Russian art and culture. Far away from the major centres the forced labour camps still operated. They visited the house of Dostoevsky, and Sartre added Khrushchev to the list of dictators he shook hands with in his life.

Their guide and interpreter was Lena Zonina, a beautiful, thirty-nine year old Russian Jewish writer. She and Sartre became romantically attached, a romance that motivated him to visit Russia no fewer than eight times over the next four years. His next visit was the following month and he was back there again in December after spending the autumn in Rome.

He arrived just after Christmas with plans to set up an international community of writers, although his main concern was to reinforce links with one lady writer in particular. Sartre was soon to dedicate his autobiography, *Words*, 'To Madame Z', a work she later translated into Russian. It was immediately following his return from Russia in mid-January 1963 that Sartre sat down to finally finish that exquisite piece of writing after ten long years of tinkering with it.

Since the days of *What is Literature?*, Sartre had insisted that writing should be functional; that only the political message matters; that crafting one's prose is a bourgeois pretension. With *Words* he returned to writing *literature*, to producing *belles-lettres*. Why did he do this?

On a practical level, he needed the money. Constant travelling was expensive and he had not written a bestseller for years. Who was going to buy *Critique of Dialectical Reason* apart from a few libraries? On an artistic level, he could not resist turning on the style one last time in order to show the world and himself that the author of *Nausea* still had it in him to write great literature. In thinking about his legacy, about posterity, he decided to play to the full the role of the ageing master craftsman. He would pull out all the stops to tell tiny Poulou's story with more style than any hack-biographer thereafter.

Yet in creating the myth of Anne-Marie's petit, pen-wielding monster, mummy's spoilt, golden-curled prodigy, *Words* is also a send-up of literature, a comment on its capacity to distort reality by transforming the most mundane situations into great adventures and portentous happenings. As Ronald Hayman and others have pointed out, no child could have been quite so precocious as Poulou is made out to be. A child's existential anxieties are real and profound, but Sartre seduces us into thinking that Poulou had analysed his human condition and developed strategies for managing his contingency to a degree worthy of a sage in his late fifties.

Words is a psychoanalytic excursion into literature by means of which Sartre diagnoses his desire to write as a neurosis, as an anxiety-reducing compulsion. Writing made him feel substantial, necessary, a *someone*, but perhaps in the end that only mattered because he believed that being a someone pleased his grandfather, pleased the whole judgemental, hard to impress, bourgeois world that his grandfather represented. Arguably, Sartre spent his entire life seeking to impress the bourgeois world that spawned him, by shocking it.

He says that he grew up free of a father's oppressive will and therefore had no superego. On the other hand, he suggests that his conscience, at least the one that made him feel guilty if he did not constantly fulfil his vocation, always spoke with Charles Schweitzer's voice. 'My grandfather's voice, that mechanical voice which wakes me with a start and impels me to my table' (*Words*, p. 104). Obliged to appease his guilt by doing Charles' bidding, Sartre was, when he reached his table, damned well going to punish Charles and his ilk by writing the kind of stuff

they were bound to disapprove of. It is revealing that he deliberately sent a copy of *The Wall*, with its various shocking passages,
to Mancy, the other disapproving, bourgeois father figure of his
young life.

A simpler explanation of Sartre is that he was just one of
those short guys who was not prepared to be looked down on.
Like all sufferers of 'small man syndrome' he had a lot to prove
in a tall man's world, so he ran away from men towards women
and his pen, towards realms more conducive to proving that he
was a giant in a small man's body, which he undoubtedly was. He
invariably sought the company of younger men and especially
younger women, and suffered in the company of older men
or male contemporaries who were of similar stature to him in
terms of their achievements. He was determined to demonize
Schweitzer, Mancy and Lanson, he ran away from Heidegger,
kept Hemingway at a distance, dismissed Camus, fell out with
Aron, largely fell out with Merleau-Ponty and so on.

It is all too easy to indulge in psychoanalytic rap when trying
to figure out what made Sartre tick, just as he got carried away
by his own free-form psychoanalysis of Baudelaire, Genet,
Flaubert and even himself. Perhaps *Words* is a send-up of the
'bourgeois ideology' of psychoanalysis as much as it is a send-up
of the bourgeois indulgence of literature.

At the end of *Words*, discovering that his choice of himself,
his insatiable urge to write, is nothing more than Poulou's

neurosis reverberating down through the decades, he renounces his vocation. 'I have renounced my vocation, but I have not unfrocked myself. I still write. What else can I do? *Nulla dies sine linea*' (*Words*, p. 157). A diagnosis is not a cure and he continued writing long after *Words* was 'completed'. Indeed, he wrote his longest work, envious of those who did not share his chronic addiction.

> Today this worn exigency strikes me as clumsy and inflexible; like those solemn, prehistoric crabs which the sea washes up on the beaches of Long Island; like them, it survives from times past. I have long envied the *concierges* in the rue Lacépède when the long summer evenings bring them out on to the pavement, astride their chairs: their innocent eyes see without feeling obliged to look.
>
> (*Words*, p. 104)

Until the summer of 1963 Sartre did little else but polish *Words* to perfection. He then headed off once again to Russia with de Beauvoir, once again the guest of the Soviet Writers' Union. Some of the Russian writers were under pressure from Khrushchev, who had become uncomfortable about allowing too much artistic freedom. Khrushchev accused Ilya Ehrenburg, author of *The Thaw*, a title that gave a name to the entire post-Stalin era, of encouraging Sartre to quit the Communist Party. Sartre, of course, was never a member.

A delegation of writers that included Sartre met with Khrushchev at his dacha in Georgia. The president condemned capitalism and praised socialism while showing off his new private swimming pool. Sartre and de Beauvoir visited various parts of the USSR before returning to Paris in September. That month André Puig replaced Claude Faux to become Sartre's third secretary.

Words appeared in *Les Temps modernes* in November, the same month as Sartre and de Beauvoir visited Czechoslovakia. They met writers, gave talks and attended the Czech premiere of *Altona*. *Words* was published as a book in January 1964, soon after their return to Paris, and received rave reviews.

Sartre must have been pleased. After all, he had poured himself into the book, and the money would be welcome. He felt obliged to say, however, that Western civilization is not to be excused its atrocities because it also produces literary monuments. It was the usual irritating bias from a writer prepared to largely overlook the atrocities of the East as he embraced a variety of bloodstained communist dictators.

His old friend from the ENS, René Maheu, had become director of UNESCO. He invited Sartre to speak in Paris in April at a conference dedicated to the work of Kierkegaard. It was an opportunity for Sartre to explore his intellectual relationship with the godfather of existentialism.

Kierkegaard, in opposition to Hegel, was interested in the

individual as a being not primarily defined by history. Sartre was interested in the relationship between the individual and history, history being the collective behaviour of single individuals. He put a lot of work into his lecture, knowing the material could be recycled for his vast consideration of Flaubert's individual place in history.

The large auditorium where he delivered the lecture was packed. Scruffy students from the Sorbonne sat in the aisles alongside smartly dressed UNESCO delegates, all eager to hear one great existentialist appraise another.

Sartre lectured in Rome in May before visiting Kiev and Moscow. He and de Beauvoir returned to Paris briefly in mid-July before heading back to Rome for their summer holiday. Settled in Rome he began work on *The Trojan Women*, his last play.

In the autumn, Sartre heard rumours that he was to be awarded the Nobel Prize for Literature. *Words* had reminded the wider world of his existence and further confirmed his literary genius. He was long overdue Nobel recognition – Camus had accepted his prize in 1957. Sounding out friends, and de Beauvoir in particular, Sartre's sense that he ought to decline the prize was confirmed.

On 16 October, in a rare effort to avoid scandal and controversy, he wrote a letter to the Secretary of the Swedish Academy politely declining the prize. This letter had to be redirected and was not received by the Secretary before it was officially announced on the 22 October that Sartre was the nominated laureate. The same day, pursued by the press, Sartre was obliged to give an official statement in which he was careful not to offend the Swedish people.

In his press statement, taken by the Swedish journalist, Carl-Gustav Bjurström, Sartre insisted that it was his policy to refuse official distinctions, that he had, for example, refused the Legion of Honour in 1945. 'The writer must refuse to let himself be transformed by institutions, even if these are of the most honourable kind, as is the case here.' The Swedish Academy had to make a second announcement stating that the nominated laureate had declined the prize. With great dignity they insisted that Sartre's refusal did not alter the validity of the nomination.

Sartre declined the prize partly because it had never been awarded to a non-dissident Soviet writer, but mainly because, as he implied in his press statement, he did not want the label 'Nobel Prize Winner' attached to all he had achieved and all he might achieve, as though his life's work had all been to that end. He had repeatedly cast aspersions on the idea of literary monuments. The last thing he wanted was to become a living literary monument himself.

Although Sartre respected most of the writers who had received the prize, he was aware that becoming a Nobel laureate undoubtedly transforms a writer, however militant, into an establishment figure, and we know how Sartre felt about the establishment. Cohen-Solal puts it well when she says, 'Sartre had refused to be embalmed alive, to be made into a living statue and prematurely canonized' (*Jean-Paul Sartre: A Life*, p. 449).

Sartre still enjoys both the prestige of having been offered the prize and the notoriety of having rejected it. No one else was offered the Nobel Prize for Literature in 1964, as they would have been forever marked out as a second choice, and Sartre's name is to be found on almost any list of Nobel winners alongside that extra, anti-establishment accolade: 'Declined'. Boris Pasternak had already declined in 1958 but that was under pressure from the Soviet government. The only force holding a gun to Sartre's head was his sense of himself.

Sartre's only regret was that the considerable prize money of 250,000 crowns would have supported various political causes, although he and Éditions Gallimard certainly reaped the profits of the priceless publicity.

23

Help of the Helpless

In March 1965, Arlette Elkaïm became Sartre's adopted daughter. The youngest of his harem became his sole executor and heir. This was how he repaid de Beauvoir for decades of personal and intellectual dedication. She had the right to expect to at least take charge of his literary legacy and that would have made sense. Then again, de Beauvoir was less than three years younger than Sartre and, as it turned out, survived him by only six years. Sartre's logic was that it makes sense to leave everything to the youngest of one's intimates: especially if it binds a charming young woman less than half your age to you for the remainder of your life.

Sartre biographers have speculated that adopting his youngest lover fulfilled a long-standing incest fantasy for Sartre. Brother-sister incest is hinted at in various places in his writings and more than hinted at in *Altona*, and his first girlfriend, Annie Lannes, was his first cousin. Arlette was not his sister, but in making his youngest lover his daughter, Sartre was, Hayman argues, 'aiming a sacrilegiously mocking blow at the institution of the family while acting out a variation on a favourite fantasy' (*Writing Against*, p. 373). It is an interesting analysis of Sartre's motives, precisely the kind of Freudian analysis of motives that Sartre himself relished and often went in for. Make of it what you will.

It is certainly interesting that he adopted Arlette rather than achieving the same legal ends by marrying her, but then we know how he felt about marriage. A married Sartre would have been a very different creature from a single Sartre in the eyes of his friends, his lovers and the whole, wide world. Indeed, a very different creature in his own eyes.

Another theory is that Sartre adopted Arlette as 'an act of solidarity with the underprivileged' (*Writing Against*, p. 373). She was thrice oppressed: female, Algerian and Jewish. In adopting her and giving her everything, the little, privileged, bourgeois champion of the world's downtrodden was striking a blow against discrimination. As to Arlette being Jewish in particular, it is argued that Sartre was doing what he could for Jews now, appeasing his guilt, having failed to do more for them during World War II. Then again, maybe it had nothing to do with Holocaust guilt. He simply liked Jewish women – Arlette, Evelyne, Lena – and at least some of them clearly liked him.

If the simplest explanations are the best then Sartre adopted Arlette for practical reasons that were of mutual benefit. If the crudest explanations are the best then he was a dirty old man and she was more than willing.

In the same month that Arlette was adopted, Sartre's last play, *The Trojan Women*, opened at the Théâtre National Populaire. Appearing six years after his previous play, the ambitious *Altona*, *The Trojan Women*, a relatively short adaptation of Euripides' tragedy, was something of an afterthought in Sartre's career as a playwright. In other respects, it neatly wrapped up his dramatic career, allowing him to end as he had begun, utilizing an ancient Greek myth to comment upon a contemporary political situation and upon war and oppression generally.

His first professional play, *The Flies*, was a comment on the Nazi occupation of Paris. *The Trojan Women*, when he started writing it, was a comment on the Algerian War. By the time it was performed, however, it was more a comment on the escalating Vietnam War.

In an interview with *Bref: The monthly journal of the Théâtre National Populaire*, Sartre says that Euripides wrote *The Trojan Women* to denounce Greek colonialism in Asia Minor. 'It was this colonialism of Greece into Asia Minor that Euripides denounced, and where I use the expression "dirty war" in reference to these expeditions I was, in fact, taking no liberties with the original text' (*Bref*, February 1965).

The Trojan Women is set outside the walls of Troy. The Greeks have finally defeated the Trojans after a siege lasting ten years. Reduced to mere spoils of war, the Trojan women and their children await their fate at the hands of the Greeks. Some are killed, most are to be taken back to Greece as slaves. The women bemoan their fate and that of their dead men-folk, cursing the Greeks and the gods. The prophetess, Cassandra, foretells the death and destruction that will befall the Greeks on their journey home.

The play ends with the god Poseidon cursing mortals for making war and inflicting suffering on themselves. In bad faith men blame the gods for war but war is the responsibility of men. War kills all in the end and brings only hollow victories.

> Idiots! We'll make you pay for this. You stupid, bestial mortals. Making war, burning cities, violating tombs and temples, torturing your enemies, bringing suffering on yourselves. Can't you see war will kill you: all of you?
>
> (*The Trojan Women*, Scene 5, p. 347)

The play, for both Euripides and Sartre, seeks to emphasize the waste, futility, injustice and depravity of war and to call into question the distinction between victor and vanquished. In bringing death and destruction to both sides, war is a means by which humankind defeats itself. This point echoes a central claim of Sartre's previous play, *Altona*: man is his own worst enemy.

From March 1965, with Algeria now independent, the Vietnam War became Sartre's number one cause. Keen to protest against increasing US military involvement in Vietnam, he cancelled a series of lectures he was due to give at Cornell University in New York. As ever, his universal condemnation of the USA was at odds with the many allowances he made for the USSR and China. In cancelling the Cornell lectures he missed a golden opportunity to criticize US foreign policy from within the USA and to forge links with the growing number of left-leaning Americans who had similar views to his on Vietnam and other issues. Perhaps he was simply fearful of running into Dolorés.

In May 1965, the soft-porn magazine, *Playboy*, published an interview with Sartre conducted by Madeleine Gobeil: 'A Candid Conversation With the Charismatic Fountainhead of Existentialism and Rejector of the Nobel Prize'. Sartre was well paid for the interview which, because it appeared in a girlie magazine, is by far the best-known interview he ever gave. In the interview, which actually took place in 1964, before the Nobel episode, Sartre speaks quite candidly about certain aspects of his life. Indeed, he says much more about his adult life than he does in *Words*.

He manages to suitably titillate *Playboy* readers by denying certain scandalous stories about himself. For example, he dismisses as a myth the story that during the height of the existentialist craze he invited a girl to his bedroom only to take an overripe Camembert cheese from a cupboard and shove it under her nose. 'Smell!', he is supposed to have demanded, before ordering her to leave.

July 1965 saw Sartre and de Beauvoir in Russia once again. As usual they were the guests of Russian writers. Brezhnev and Kosygin had replaced Khrushchev in October 1964 and on one level had relaxed censorship controls: some books that had been banned were now available. An increasing number of writers were, however, being arrested for publishing anti-Soviet books abroad, while those writers who tried to defend them were being silenced and threatened by the authorities.

In the middle of July, Sartre flew the relatively short distance from Leningrad to Helsinki to attend the communist-backed 1965 World Congress for Peace. His speech affirmed his support for the Soviet-backed North Vietnamese and called for the complete withdrawal of US armed forces from Vietnam.

Alongside his ceaseless travelling and political campaigning, Sartre was working hard on his psychoanalytic biography of Flaubert, *The Family Idiot*, a work that would grow to massive, preposterous proportions over the coming years. He found it easier to write while travelling. Paris meant constant interruptions.

Paris also meant the latest developments in continental philosophy, which were largely passing him by. He was too busy living the cosmopolitan life, too busy totalizing Flaubert, too busy politicking to know or care much about structuralism, post-structuralism and the whole tedious linguistic turn in French philosophy. In 1965, it was Lévi-Strauss, Barthes and Foucault who were cutting edge among the Parisian intelligentsia, not Sartre.

It was, however, Sartre's Marxist existentialism that was helping to inspire and give voice to a rapidly growing number of impoverished, marginalized, disaffected students seeking radical change. The student population in France had grown massively since the late 1950s, but the education system had not kept pace. There was overcrowding, poor facilities, lack of funding, lack of teachers and, above all, a sense that an education was no longer a passport to a brighter future.

Even if Sartre himself was often absent from France, addressing a writers' conference or holed up in some foreign hotel room with Flaubert and a tube of Corydrane, his brand of Marxism spoke to students in a way that structuralism could not. Above all, his radicalism spoke to the student leaders of the increasingly powerful student unions. Sartre quotations and jargon appeared constantly in student union pamphlets and magazines of the time, and when student disaffection finally exploded in the protests of 1968, some called it a 'Sartrean rebellion'. This is an exaggeration.

Sartre was an inspiration – as were many others, including Nizan – but the real catalyst of the 1968 uprising was the Vietnam War. The students knew that the American-led, capitalist establishment did not give a damn about them: the young adults who were supposed to be its future. It was too busy dropping napalm on children. In their anger towards the establishment the students felt a sense of solidarity with the victimized Vietnamese. For most students the protests were about resentment rather than ideology, but whatever the prime motivation, Vietnam was the final straw.

Sartre and de Beauvoir returned to Russia in May 1966 to find that the government was continuing to turn the screw on intellectuals. Some of their fellow writers were being 're-educated' in labour camps while the rest were living in fear of arrest.

Sartre wanted to meet the great Russian writer, Aleksandr Solzhenitsyn, some of whose work had recently been de-censored in the USSR. Despite Lena Zonina's efforts to charm and persuade him, Solzhenitsyn refused. The reason he gave was that it would sadden him to meet a writer who enjoyed freedom of speech. He later admitted that he resented Sartre's support for the writer, Mikhail Sholokhov, a pro-establishment figure and member of the Supreme Soviet who had slated Solzhenitsyn's classic, anti-Stalinist, labour camp exposé, *One Day in the Life of Ivan Denisovich.*

Sartre returned to Paris for a few weeks before spending July and August in Greece and Italy. On the 18 September 1966, he and de Beauvoir began a month-long tour of Japan as the guests of Kyoto University and his Japanese publisher. Their arrival was akin to Beatlemania. Two hundred photographers and over a thousand students besieged them at the airport where they gave a press conference.

Unlike in China, where the people had never heard of him despite his ultra-left politics, Sartre was hugely popular in capitalist Japan. All his works had been translated into Japanese and were taught in the universities by professors who had assisted at the ENS. Japan had a huge appetite for all things French. The Japanese press named Sartre one of the three best-known Frenchmen in Japan, alongside Napoleon and de Gaulle.

They appeared on TV, lectured, addressed an anti-war rally, visited Nagasaki and generally took every opportunity to condemn US imperialism in a country that was wholeheartedly embracing US capitalism. They survived a typhoon and Sartre was violently sick after a meal of sushi. On their way back to Paris they stopped off in Moscow for a few days.

In mid-November, Sartre's opposition to the Vietnam War found its focus in the Russell Tribunal. The British philosopher, Bertrand Russell, now in his nineties and having published a book on the subject, convened an international tribunal to investigate US war crimes in Vietnam. Although a private organization that the US government chose to ignore, the tribunal, conducted on the same model as the Nuremberg trials, did much to turn worldwide opinion against the war.

Sartre became a central figure of the tribunal, sometimes called the Russell-Sartre tribunal. He attended its founding session in London in 1966 and was among those who presided over its two main sessions in Sweden and Denmark during 1967.

Overwhelming evidence of US atrocities in Vietnam was brought before the sessions of the tribunal, some of it by former American servicemen. The tribunal gathered evidence of torture, systematic poisoning of crops and the annihilation of whole villages of civilians. It even examined, in the flesh, children hideously scarred by napalm. The tribunal concluded that US military activities in Vietnam amounted to nothing less than genocide.

A few days after the founding session of the Russell Tribunal ended, Sartre received news that Evelyne Rey had cut short her moderately successful stage and film career by committing suicide.

Some critics blame Sartre for Evelyne's overdose, claiming she ended her life in response to his ending their relationship. In truth, their relationship was always clandestine and part-time and she had many other lovers and issues besides Sartre, who had become essentially a sixty-one year old father figure to her by the time she died.

As Rowley points out in *Tête-à-Tête*, Evelyne was anxious about her career – according to her brother she was afraid of theatre audiences – and in early 1966 she contracted pleurisy which left her tired and depressed with only one functioning lung (*Tête-à-Tête*, p. 295).

Sartre suffered stomach cramps on hearing the news of Evelyne's death. He also expressed guilt, not because he felt directly responsible for her demise but because he, along with others, including her brothers, had failed to do more to help and protect a young woman whose beauty masked a deep vulnerability.

As though his Vietnam War activities were not enough, in February 1967 Sartre decided to plunge headlong into the Arab-Israeli conflict by visiting both Egypt and Israel.

He, de Beauvoir and Lanzmann visited the ancient sites of Egypt and took a boat trip down the Nile. They viewed a Palestinian refugee camp and had an audience with President Nasser. They were keen to do what they could to improve Arab-Israeli relations but the general feeling was that the Jews should be forced out. Many Arabs Sartre met expected him to sympathize with this position given his support for Algeria during the war of independence, but as we know, Sartre had long-standing and deep-running sympathies with Jews. His own 'daughter' was Jewish.

Arlette met Sartre and de Beauvoir for a tour of Israel. They visited several kibbutzim and spoke at numerous meetings, some about Vietnam, some about local tensions. On their final day they had an audience with Prime Minister Eshkol.

Sartre left the region, as so many have done since, under no illusions about the profound difficulties of satisfying both Palestinian and Israeli interests. Here was a conflict where it was not so easy for Sartre to find the moral high ground. Soon after, he declared that he was both a friend of Arabs and a defender of Israel's right to exist as a sovereign nation. Most Arabs concluded from this declaration that he was on the side of the Jews.

The Russell Tribunal wanted to hold its first main session in Paris at the beginning of May but key figures were denied visas to enter France. Sartre wrote a terse letter to President de Gaulle, on squared paper, speaking of injustice and asking if the French Government intended to ban the tribunal. De Gaulle wrote an equally terse reply. It began, 'Mon cher Maître', implying that Sartre considered himself to be de Gaulle's master and teacher. De Gaulle said that he would not take lessons from Sartre on the nature of justice. The venue for the tribunal was moved to Stockholm.

Following the first session of the tribunal in May, Sartre and de Beauvoir were expected to make one of their regular visits to Russia. They had been invited, as ever, to attend the conference of the Soviet Writers' Union. They chose to decline the invitation in protest over the worsening treatment of Russian intellectuals by the authorities. It was a protest long overdue. As they well knew, many Russian writers had been subject to arrest and 're-education' for a long time. Seemingly, Sartre was less keen to see Lena Zonina than he had been in the past.

The second session of the Russell Tribunal took place in November at Roskilde near Copenhagen. It found the USA guilty of terrorism and genocide in Vietnam in clear violation of international law. Sartre was prepared to go along with this verdict, although he struggled with the whole notion of international law, viewing it as a bourgeois concept and convenience.

The countries that were developing structures of international law were also brutal colonialists and neo-colonialists. The USA in particular was quick to charge other countries with breaches of international law, as at Nuremberg, but not at all ready to recognize its own breaches. For Sartre, only the worldwide triumph of Marxism could bring about true international law.

The year 1967 ended with Sartre hearing of the death of another of his old lovers. This time, it was the former actress and socialite, Simone Jollivet, otherwise known as Toulouse or Camille – the *other* Simone – whose great beauty, vivacity and egoism had so bedazzled him in his student days. She died in poverty in her mid-sixties on 12 December. She had lost the great love of *her* life, the charismatic actor and director, Charles Dullin, eighteen years earlier.

24

Revolution in the Air

Sartre began 1968 with arteritis – inflammation of the walls of the arteries – and was forced, by his standards, to take it easy. He was, nonetheless, in reasonably good shape for his age given the unreasonable demands he had placed on his health for many years.

As he recuperated, momentous events began taking place in Czechoslovakia. Alexander Dubček, First Secretary of the Czechoslovakian Communist Party, initiated the 'Prague Spring' which ushered in a series of liberal reforms: decentralization, democratization, freedom of speech and travel. As the liberalization progressed, communist leaders in neighbouring countries, particularly the USSR, grew increasingly uncomfortable about the example Czechoslovakia was setting. It threatened to encourage their own people to seek to throw off the yoke of communist oppression.

Yet the country in Europe that most caught the revolutionary bug from Czechoslovakia in the spring of 1968 was France.

The roots of France's May uprising lay in poor student conditions and prospects. The young were further galvanized by their disgust with Western governments over the Vietnam War. When student anger finally erupted, large sections of the wider population were inclined to be sympathetic. Millions of workers throughout France were up for any fight that might secure them better pay and conditions, and thousands of Parisians, outraged by police brutality towards the student protesters and their supporters, were goaded into action themselves.

Trouble began on the 22 March at the recently built University of Nanterre in the western suburbs of Paris. The place soon became known as 'Red Nanterre' or even 'Mad Nanterre'. The leading Marxist thinker, Henri Lefebvre, allowed his philosophy and sociology students to discuss their militant views in class. When these students heard that local members of the National Vietnam Committee had been arrested they immediately occupied the Nanterre administration building in protest.

The students demanded reform of the French education system in particular and French society in general, and then left the building peacefully after the police arrived. Encouraged by the right-wing establishment, the university authorities sought to round up and discipline those they perceived to be the ringleaders of the protest. This intimidation obliged those who had taken part in what was a spontaneous demonstration to identify themselves as a group and to put forward a spokesman,

Daniel Cohn-Bendit, to assert that they had no leaders. By this process an unorganized group of students acting on impulse soon crystallized into the militant organization, Mouvement du 22 mars (M22M).

Trouble rumbled on at Nanterre until the 2 May when the authorities finally closed the university to prevent a three-day 'teach-in': students barricading themselves inside lecture theatres rather than seeking to flee lessons early as they normally do.

The closure of Nanterre triggered an initially peaceful demonstration at the Sorbonne on 3 May where a large crowd of onlookers witnessed the heavy-handed arrest of five-hundred students. Shocked by the behaviour of the police, the onlookers shouted in support of the students until the situation exploded in violence with the police attacking the onlookers.

Over the next few days the trouble escalated into widespread rioting as the police became locked in a vicious struggle with the students and their supporters. The police resorted to tear-gas and water cannon while the protesters hurled paving stones and Molotov cocktails.

Keen to encourage a wider rebellion, Sartre entered the fray on the 7 May. Along with de Beauvoir and other intellectuals, he signed a manifesto condemning police brutality and calling upon the workers of France to support the students. In a Radio Luxembourg interview given on 12 May Sartre said, 'The only relationship they can have to the university is to smash it.'

Once more he was giving voice to the young. His message soon appeared on leaflets and posters.

The workers' unions were not keen to be led to revolution by bourgeois students and intellectuals. Meanwhile, the PCF, that ultimately conservative organization, argued that genuine revolution could only originate in a proletariat organized by the PCF. The proletariat, however, were not prepared to be held back by conservative communists and their own unions. Strikes and factory sit-ins all across France began to paralyse the country.

Despite de Gaulle agreeing to reform the education system and the unions seeking to calm workers by successfully negotiating considerable improvements in pay and conditions, an estimated nine million people were on strike by the 24 May. It is not an exaggeration to say France was on the brink of its second revolution. In some respects the events of May 1968 *were* France's second revolution, as huge political and economic concessions and changes had to be made, and made quickly, in order to pull the nation back from the brink.

Fear of an all-out revolution became so real that the wealthy began to flee Paris with their children. On the 29 May it was rumoured that the government had collapsed when President de Gaulle temporarily disappeared.

The master tactician had travelled in secret to the French military base at Baden-Baden, just over the border in Germany, to receive personal assurances from the seasoned campaigner,

General Massu, that the French Army still backed him. Part of de Gaulle's motivation for disappearing was to absent himself from the Élysée Palace to reduce the likelihood of it being attacked by protesters. Perhaps, in the back of his mind, he was also eyeing Germany as a personal refuge if the situation in Paris further deteriorated.

De Gaulle's disappearance proved to be a smart move as it caused protesters to pause while they speculated as to what on earth was going on and to succumb to the belief that they had already succeeded in bringing him down. It also forced many less genuinely militant people in France, who were caught up in the heady atmosphere of rebellion, to consider the stark, long-term consequences of all-out revolution: domination by the far left, loss of the comforts of capitalism and so on. In de Gaulle's absence the French people blinked, concluding that it is better the devil you know.

De Gaulle was back on the scene with a vengeance the following day. Knowing he had the backing of the army, he dissolved the National Assembly and called an election. This did much to defuse the situation. The students continued to campaign, calling on the people to boycott the elections, but the revolutionary momentum had gone. Disagreements between the students, the unions and the PCF became outright splits. The workers took their pay rises and returned to work. By the time the Sorbonne fell to the police on the 16 June it was all over. In the elections that took place on the 23 and 30 June the Gaullists strengthened their position, winning 358 of 485 seats.

Sartre spoke up for the students, for the young, blaming the failure of the revolution on the PCF and the unions who had failed to seriously back it, rather than on the fundamental, small 'c' conservatism of the vast majority of French people – carnivals of rebellion aside.

Sartre had fallen out with the PCF long ago, but despite condemning the crushing of the 1956 Hungarian Revolution and the treatment of Russian writers, he had retained some degree of sympathy towards the Soviet Communist Party. This was about to change.

While France was in uproar, the 'Prague Spring' had been progressing too well for the Soviet system to continue to ignore it. In August, during the long summer recess, as France slept off its revolutionary hangover, the USSR invaded Czechoslovakia with 200,000 troops and 2,000 tanks. Many tanks rolled into the heart of Prague, crushing the 'Spring' beneath heavy tracks.

Although the Czechs could only offer token resistance, the liberalizing spirit of the 'Prague Spring' endured and spread. It ultimately proved stronger than the Soviet system, which collapsed less than twenty-five years later, morally and economically bankrupt.

Sartre, on holiday in Rome, condemned the invasion of Czechoslovakia as he had condemned the invasion of Hungary, but this time he did not proceed to find complex excuses for the conduct of the USSR: blaming Khrushchev's mismanagement of an otherwise sound regime then hobnobbing with the Soviet leader on a couple of occasions in the early 1960s.

Sartre was finally finished with the Soviets, had finally outgrown his hopes, as stubborn as they were naive, that Soviet communism could somehow pave the way towards equality and justice for all men. On the 25 August, he told the Italian communist newspaper, *Paese Sera,* that although he was in no way an anti-communist, 'the Soviet example, smothered as it is with bureaucracy, is no longer valid'.

In October, he joined forces with philosophers Bertrand Russell and Herbert Marcuse to reprove the Soviet oppression of Czechoslovakia and demand the immediate withdrawal of all Soviet troops. At the end of November he reinforced his solidarity with the Czech people by visiting Prague to watch the Czech premiere of *The Flies.*

Sartre's mother still lived in the hotel on the Boulevard Raspail where he had placed her in 1962 so that she would not be blown apart by the OAS. Now eighty-six, Anne-Marie was in poor health with a list of ailments similar to those her son had inflicted upon himself: heart problems, high blood pressure, headaches. She was well enough to toast Christmas 1968 with champagne in the company of Poulou and de Beauvoir, but by New Year she was seriously unwell.

Hospitalized by a heart attack on the 3 January, she suffered a stroke the following week that paralysed her right side, contorted her lips and plunged her into a coma. Sartre spent the greater part of the next two weeks at her bedside, surrounded by instruments, awaiting each of those few precious moments when she would stir enough to squeeze his wrist with her good hand.

On the 30 January, the hospital contacted him to say she was sinking fast. He and de Beauvoir rushed to be at her side but were still half an hour away when she quietly died. They arrived to find a very white body with a face that was no longer contorted.

25

Ultra-Lefty

Anne-Marie had felt that her son misrepresented his childhood in his autobiography. Following her death Sartre did not begin a second volume of *Words* to say all the things he was reluctant to say while she was alive. Instead, he pressed on with his biography of Flaubert, which some have argued is his autobiography in disguise. For example, it is said that in writing about Flaubert's bourgeois, conservative father, Achille-Cléophas, Sartre was really writing about his own grandfather, Charles. Certainly, the two characters are similarly drawn, but perhaps that is because the two grandees really were similar.

Sartre thought that every good biographer should use his imagination to breathe life into his subject, to access his subject's subjectivity and the true psychological motives behind his actions. When there is far more imagining and psychoanalysing than there is research into hard facts, however, when certain salient facts are ignored or dismissed, as is the case in all of

Sartre's pathographies, a certain drift towards autobiography is inevitable. A biographer has to be constantly on his guard against turning his subject into himself, precisely because his own fears, hang-ups, motives and preferences are too readily available as a basis for interpretation. The psychoanalyst, being a kind of biographer, is in exactly the same position in relation to his client.

Sartre, of course, knew all this, knew what an accurate and fair biography, an ordinary biography, ought to guard against. But *The Family Idiot* is no ordinary biography. Along with everything else that it is, it is an exploration of Sartre's complex relationship with Flaubert, a relationship that became more complex the longer the book became. A biographer rarely picks his subject in cold blood. Sartre picked Flaubert because he already had a raft of Flaubert-related issues, a lifelong love-hate relationship with the novelist and all he stood for. What did Flaubert stand for? In starting 'the Flaubert' Sartre was deliberately opening the biggest can of worms he could think of to see what would emerge. He ended up challenging himself to see how many more worms he could stuff in there.

Sartre wrote nothing else of philosophical significance in the late sixties and early seventies because *The Family Idiot* was made to be the receptacle of everything of philosophical significance that he wrote. Ideas on psychology, sociology, history, politics, economics, ethics and literature were all poured into *The Family*

Idiot in an over-ambitious effort to totally understand one man. In contemplating *The Family Idiot*, Hayman says, 'The importance of Sartre's gigantic, unbalanced, unfinished, almost unreadable book may turn out to reside in the sheer quantity of the energy it throws into a raid on the unknowable' (*Writing Against*, p. 383). For all its insight into Flaubert's life and times, *The Family Idiot* may still reveal more about Sartre's own ruling neurosis.

In the spring of 1969, while Sartre was busy raiding the unknowable, that grandest of grandees in his life, de Gaulle, finally fell from power. Seeking further constitutional reforms, de Gaulle asked the French people to back him yet again or he would resign. It was a referendum too far. Fifty-three per cent of the voters defied him and on 24 April he stepped down. He died the following year, a couple of weeks short of his eightieth birthday. Asked for a few generous words on a statesman who had, in many ways, been his 'opposite number', Sartre simply replied that he had never thought much of him.

In a letter published in *Le Monde* in May, Sartre, de Beauvoir and other notable left-wing intellectuals backed the Trotskyist, Alain Krivine, the presidential candidate for the Ligue communiste révolutionnaire. Sartre did no campaigning for Krivine, however, and when it came to the presidential election, won by Pompidou, he chose not to vote. Over the next few years Sartre's politics shifted way beyond seeking to bring about change through the existing political system: way beyond communism to the ultra-left, to Maoism and the fringes of anarchism.

Bitter towards the communists for failing to seriously back the May 1968 uprising, he increasingly aligned himself with the *gauchistes*, with the young radicals of the extreme left. He strove with them to revive the revolution. Most people become more conservative as they grow older, more resigned to the status quo. Sartre consciously went in the opposite direction in an almost desperate effort to prove to himself and the world that old age need not be characterized by quietism and an acceptance of bourgeois values.

Not least, running around with a bunch of radical young lefties, protesting against every injustice under the sun, gave him the buzz he was finding it increasingly difficult to get from his writing. Sustained concentration was not as easy as it used to be, largely because amphetamine abuse was not as easy as it used to be. As his long-mistreated body began to wear out it could no longer cope with Corydrane or supply his brain with quite enough oxygen. One way and another, his still-great mind was beginning to fray at the edges.

He spent the summer of 1969 in Yugoslavia and then Italy, where he took the opportunity to meet with student leaders. Returning to Paris he continued working on *The Family Idiot*. By the end of the year he had made significant progress with the third volume.

Opposing the Vietnam War was still top of Sartre's list of causes. On 11 December 1969, he appeared on French television to condemn the My Lai massacre: the slaughter of several hundred unarmed South Vietnamese men, women and children by US troops. Many of the bodies were mutilated and some of the women had been gang-raped. The atrocity occurred in March 1968, but it did not become public knowledge until November 1969, largely due to US efforts to cover it up.

News of the massacre and the cover-up greatly increased opposition to the war, particularly within the USA, and it confirmed the conclusion of the Russell-Sartre tribunal of 1967 that in Vietnam the Western, capitalist, neo-colonialist establishment was committing nothing less than genocide.

The 1970s began with Sartre stepping up his political activism. By the spring, he had signed statements, addressed meetings and given interviews condemning injustices in Biafra, Brazil and Mexico. He also joined a committee of far-left militants who believed they could influence relations between the Israelis and the Palestinians.

In April, he had a working lunch at the Coupole with Benny Lévy, Alain Geismar and other leading figures of the Gauche prolétarienne, a radical group that had evolved to some extent from Cohn-Bendit's M22M. The group had taken over a newspaper, *La Cause du peuple*, that sought to promote militant activity by serving as a channel of communication between those plotting strikes, demonstrations, sit-ins and sabotage.

The paper was primarily a bridge between intellectuals and workers: a means by which intellectuals could help workers achieve their revolutionary aims. Although the authorities resisted making the paper more attractive by declaring it illegal, copies were regularly seized by the police, and two of its previous editors, Jean-Pierre Le Dantec and Michel Le Bris, were facing trial for subversion. They were eventually sentenced to one year and six months' imprisonment, respectively.

Sartre enthusiastically agreed to give the paper his protection by becoming its editor-in-chief. Ten years earlier de Gaulle had declared, 'You do not imprison Voltaire.' Though the establishment despised him – the right-wing weekly, *Minute*, called him 'the nation's red cancer' – they were not prepared to give the *gauchistes* the oxygen of publicity a Sartre trial would supply. As ever, prosecuting Sartre would, at the very least, spark serious unrest. Sartre, of course, wanted to be prosecuted for this very reason, but if the authorities insisted upon granting him immunity then he would exploit it by bringing *La Cause du peuple* under the wing of that immunity.

The police continued to seize copies of the paper from street distributors and to take the distributors in for questioning, but its CEO, whose name appeared on every page alongside de Beauvoir's, was untouchable. What would happen if Sartre distributed the paper himself? On 20 June, wearing his trademark old coat with its fake fur collar, he descended to the streets of Paris to find out.

While friends, supporters, journalists and a photographer from Gallimard lurked anonymously in the background, the great writer began hawking the amateurishly produced radical magazine. Initially timid, he warmed to his task, shouting 'Read *La Cause du peuple*' at the top of his voice as he pressed copies into the hands of passers-by. A policeman confronted him and was about to lead him away to the station when someone yelled, 'You're arresting a Nobel Prize.' Realizing that his detainee was none other than the famous Nobel Prize-declining author and red menace of France, the policeman scurried away. 'You do not imprison Voltaire.'

The stunt was repeated six days later with more success. This time Sartre managed to get himself arrested but was released after ninety minutes of what he later described as polite questioning.

Sartre had not enjoyed being in Paris so much for years but he was not prepared to abandon his summer holiday plans. He toured Scandinavia with Arlette before heading down to his beloved second city of Rome to meet de Beauvoir.

Returning to Paris in September he picked up where he had left off. He allowed his name to be used – exploited – by every ultra-left cause that wanted to take advantage of it. Some of them did not even ask him first. By the end of the year he was the nominal editor of a host of extremist rags, some of them advocating anarchism, even terrorism: all of them seeking to coat themselves in Sartrean Teflon. He believed that if his name could help any activism that helped bring about the revolution then he had no right to refuse. He nonetheless admitted to the paper, *L'Idiot international*, that the bourgeois papers were better written and produced and even that they were more truthful.

Sartre had, not surprisingly, moved *Les Temps modernes* further to the left, prompting resignations among long-standing staff. His young Maoist friends declared, however, that the journal had become an *institution* and therefore part of the established order. Sartre was inclined to agree that his baby had grown up, that there could no longer be anything particularly revolutionary about it.

In early October, he submitted volume three of *The Family Idiot* to Gallimard. The publication of volumes one and two was still some months away. Despite being nearly 3,000 pages long the biography was, of course, unfinished. Having decided that Flaubert could not be totalized without a detailed analysis of his most famous novel, *Madame Bovary*, Sartre began planning a fourth volume.

Sartre's health had not been great for a long time. Nonetheless, he was showing remarkable stamina in maintaining an exhausting schedule and a forty-a-day cigarette habit. He had suffered occasional giddy spells for years, drink and drugs more often than not the cause, but in mid-October, tests prompted by bouts of staggering and dizziness the previous month revealed that he had constricted arteries and asphyxia of the brain. In short, he was a walking stroke and heart attack time bomb. He was prescribed medicine to reduce his blood pressure and improve his circulation.

He knew no other way to live than to keep himself busy. Given that the health benefits of remaining active are not to be underestimated, busyness was not the main risk he ran. That lay in the cigarettes and alcohol. Although he cut down a little, at least on the drink, and generally tried to take better care of himself, he became more or less resigned to dying before he reached his seventies. What could he do? As the 'bible' of existentialism preaches, life is a finite project. Whatever measures he took he was not going to live forever. What matters is how you live, not how long you live.

On 21 October, Geismar went on trial for his part in a demonstration that took place back in May on the evening of the trial of Le Dantec and Le Bris. Sartre decided that rather than attend a trial with a foregone conclusion – Geismar was given an eighteen-month prison sentence – he would address workers outside the Billancourt Renault factory. There was a chance, perhaps, that the Geismar trial had feelings among the proletariat running so high that he could rekindle the 1968 uprising, or at least the alliance that had existed back then between workers and intellectuals.

He stood on an oil barrel in order to be seen, his famous face, eleven years more worn than when Huston had criticized it so cruelly, protruding from his fake fur collar. Megaphone in hand he addressed a small crowd, consisting almost entirely of journalists and Maoists who had followed him there. He declared that the role of the intellectual is to be the ally of the people. The people, as represented by car workers leaving the Renault factory, largely ignored him. There was not going to be a revolution that day.

The press found the spectacle depressing, the message as tired as the man. Surely, such an eminent figure, the spokesman for a generation, for several generations, need not resort to a barrel in a factory car park. Sartre's reputation was assured, but the old man himself was surely losing it, becoming a caricature.

Yet, looking back, there is now something quite poignant and powerful about this Renault episode, more so than had he addressed one of the large crowds he usually attracted. The event has become a key element in the folklore of the later Sartre, a crucial piece of the Sartre jigsaw. A Socrates moment, maybe even a Jesus moment. Sartre crucified on top of a barrel at Calvary-Renault, just outside the walls of Paris: 'People, why hast thou forsaken the revolution, why art thou so far from helping yourselves, and from the words of my roaring.'

Undaunted, Sartre continued his militant activities into 1971. In January, he spoke at a protest about the treatment of Jews in Russia, and the following month he joined Maoists occupying the Sacré Coeur to publicize an incident in which a young leftist militant, Richard Deshayes, was mutilated by a tear-gas grenade. Posters of the young man's maimed face appeared all over Paris. In April, Sartre broke with Castro over civil rights abuses in Cuba, accusing him of behaving like Stalin.

Returning from a spring holiday in the French Riviera with Arlette, de Beauvoir and Sylvie Le Bon, whom de Beauvoir later adopted, Sartre was pleased to discover advanced copies of *The Family Idiot*. The first two volumes were published on 14 May 1971. The third volume appeared the following year.

The work aroused some interest because of its length, because it was one great French writer contemplating another and because it was a long time, by Sartre's standards, since he had published anything significant. This interest did not, however, translate into high sales. It was just too long for anyone but the most masochistic Sartre enthusiast to contemplate reading. Knowing there would be a third and possibly a fourth volume to wade through hardly helped. Most reviewers were similarly put off. By 1985, Gallimard had sold 27,000 copies, which is actually not bad considering. Early in that same decade Carol Cosman began translating the work into English for University of Chicago Press, a mammoth task she finally completed in 1993.

As with Sartre's other works about writers, *The Family Idiot* is not so much a biography of Flaubert, detailing the main events of his life in chronological order, as an exhaustive psychological study of Flaubert, an exercise in existential psychoanalysis. It is also and at the same time an exhaustive sociological study from a Marxist perspective that seeks to explain Flaubert as both a product of, and a reaction to, the immediate social circumstances of his family life and the broader social circumstances of his age and culture. Sartre's aim is to deftly merge these psychological and sociological perspectives in order to understand Flaubert as a totality.

As to the previously mentioned thesis that *The Family Idiot* is really Sartre's autobiography in disguise, the sequel to *Words*, Sartre rejected it, pointing out that his childhood was unlike Flaubert's. He, for example, was doted on while Flaubert was 'underloved'. Far from seeing himself in Flaubert, Sartre claims he was fascinated with Flaubert as his opposite. Sartre, for example, was prolific: he wrote quickly and always had more than one project on the go. Flaubert, on the other hand, was painstakingly slow, he could take years to write a book, endlessly researching and revising it.

It remains a matter of debate how much of himself Sartre projects onto Flaubert, both intentionally and unintentionally, but what is certain is that 'the Flaubert' returns to the central theme of *Words*: writing as a choice of being. The thesis that *The*

Family Idiot is Sartre's autobiography in disguise is not really credible, but it is a work in which Sartre is obsessed with the *choice* to be a writer, a choice of self that was very much his own.

Sartre likens the young Gustave Flaubert's family to a deep well. Gustave can rise up the well from the bottom, but he remains imprisoned within it. The walls of the well were built before he was born. His mother wanted a daughter, a female companion to compensate for her lonely childhood, so Gustave was a disappointment. Not only that, given that the two siblings immediately preceding him had died, he was not expected to survive.

There was, therefore, little maternal affection in the care that the disappointing, futureless child received; it aimed only at pacifying him. Sartre identifies Flaubert's passivity as his fundamental choice of himself, at least until he underwent a radical conversion in his twenties. Pacified, overlooked as a person, Gustave's intellectual development was slow. He was, according to Sartre, unable to read at the age of seven, though other biographers of Flaubert dispute this. His family further reinforced the low self-esteem at the heart of his ennui by viewing him as an idiot. Gustave was, according to Sartre, eventually taught to read by the local priest.

The defining moment of Gustave's life occurred in 1844 when he suffered an incapacitating nervous crisis, possibly an epileptic fit, that left him unable to pursue the legal career his father had chosen for him. Gustave's crisis, arguably self-induced, allowed him to free himself from his father's domination and become a writer. The invalid, being no good for anything better, was left to write. The idiot was at last free to transform himself into a genius.

For Sartre, Flaubert's crisis was a radical conversion to authenticity, an act of self-assertion in which he finally dispensed with his passivity, his choice not to choose, his bad faith. Through an act that had the outward appearance of a nervous breakdown, but was in fact a positive affirmation of freedom, he ceased to exist primarily for others and began to exist for himself.

To some, *The Family Idiot* is Sartre's crowning glory, a work in which he brilliantly fuses together all the key elements of his life's work. To others, it is a self-indulgent monstrosity that cobbles together a grotesque portrait of Flaubert with little regard for established facts. Oddly enough, there appears to be some credibility in both these views, though the real truth lies somewhere in between. As Julian Barnes wrote in the *London Review of Books* on 3 June 1982, 'This book is mad, of course. Admirable but mad.'

Inspired by the publication of volumes one and two, Sartre soon began working on volume four and even contemplated writing a play or a novel. Neither the play nor the novel ever materialized, however, and circumstances soon forced him to abandon volume four. His phenomenal career as a writer, as several great writers in one, was all but over.

On the night of the 17 May 1971, a few days after the publication of *The Family Idiot*, Sartre had a stroke while sleeping at Arlette's. The following morning his mouth was twisted and he could hardly walk. He was still in this state when he arrived at de Beauvoir's flat in the evening. In her book, *Adieux: A Farewell to Sartre*, which movingly documents the last ten years of his life, de Beauvoir writes:

'How are you?' I asked in the ordinary, rather casual way. 'Well, not so good.' And indeed his legs were giving way under him, he spoke indistinctly, and his mouth was a little twisted. I had not noticed that he was ailing the day before, because we had been listening to music and had hardly talked at all. But that evening he had reached Arlette's in a bad way, and he had awakened this morning in the state in which I saw him now; obviously he had had a slight stroke during the night. I had dreaded an occurrence of this kind for a long while, and I had vowed I would keep my head … I had to make a great effort not to let my panic show. Sartre insisted upon drinking his usual dose of whisky.

(*Adieux: A Farewell to Sartre*, p. 17)

A visit to the doctor the next day revealed that the blood supply to his brain had further deteriorated. His blood pressure was an alarmingly high 180 and he had not been taking the medicine prescribed back in October.

He started taking his medicine again and within a few days he had bounced back once more. He took control of yet another radical publication and began making plans to put the police 'on trial' before a people's tribunal. He was in good spirits when he celebrated his sixty-sixth birthday on the 21 June.

In Switzerland in July, again with Arlette, he had another stroke. Again he bounced back, enough to meet Wanda in Naples and visit Pompeii. By the time he reached Rome the effects of an abscessed tooth were troubling him more that the after-effects of the stroke. His teeth were in a terrible state. He had not taken care of them any better since the Irish dentist incident of 1959.

As a way of warning him off conducting his people's tribunal, the authorities had started libel proceedings against him based on claims made in a couple of *La Cause du peuple* articles. He had already shelved his tribunal plans in favour of meetings and press conferences about police activities, but on the 24 September he had to appear before two judges. The judges threw the case out. 'You do not imprison Voltaire.'

Half expecting to die at any moment, Sartre continued acting up. In October, he joined an anti-racist demonstration alongside Genet and Foucault, and in January 1972 took up the cause of improving prison conditions. He, Deleuze, Foucault, Michelle Vian and François Mauriac's son, Claude, were evicted from the Ministry of Justice for trying to hold a press conference on injustices in the prison system.

On the 14 February 1972, Sartre, several journalists and the singer, Colette Magny, were similarly evicted from Renault after a van smuggled them into the workshop to distribute leaflets. At the ensuing press conference, Sartre argued that, 'Since Renault has been nationalized one should be able to walk about there freely. We were unable to speak to the workers. That proves that Renault equals fascism' (*Adieux: A Farewell to Sartre*, p. 27).

In Brussels in late February, dressed in a scruffy, black pullover, he talked down to a room full of smartly dressed, middle-class lawyers, explaining to them that the bureaucratic justice they peddled was an oppressive force that needed to be replaced by a true justice of the people. The philosophical complexity of his thesis 'floated over the heads of his listeners' (*Adieux: A Farewell to Sartre*, p. 26), who, for the most part, had sufficient mental capacity only to be offended that he was far less smartly dressed than his audience. 'As everybody was leaving, a woman looked at Sartre and said angrily, "It wasn't worth dressing up," and another, "When you speak in public you make an effort; you put on proper clothes"' (*Adieux: A Farewell to Sartre*, p. 26).

Perhaps Sartre on his barrel outside Renault in October 1970 had sown more seeds of discontent than the press gave him credit for. Maoists had been leafleting at the factory gates since January and some militants within the workforce had been sacked. While Sartre was haranguing sharp-suited lawyers in Brussels, a demonstration at the factory about the sackings turned nasty. A fight broke out between Maoists and armed security guards, culminating in the fatal shooting of Pierre Overney, a worker who had been sacked from the factory some months before. The killing moved 30,000 people to march in protest a few days later and the following week over 160,000 people, including Sartre, marched before Overney's funeral.

Notable by their absence from the reaction to the Overney killing was the PCF. Sartre accused them of perverting the communist ideal and of being in league with the government. There was no greater hatred in French politics than that between the Maoists and the PCF. Cohn-Bendit had launched the first salvo back in May 1968 when he described the PCF as 'Stalinist filth'.

In revenge for Overney's killing, an ultra-ultra-left underground faction of the ultra-left Gauche prolétarienne kidnapped Robert Nogrette, assistant head of personnel at Renault. They held him for forty-eight hours before releasing him unharmed. They had made political demands but without attaching conditions to them and they received no ransom. Sartre was careful not to condone the kidnapping but he said in so many words that it was to be expected. He was now operating on the fringes of terrorism.

In the spring, he took another holiday in the south of France with de Beauvoir and Sylvie – more than most of the workers at Renault could afford to do. Upon his return to Paris he continued ticking the usual boxes of left-wing indignation by campaigning for squatters' rights. He also wrote the preface to a book accusing psychiatrists of oppressing their patients. He argued that what was needed was a dialogue between equals, something that has now become standard practice in many areas of mental health therapy, particularly existential counselling.

Although his militancy was undiminished, cracks were beginning to show in his relationship with the Maoists in general and the editors of *La Cause du peuple/J'accuse* in particular – the paper had changed its name somewhat since its merger with another radical publication. When the paper declared that a lawyer accused of a murder should be taken by the balls, cut up with a razor and lynched, Sartre reminded its editors that it was a fundamental principle of justice that people must be presumed innocent until proven guilty. He knew the paper was narrow-minded and unreasonable yet he did what he could to keep it going.

Despite all his campaigning efforts, Sartre's young Maoist friends increasingly nagged him to give up writing about a figure of the last century – he was still making some effort with 'Flaubert 4' – and to write a popular, contemporary novel instead, something to inspire the revolution. Sartre argued that he was committed to 'the Flaubert', that he was unsure what constituted a popular novel in 1972, that it was unclear a novel would make any difference and that a decent novel takes time.

In truth, he no longer had the capacity to write a novel, and as genius is as genius does, it was not the case that he had another novel in him that his poor health was holding back. 'Why should we attribute to Racine the capacity to write yet another tragedy when that is precisely what he did not write?' (*Existentialism and Humanism*, p. 42). His oxygen-starved brain was hardly up to plodding on with *The Family Idiot*, let alone creating believable characters and coordinating them in a meaningful plot. He had not published a novel since 1949, had not taken the trouble to write one even when it was well within his powers. Now, sadly, it was well beyond his powers. Even another turgid play was well beyond his powers.

His teeth and gums were giving him hell, his sight and hearing were poor, his legs ached and he was sleeping badly. At times he was little better than a dribbling wreck. '"Yes, I dribble. For a couple of weeks now I have been dribbling." I had not mentioned it, for fear of embarrassing him, but he attached no importance to it. What did displease him a little was his drowsiness' (*Adieux: A Farewell to Sartre*, p. 62). Worst of all, as regards any aspiration to write a novel, his memory was going.

One afternoon in Rome in the autumn of 1972, as they were walking past the Pantheon, he told de Beauvoir and Sylvie that some cats had urinated on his trousers from a balustrade.

Perhaps, in his dotage, he believed this to be the case, but de Beauvoir guessed the truth. 'Sylvie believed him and laughed about it. For my part I knew what was the matter, but I said nothing' (*Adieux: A Farewell to Sartre*, p. 34).

So, the great man was now inclined to piss his pants in the street, especially when he was a little pissed himself, which was often the case. Or, if you prefer not to snigger, a sixty-seven-year old man in poor health, who had suffered several strokes, had become bladder incontinent, particularly when under the influence of even a small amount of alcohol. It comes to most people in the end, even those who are not partial to a stiff whisky or two.

Such deterioration seems more shocking in Sartre's case than in most other cases, partly because he had always been so physically tough and resilient, not least in coping with his own excesses, partly because it underlines the existential truth that even the greatest minds, the greatest men, are utterly dependent on the fragile flesh that sustains their greatness. There is a lot of truth in Huston's claim that only the mind mattered to Sartre, but he was wrong that the physical universe did not exist for him.

Then again, Sartre's greatness now resided in writings that had entirely transcended his deteriorating body. He was only a little old man in a very limited sense. His real bones were paper, ink and glue, duplicated to virtual indestructibility on countless bookshelves. He had needed his body to achieve that end and it had served him well. Now he had achieved that end his body was in the way. He would go on living out of habit, doing what he could, waiting to become what he had dreamed of becoming since childhood: a great, dead writer.

> My bones are leather and cardboard, my parchment flesh smells of glue and mildew, and I strut at my ease across a hundredweight or so of paper … My consciousness is in fragments: all the better. Other consciousnesses have taken charge of me. They read *me* and I leap to their eyes; they talk about *me* and I am on everyone's lips, a universal and singular language; I have made myself a prospective interest for millions of glances … I exist nowhere but I *am*, at last! I am everywhere: a parasite on humanity, by my good deeds I prey on it and force it endlessly to revive my absence.
>
> (*Words*, p. 122)

26

The Long Road Down

Sartre was resigned to his body dying before he reached his seventies, but the road down was longer and in some ways crueller than he envisaged. He was ailing but nonetheless remarkably resilient. As the saying goes, there was life in the old philosopher yet.

An old man can live with occasionally pissing his pants but constant toothache is unbearable. Hell is bad teeth! Having all his teeth removed had been the obvious answer for years but he was concerned that false teeth might prevent him from speaking clearly in public and shoot from his mouth when he tried. When he finally took the plunge towards the end of 1972 he was pleasantly surprised at how quickly he got used to dentures. Best of all, he had no more painful abscesses. As de Beauvoir writes:

> Two days later he came home at about half past five in high spirits. His new teeth did not bother him at all – no difficulty

in speaking and he chewed better than before. Later, when he came to my apartment about midnight, I asked him how the evening had gone – an evening that he had expected to be boring. 'It was dreadfully dull,' he said. 'But I thought about nothing but my teeth and I was so pleased!'

(*Adieux: A Farewell to Sartre*, p. 35)

Relief from toothache gave him a new lease of life. Aware of the amateurish journalism and print quality of all the ultra-left publications he had under his wing, he continued planning a quality ultra-left journal to be called *Libération*. Quality required money and he ploughed a considerable amount of his own into the project.

To raise more money he began a new book, one that would involve little writing. *It's Right to Rebel*, started in November 1972 and published in 1974, is a script of conversations between Sartre, Philippe Gavi and Pierre Victor, the last name being the pseudonym of Benny Lévy.

Much to the consternation of de Beauvoir and other of Sartre's old allies, the young, demagogic Lévy soon became Sartre's secretary, reader and spokesman. To some extent, Lévy began putting alien words into Sartre's mouth and even alien ideas into Sartre's increasingly addled brain. But Sartre liked to have Lévy around as a sort of ultra-left attack dog, lest the bourgeoisie try to claim him in the King Lear phase of his life.

As 1973 got underway Sartre threw his remaining strength behind the *Libération* project. On 7 February, he appeared on TV, where he ducked questions about his life and work to plug the forthcoming newspaper.

The following month, after suffering a bout of bronchitis and pushing himself to finish an article for *Libération*, he suffered what was probably yet another small stroke. A series of injections alleviated the paralysis in his face and arm but he was also left disorientated and struggling to remember who people were.

Various symptoms of vascular dementia persisted during an early spring holiday in the south of France that Arlette had begged him to take. He kept mistaking one person for another and even started to believe that fictional characters were real. Reduced to reading detective stories, he awaited the arrival of Hercule Poirot. Mercifully, he did not begin to expect the imminent arrival of his old adversary, the lurking lobster. When he joined de Beauvoir in Avignon he kept confusing her with Arlette. It must have taxed his brain at the best of times to keep track of which of his many women he was with; in his current state it was all but impossible.

May 1973 brought the best of news and the worst of news. The good news was the successful launch of *Libération*. The first issue appeared on 22 May. The creation of this quality far-left newspaper, in collaboration with Serge July, was one of the great triumphs of the later Sartre. The paper survives to this day, though is now centre-left in its politics. Sartre would not be amused to know that today a significant share of the paper is owned by the super-rich Rothschild dynasty.

The bad news was that the vision in his 'good eye' was rapidly deteriorating. Veins at the back of his left eye were clotting and haemorrhaging. Treatment temporarily improved the situation, but not enough for him to read what he wrote. He was finally forced to abandon *The Family Idiot*. By August, his sight was worse than it had been in the spring. His ophthalmologist also discovered that he had glaucoma. His visual impairment was officially declared irreversible in October when his retina was found to be permanently scarred near the centre.

Despite the diagnosis, he could not help hoping that his vision would somehow normalize enough for him to read his own writing. He tried various visual aids but these required such a level of magnification that he could only view one word at a time and so lost the gist of the sentences. 'The words went by so slowly that he preferred hearing them read aloud – so slowly that it was impossible for him to revise and correct his own texts' (*Adieux: A Farewell to Sartre*, p. 59).

It was torture for a man who had written for many hours every day for most of his life to suddenly be robbed of his occupation. Listless and depressed, he spent hours listening to a transistor radio or simply starring into space, light being just about the only thing he could see. His only relief was sleeping, which he often succumbed to thanks to his frailty and the limited supply of oxygen to his brain.

Sartre was paying the price of forcing his body for so many years to make his mind more productive. He had enlivened himself for decades with a range of stimulants, the most damaging of which was not Corydrane but tobacco, and now he had the cardiovascular system of an unhealthy centenarian. He also had diabetes.

As a writer, he had run many marathons at a sprint, but had he taken better care of his health, he probably could have run several more marathons than he actually ran. He certainly lived on for seven long years unable to write anything of significance. It seems crass to charge Sartre, of all writers, with not writing enough, but as a writer who was always most interested in what he was *going* to do, he certainly levelled this charge against himself. He might have kicked himself but smoking had hardened the arteries in his legs, rendering them stiff, weak and painful. In carrying on smoking, even though he had cut down a fraction, he was running the risk of having both legs amputated bit by bit.

As he reluctantly began to accept that his blindness was permanent, he told an interviewer:

My occupation as a writer is completely destroyed ... The only point to my life was writing ... What will no longer be accessible to me is something that many young people today are scornful of: style, let us say the literary manner of presenting an idea or a reality. This necessarily calls for revisions ... I can no longer correct my work even once, because I cannot read what I have written'

(quoted in Cohen-Solal, *Jean-Paul Sartre: A Life*, p. 489).

It came almost as a welcome distraction when, in October 1973, the right-wing paper, *Minute* finally brought him to court on charges of libel for comments made years earlier in *La Cause du peuple* and elsewhere. His lawyer was given the opportunity to reiterate at length Sartre's accusations that the editorial staff of *Minute* were thugs who had actively supported the OAS. 'Gisèle Halimi spoke for more than an hour. She drew up a pitiless indictment of *Minute* – its references to the OAS, its incitements to murder, its racism. From time to time the judge reminded her that the question lay elsewhere, but he let her go on' (*Adieux: A Farewell to Sartre*, pp. 57–8). Sartre was fined 400 francs and *Minute* received a derisory sum of 1 franc in damages.

The popular press who came to report on the court case were more interested in how ill Sartre looked. Shamelessly, 'with man-eating expressions on their faces' (*Adieux: A Farewell to Sartre*, p. 58), they asked Halimi to let them know immediately if and when Sartre took a turn for the worse.

No longer able to live alone, nor indeed in an old building

where the lift was always out of action, he moved to a modern apartment on the Boulevard Edgar-Quinet, near the Montparnasse Cemetery and the Montparnasse Tower. The great advantage of the Montparnasse Tower, some say, is that it offers spectacular views of Paris that do not include the Montparnasse Tower. Sartre was indifferent on this issue, being unable to see either the tower or the views from it.

He accepted the necessity of the move but took little interest in his new accommodation, later referring to it as 'the place where I don't work anymore' (*Adieux: A Farewell to Sartre*, p. 64). His women took care of everything and willingly became his care workers, probably the most intellectual bunch of care workers an old man ever had. They helped him dress and eat and even cleaned him up when he lost control of his bladder or bowels. De Beauvoir slept five nights a week in the spare room, Arlette the other two.

Lévy became what Hayman describes as Sartre's 'intellectual nurse' (*Writing Against*, p. 426): reading to him, pushing him to complete *It's Right to Rebel* and stirring his mind with challenging questions. It was a tough job that he did well, though on occasion he felt like quitting. He did not quit partly because of his deep admiration for Sartre's work and partly because he owed the old philosopher a debt of gratitude. As an Egyptian Jew, Lévy was stateless. As Sartre's employee he was entitled to live in France.

In 1974, Sartre appealed by letter to President Valéry Giscard d'Estaing on Lévy's behalf. The president, who was either a Sartre fan or knew the value of having him as an ally, replied immediately and soon pulled strings to grant Lévy French citizenship.

De Beauvoir came to hate Lévy: his influence over Sartre and Sartre's increasing dependence upon him. When Lévy arrived each day in his role as Sartre's secretary, de Beauvoir had always already departed. As Lévy shifted from Maoism to a profound interest in Judaism, she felt he was increasingly leading the old existentialist and arch-atheist to endorse certain metaphysical and even religious views. Sartre was King Théoden of Rohan and, for all his genuine support, Lévy was something of a Gríma Wormtongue whispering in the old king's ear.

De Beauvoir worried about the damage Lévy would do to Sartre's intellectual legacy but the truth is that nobody takes too seriously the work that the senile Sartre produced with Lévy's collaboration. *Being and Nothingness* it is not. No, nor *Nausea* neither. Rather, it is largely the inconsequential by-product of a therapy programme aimed at saving Sartre's mind from total stagnation.

For her part, Arlette liked Lévy. They were both young, both from North Africa, both of Jewish descent. They even studied Hebrew together under the tutelage of Shmuel Trigano. Not least, they formed the core of an alliance of young Sartre disciples opposed to the senior disciples led by de Beauvoir.

It's Right to Rebel was published in May 1974. To promote the work, Sartre, Gavi and Lévy took part in a conversation with Herbert Marcuse that was reported in *Libération* by Hélène Lassithiotakis (aka Melina), a young Greek woman who had first introduced herself to Sartre in 1972 and with whom he had the last of his many romances.

The old charm was still there and the old wallet was still open where an attractive girl was concerned. Although his means were stretched – he had sunk a lot of money into getting *Libération* off the ground – he started paying her an allowance to live in Paris and study philosophy. He also visited her several times in Greece after she returned there following a mental breakdown. He was also keeping Arlette, Wanda and Michelle, who were, of course, far from being girls by that time. De Beauvoir had her own money.

Despite his poor health, he continued to travel. It gave him something to do. As well as visiting Greece, Portugal, Switzerland, Germany and Israel, there were regular excursions to Junas in the south of France with Arlette and long stays in his beloved Italy with de Beauvoir.

In the summer of 1974 de Beauvoir collected him from a Florence hotel, where he had been staying with Wanda, to take him by train to Rome. He was sporting a scruffy white beard that he could not see to shave off. It suited him no better than the Phoney War beard of 1939 and de Beauvoir determined, as she had back then, that he should lose it as soon as possible. She had the hotel barber shave it off as soon as they reached the Eternal City. Meanwhile, Sylvie, who was due to arrive in a few days from her father's funeral in Brittany, was issued with strict instructions to purchase an electric razor.

Lévy, who often chose what he read to Sartre, helped keep him in touch with the latest left-wing causes. Both men were sympathetic towards The Red Army Faction or Baader-Meinhof Gang, a communist, West German, terrorist organization opposed to imperialism and the continuing domination of German politics by ex-Nazis. On 4 December 1974, Sartre, Lévy and Cohn-Bendit, who acted as interpreter, visited the leader of the group, Andreas Baader, in Stammheim-Stuttgart prison.

Sartre's main aim was to publicize the issue of the psychological torture of political prisoners. He attempted to make clear to the German press and TV that he did not approve of the group's use of extreme violence. The distinction was lost on the German media who were scathing about his intervention. For his part, despite the heavy criticism he received, Sartre was happy to be ticking the ultimate tick-box on the list of ultra-left-wing causes: campaigning for the rights of terrorists and mass murderers. One is reminded of the ageing Lord Longford's absurd efforts on behalf of the serial killer, Myra Hindley.

The year 1975 began with Sartre and his entourage stepping up plans for a ten-part TV series on twentieth-century history from Sartre's perspective. Each programme was to conclude by linking the historical period covered to contemporary issues. It was a great idea. After all, few people had lived, contemplated and sought to influence the main events of the twentieth century to the extent Sartre had. Nobody could accuse him of not striving to make the century his own. Now, as he approached his seventieth birthday, he was a kind of living embodiment of his century.

Historians were employed to research and gather material for each programme, while Sartre, with Lévy constantly at his side, fought constant tiredness and exhaustion to coordinate the project. By September, however, it became clear that the TV channel, Antenne Deux, had developed cold feet.

André Vivien, a government official charged with relations with France's national broadcasting agency, the Office de Radiodiffusion Télévision Française, had submitted a copy of the series synopsis to Prime Minister Jacques Chirac who was concerned about such a far-left view of history going to air. It was seven years on from the near revolution of 1968 but the French authorities were still twitchy.

On 21 September, Sartre called a press conference, which he subtitled: 'A Problem of Television Censorship'. With all the anger his frail body could muster he declared that he had been forced by indirect censorship to give up his TV series. '"It has been said 'Sartre is giving up.' No. I have been *made* to give up. It is a case of categorical indirect censorship"' (*Adieux: A Farewell to Sartre*, p. 88).

Wrangles and angry exchanges over the TV series did nothing for his health, which had been surprisingly good during a long summer vacation in Greece, and in October 1975 he collapsed several times. His blood pressure was sky-high and he was barely able to avoid succumbing to a wheelchair. Fear of having his legs amputated led him to make a genuine effort to give up smoking cigarettes. He was unable to kick the Boyards completely until March 1977 but at least trying to give up constituted cutting down. Each morning it took him an age to shake off a paralysis that numbed his mouth and gripped his throat. He dribbled his juice as he attempted to watch movies on a hired TV set by sitting a few inches from the screen.

Feeble though he was, some right-wing groups still considered him sufficiently dangerous to be worthy of occasional death threats. Following the receipt of one particularly menacing letter, de Beauvoir had his apartment fitted with an armoured front door. Despite having been the target of two OAS bombs in the early sixties, Sartre was unconcerned by the threats.

In 1976, he began supporting a campaign against his once beloved USSR. In January, he backed protesters who had been jailed for occupying the Soviet embassy in Paris to publicize civil rights abuses in Russia. By February, he and de Beauvoir had managed to persuade fifty Nobel Prize winners to sign a petition that appeared in *Libération* and *Le Monde* calling for the release of Russian dissidents.

He was well enough to spend most of the summer travelling, visiting Venice, Capri and Rome before flying to Athens to hook up with Hélène. He managed to do a fair amount of very slow walking in these places and apologized to the women for impeding them. When he returned to Paris in the autumn, Lévy persuaded him to resume attending *Les Temps modernes* editorial meetings. He had forsaken this duty for some time, partly because he was more interested in his new publication. It all helped to get him out and about and keep his mind and body active.

The movie, *Sartre by Himself*, was released on 27 October. Filmed in 1972 by Alexandre Astruc and Michel Contat, this 190-minute film documentary features a chain-smoking Sartre talking from behind large glasses about his life and work to a group of chain-smoking friends gathered in his book-lined study. A marathon if watched all at once, the film nonetheless offers a golden opportunity to get up close and personal with the great man and some of his inner circle. According to de Beauvoir, 'Once again the critics praised Sartre enthusiastically and the public flocked to see it' (*Adieux: A Farewell to Sartre*, p. 96).

In November, Sartre broke his rule of not accepting honours and attended the Israeli embassy, Paris, to receive an honorary doctorate from Hebrew University, Jerusalem. As ever, he made every effort to be even-handed about the Arab-Israeli conflict. He affirmed his friendship for Israel while raising concerns about Israel's mistreatment of the Palestinians. 'He spoke of his travels in Egypt and in Israel in 1967 and said that if the university of Cairo offered him a degree he would accept it' (*Adieux: A Farewell to Sartre*, p. 97).

Sartre nearly died in January 1977 after a Saturday evening of heavy drinking with Michelle. She sometimes stopped at his place on Saturdays to relieve the others. Michelle was the least stringent when it came to his alcohol consumption – Sylvie, with de Beauvoir's approval, had been watering down his bottles of whisky for some time. By the following evening, his blood pressure was so high – 250! – that de Beauvoir had to phone the emergency services who stabilized him with an injection. Michelle, who made the excuse that she was allowing him to die happy, was forbidden by the queen bee to stay with him again. Years later, Michelle told Rowley in an interview that de Beauvoir was his mama, the only one allowed to give him his bottle (*Tête-à-Tête*, p. 334).

February saw him heading to Athens with Lévy to spend a week with Hélène. During his stay he was well enough to lecture to a huge audience on 'What is philosophy?' Hélène turned up in Paris a couple of weeks after his return and for a while they spent a lot of time together. He told her she had the power to rejuvenate him and make him feel young again.

In reality, he was continuing to decline. Circulation in his legs was down to 30 per cent and he was advised that even a short walk might induce a stroke. He made it to Venice with de Beauvoir but was reduced to a wheelchair to get about. Despite his condition, he travelled for much of the summer. When he reached his regular haunts, however, he was unable to do little more in them than sleep and listen to music.

Junas in July with Arlette was followed by two weeks in Venice with Wanda then over a month in Rome with de Beauvoir. He did some of his travelling by train and plane but it is remarkable that he had both the stamina and the desire to spend so much time sitting in a hot car feeling like death warmed up when he could not even see the view. Anything was better than sitting at home in Paris feeling sorry for himself.

Back in Paris, at the end of the summer, he dumped Hélène, telling her that she no longer had the power to rejuvenate him and that he no longer loved her. He sought to soothe her tears with the promise that he would continue paying for her to live in Paris for a while. He told de Beauvoir that he had called the affair off because "'She is too self-seeking; she's not worthwhile. She no longer means anything to me'" (*Adieux: A Farewell to Sartre*, p. 107). Seemingly, Hélène was simply getting on his ageing nerves. After all, he had enough women mithering him as it was. Possibly, he was also seeking to spare the emotional and somewhat mentally unstable young woman from bearing close witness to his endgame, which surely had to come soon.

Relations between Israel and Egypt had been moving towards a peace treaty that was eventually signed in 1979 by Presidents Begin and Sadat and witnessed by US President Carter. In February 1978, Sartre travelled to Israel with Lévy and Arlette to do his bit for the process.

The trip resulted in an article about the Arab-Israeli situation written largely by Lévy and signed off by Sartre. In true Lévy style the article was rambling, poorly written and slightly weird, with an undertone of Zionist mysticism. Lévy (Victor) addressing Sartre in the article: 'Since you are neither Solomon nor a universal consciousness, from what place do you speak?' The place turns out to be Paris during the French Revolution.

The article was sent to *Le Nouvel Observateur* where it was read with horror by Bost. De Beauvoir was equally alarmed when she read it and strongly advised Sartre to withdraw it. Sartre was happy to comply but Lévy was furious. It was the final showdown between the junior and senior Sartreans.

A blazing row followed at a *Les Temps modernes* meeting, in which Jean Pouillon, André Gorz and other senior members of the editorial staff rubbished Lévy's article and criticized his effrontery in trying to pass it off as Sartre's work. The hot-headed Lévy retaliated by calling them a bunch of corpses and never showed his face at the *Les Temps modernes* offices again. Perhaps the senior Sartreans should have let the article appear. After all, the bonkers ramblings of Nietzsche's twilight years have never done *his* reputation any harm. But then they were at least Nietzsche's *own* bonkers ramblings.

In her analysis of Lévy in *Adieux*, which immediately follows her account of the row over the article, de Beauvoir is scathing. How dearly she would have liked to rid Sartre of Lévy's influence, but Sartre liked him for the very same reasons that de Beauvoir hated him:

> Victor had been one of the leaders of the *Gauche prolé-tarienne* and he had retained the 'little boss's' state of mind – everything had to give way before him. He moved easily from one conviction to another, but always with the same obstinacy. From the ill-governed intensity of his various enthusiasms he derived certainties that he would not allow to be called into question. This gave his words a vigour that some people found stimulating, but writing calls for a critical attitude of mind that he did not possess.
>
> (*Adieux: A Farewell to Sartre*, p. 110)

In the spring of 1978 Sartre told de Beauvoir that he could not afford a new pair of shoes, yet he was still able to spend Easter in northern Italy with her and Sylvie. Perhaps de Beauvoir paid.

Despite the revenue that flowed from his publications worldwide, Sartre owed Gallimard money. Over the years his publisher had become his personal loan company, willing to advance him cash on his next book even when they had no idea what it would be. Gallimard still did very well out of him thanks to various re-releases, new editions, paperback versions and translation rights, but with nothing new for several years except the Lévy collaborations, they could not afford to be as generous as they once were.

Sartre had a decent income by most people's standards but his expenditure was enormous. The travelling was one thing and his many political causes another, but the main drain on his finances was all the hangers-on he was prepared to support. He was generous to a fault and usually had pockets full of cash that he was happy to spend picking up the tab. To his credit, he never amassed a personal fortune by hoarding his money, by investing it or by selling out his artistic integrity to the highest bidder. Any such action would have been far too bourgeois.

As 1978 progressed, Sartre continued to travel when he could – to languish and doze in a series of European hotel rooms. He also continued deluding himself that he was doing worthwhile work with Lévy in the form of a long, confused work, *Power and Freedom*, that they were concocting in the same manner as *It's Right to Rebel*.

When de Beauvoir finally read the work in early 1980, she was horrified by how unrepresentative and unworthy of Sartre's philosophy it was and the arrogant superiority of the unknown Lévy's tone towards the great thinker. All the other leading Sartreans felt the same. Sartre nonetheless insisted on the publication of an outline to *Power and Freedom* titled 'Hope Now'. These discussions with Lévy ran in *Le Nouvel Observateur* shortly before Sartre died. Sartre was distressed and disappointed by the universally negative reception his friends gave 'Hope Now', a hurt that helped precipitate his end.

Returning from Provence at the end of Easter 1979, Sartre was slashed across the hand by Gérard de Clèves, a Belgian poet with mental health issues. Sartre was in the habit of inviting de Clèves in and giving him money when he came begging at his door. Tired of the poet's all-too frequent visits, Sartre finally told him, keeping his armoured door on its chain, to go away and not come back. De Clèves lost his temper, slashed Sartre's hand through the gap allowed by the chain and before the police arrived nearly managed to batter down a door designed to withstand plastic explosives. Sartre refused to press charges against de Clèves.

Sartre's heavily bandaged hand can be seen in photos of him leaving the Élysée Palace on the 26 June 1979 after President d'Estaing personally thanked him for his fund-raising efforts on behalf of Vietnamese 'boat people'. Also in the photos is Sartre's onetime friend and long-time adversary, Raymond Aron. Sartre and Aron had shaken hands earlier for the sake of appearances but there was to be no rapprochement between the two old men.

To Aron's, 'Bonjour, mon petit camarade!', Sartre replied only with an abrupt, 'Bonjour'. When Aron tried to embrace him he recoiled.

Clearly Aron was prepared to forgive years of very public disagreement but Sartre was not. To Aron, Sartre was a well-meaning but naive old communist. To Sartre, Aron had sold out to the bourgeoisie in the late forties, confirming his right-wing credentials in 1955 with the publication of his anti-Marxist polemic, *The Opium of the Intellectuals*.

They had exchanged fire again in 1968. Aron, who was openly opposed to the student protests, had mocked the idea put forward by Sartre and other ultra-lefties that France should help fund universities in Cuba. Sartre had retaliated with a withering attack on Aron, accusing him of being typical of pompous university professors who peddle the same tired thesis for decades, as though it were gospel, to students who are not allowed to seriously question them.

> When an ageing Aron endlessly repeats the main tenets of a thesis he wrote in 1939 to his students, without letting them express any criticism whatsoever, then he is exercising a real power that, however, has nothing to do with anything worthy of the name of knowledge.
>
> (*Le Nouvel Observateur*, June 1968).

Sartre had sufficient wits about him even in the summer of

1979 to refuse to forgive Aron the anti-revolutionary stance he had taken in 1968, even if Aron's stance had more to do with preaching reason and moderation than with Gaullism. To a man who had directed most of his energy since 1968 to reviving the revolution, Aron was and remained a traitor, a collaborator. He was certainly not Sartre's comrade. Sartre was always wary of nostalgia and was not prepared to soften over distant memories of apricot cocktails at the Bec de Gaz or whatever the hell it was they drank that fateful day in the spring of 1933 when Aron introduced Sartre to phenomenology.

The past had come to say goodbye, to request reconciliation at the eleventh hour, but Sartre was having none of it. He knew where he stood, where he wanted to be standing after his worn-out body had departed the scene. Both men had made their own bed and now they were going to have to die in it. They were friends in a former life, but now, certainly as far as Sartre was concerned, they were enemies to the last.

Over the next few months, Sartre travelled a little more, drank a little more, campaigned a little more and physically deteriorated a little more. His capacity to continually deteriorate without dying far sooner than he did is as remarkable as his many other remarkable achievements. But of course, he was not one of his great works and so could not remain perpetually unfinished.

27

Immortality

Blood circulation problems had damaged his legs, arms, heart, eyes and brain. His lungs, the means by which he had drawn smoke from a million Boyards cigarettes and a plethora of pipes into his small body, had held up remarkably well. On the 20 March 1980, however, his respiratory system began to suffer severe circulation problems too. He had developed pulmonary oedema: not enough blood was getting into his fluid-filled lungs and therefore not enough oxygen was getting into his blood.

When de Beauvoir found him at nine in the morning he had been sitting on the edge of his bed since five, gasping, unable to call for help. Due to an unpaid bill his phone had been cut off and she had to leave his flat to call the doctor. The doctor soon arrived and immediately called the emergency services. It took almost an hour to stabilize him before he could be stretchered to an ambulance and taken to the intensive care unit of the nearby

Broussais hospital. The paparazzi took photos from an adjacent rooftop of him lying in bed.

Oxygen starvation led him to imagine that he had already died and that he and Arlette were in an *In Camera* type situation. He asked her how it had felt to be cremated. Regaining his lucidity after a few days, he was allowed to sit in a chair to eat before nurses returned him to bed. He received a steady flow of visitors, one at a time. His circulation was now so poor that his kidneys began to fail and his bed sores to turn gangrenous.

When Pouillon passed him a drink of water he tried to be cheerful: "'The next time we have a drink together, it'll be at my place and it'll be whisky!'" (*Adieux: A Farewell to Sartre*, p. 123). De Beauvoir insists that these were not, as some have claimed, Sartre's last words. The following day, no longer trying to be cheerful, he asked her how they would pay for the funeral. Drifting in and out of consciousness as mid-April approached he took de Beauvoir's wrist and said: "'I love you very much, my dear Castor'" (*Adieux: A Farewell to Sartre*, p. 123). These were just about his last meaningful words.

On Monday 14 April, too weak to open his eyes, he uncharacteristically puckered his swollen lips to be kissed a final farewell. De Beauvoir kissed him tenderly on lips and cheek. As evening drew on he sank into a coma from which he did not emerge. A little over twenty-four hours later at 9 pm on Tuesday 15 April 1980, with Arlette at his bedside, he died. 'At nine the telephone rang. She said, "It's over." I came with Sylvie. He looked just the same; but he no longer breathed' (*Adieux: A Farewell to Sartre*, p. 124).

His abused, worn-out body was finally a corpse, finally out of his way. 'I exist nowhere but I *am*, at last!' (*Words*, p. 122). A living human being never *is*. He is only ever a lack of being in process of becoming. Now forever dead he was complete in his absence, free to be immortal. 'Only the dead can enjoy immortality' (*Words*, p. 124).

Arlette, de Beauvoir, Sylvie, Lanzmann, Bost, Pouillon and Gorz, but not Lévy, kept a night vigil around his body, drinking whisky, talking about old times and his final days, whispering their last goodbyes and protecting him from press intrusion. Left alone with him for a while, de Beauvoir lay down beside him. She attempted to get beneath the sheets but a nurse stopped her, concerned about gangrene infection. Two hours before dawn orderlies covered and removed him.

De Beauvoir viewed his body on Friday and again on Saturday morning before the funeral. His face had been made up and he was wearing a maroon corduroy suit. 'Sartre was laid out, his face uncovered, stiff and cold in his fine clothes' (*Adieux: A Farewell to Sartre*, p. 126). On her Saturday viewing, she asked a friend to take photographs of the body. Overwhelmed by the occasion, he dropped his camera on the coffin before managing to get a few shots.

Despite being heavily sedated with Valium, de Beauvoir's tears flowed freely as she caressed his forehead and gazed upon his face for the last time. He had not been as good or as loyal to her as he might have been but they had enjoyed a unique and unbreakable relationship: a great, creative romance lasting over fifty years. The stuff of legend.

President d'Estaing visited the body too. He stayed for an hour, as if to underline the historical importance of Sartre's passing. Sartre was joining the likes of Descartes, Pascal, Voltaire, Diderot and Bergson: great French philosophers whose ideas have shaped the history of the world.

The large hearse left the hospital at 2 pm behind a Citroen truck piled high with huge wreaths and bouquets. Apart from the coffin, the hearse carried de Beauvoir, Poupette, Arlette and Sylvie. The two vehicles pushed their way slowly through the vast crowds gathered on that murky, slate grey, Paris afternoon. Fifty thousand Parisians joined Sartre in one last street demonstration to protest peacefully against the fact that the old thinker and provocateur was finally dead.

Where else but France could the death of an intellectual stir such emotion? But then Sartre was no ordinary intellectual. He was loved and hated in equal measure by the people of France, but to all of them he was the years between the world wars, the overthrow of France, the Occupation, the Resistance, the liberation, the major exponent of a philosophy that helped give

France a new direction in the post-war period, the struggle over Algeria, the outrage over Vietnam and the 1968 uprising. All that history condensed into a small wooden box, making its final journey through *his* Paris, past *his* cafés and restaurants, to the Montparnasse Cemetery.

The vast crowd following the hearse merged with the vast crowd already gathered in and around the cemetery. They lined the walls, stood on graves and gravestones, pressing and surging to glimpse the end of an era. One man was accidentally pushed into the hole reserved for Sartre, others were injured in the general crush. Police and undertakers struggled to make room for the coffin and the chief mourners to emerge from the hearse.

'Atheism is a cruel, long-term business: I believe I have gone through it to the end' (*Words*, p. 157). There were no religious words or gestures as they lowered the devout non-believer into the ground. There was, in fact, no ceremony or speech of any kind.

Sartre was making the point that there was nothing to say, emphasizing the existential truth that one's own death is not something one can experience, but rather the limit of all experience. 'Death is not *my* possibility' (*Being and Nothingness*, p. 568). Or to put it another way, life has no outside. His death was a major event for the thousands gathered, but for him it was an absolute non-event, and therefore it would have been absurd to utter incantations of any kind over his already rotting corpse.

It is the irony of Sartrean ironies that a man utterly convinced that death is the end spent so much of his life striving to immortalize himself as a writer, as though he would somehow be present to enjoy his immortality. He became aware of this irony, this absurdity, but every person has to have some sort of goal in life. At least he could enjoy, while alive, the idea that he would be immortal. 'It is absurd that we are born; it is absurd that we die' (*Being and Nothingness*, p. 567), but the real existential problem, as Sartre well knew, is how we occupy ourselves in between.

A chair was found for de Beauvoir who was too grief stricken to stand. The crowd made just enough room for her to sit at his graveside; a small, forlorn figure devastated by Valium and inconsolable sorrow. As cameras clicked incessantly the other women tended her, kept a gentle hold on her, as though fearful she might try to follow him, her beloved other half, into his grave.

> His death does separate us. My death will not bring us together again. This is how things are. It is in itself splendid that we were able to live our lives in harmony for so long.
>
> (*Adieux: A Farewell to Sartre*, p. 127)

Sartre's body was exhumed a few days later for cremation at the Père Lachaise Cemetery. It was his express wish not to be buried at Père Lachaise between his mother and Mancy. His ashes were returned to the grave at Montparnasse, a popular site of pilgrimage to this day.

28

A Kind of Conclusion

If you are a person who thinks a biography should end abruptly with the death of its subject, or at most with the disposal of his corpse, then you need not trouble yourself to read this conclusion.

One reason why so many of Sartre's works remained unfinished is that he disliked writing conclusions. Obviously, he possessed the skill to concoct a conclusion, but he felt conclusions were artificial, a literary device by means of which a writer gives the reader the comforting impression that he has said all he could say on a given topic.

A work of philosophy, in particular, is never complete. However it is made to appear at its close, however neatly it is tied off with grand phrases, there is always more a work of philosophy could have said. Every work of philosophy is, in reality, open-ended, part of an ongoing historical process. Sartre knew this, and certainly the open-endedness of his works is an open invitation to continue the debate.

In so far as a biography is a summary of a life, a conclusion to a biography is in danger of being a summary of a summary, an exercise whereby the biographer directs the reader, like a judge directing a jury at the end of a trial, towards what he or she ought to think of the biography's subject *overall*, when all is said and done. I am reluctant to do that, to pretend to do that, because having studied Sartre's life and philosophy for many years I am still unsure what to make of him *overall*.

How can I say such a thing? Surely, this biography *is* what I make of Sartre. Well, yes and no. My view of Sartre changed continually during the writing of this biography, as I came to know more and more about his life, and would undoubtedly continue to change if I rewrote the whole thing again from scratch. Further reflection would surely produce a somewhat different biography.

If I rewrote this biography ten times over, made it ten, twenty, fifty times longer, conducted a hundred times more research, would I then finally grasp Sartre's true essence? Probably not, because, as was said at the outset, a person's life, both during and after it, is open to constant interpretation and reinterpretation. Every biography of a life is one more attempt to penetrate a life that produces one more layer of interpretation for others to penetrate. As the novelist and biographer, David Lodge, is fond of pointing out, 'Every decoding is another encoding.' Perhaps Sartre's 'admirable but mad' attempt to totalize Flaubert was in fact a very sane attempt to demonstrate that totalization is unachievable. Recall what Hayman said about a raid on the unknowable.

The basic facts of Sartre's life are the basic facts, dates and so forth set in stone for all time, but all the rest is still more or less up for grabs. I leave you, therefore, to make up your own mind about Sartre based on the relatively little I have said. Alternatively, do not make up your mind, or make it up when you have read every biography of Sartre ever written. There is certainly enough material out there and in the imagination for you or anyone else who can face the task to write a Sartre biography, pathography or hagiography that dwarfs *The Family Idiot*. Its title: *The Family Genius*.

It remains only for me to say by way of concluding clichés that Sartre lives on, as he always wanted to do, through his profound and still hotly debated works, and through the interest you, and I and many others continue to take in his fascinating and ongoing journey. This biography and your reading of it add a few more small steps to that journey, a few more facets to an already infinitely faceted phenomenon.

Despite his neurotic desire to become one of the gods and immortals of philosophy and literature – his desire to become a name to conjure with like Plato, Descartes, Nietzsche, Proust, Flaubert or Dickens – Sartre was wise and realistic enough to comprehend that there is no such thing as true immortality.

In *Words*, Sartre accepts that the so-called immortality of any writer and thinker, any philosopher, depends entirely on future generations of mortals being influenced by his life and work, by his contribution to the history of ideas. For Sartre, there is no afterlife for anyone beyond the minds of living men and women who recall the deceased, no eternal metaphysical realm where minds and their ideas dwell. So, when the human race is no more, Sartre's legacy, his *relative* immortality, will cease to exist. Until then, his ideas will inevitably play a role in shaping the world of the future, just as they have played a role in shaping the world of our recent past and our present day.

To end on a much lighter note, five words that encapsulate my *current* view of Jean-Paul Sartre are: genius, tenacious, industrious, moralizing and charismatic. What are yours?

BIBLIOGRAPHY

Works by Sartre

The Age of Reason, trans. David Caute (London: Penguin, 2001).

Anti-Semite and Jew, trans. George J. Becker (New York: Schocken, 1995).

Baudelaire, trans. Martin Turnell (New York: New Directions, 1967).

Being and Nothingness: An Essay on Phenomenological Ontology, trans. Hazel E. Barnes (London and New York: Routledge, 2003).

The Childhood of a Leader, in Sartre, *The Wall and Other Stories*, trans. Lloyd Alexander (New York: New Directions, 1988).

The Communists and Peace (New York: George Braziller, 1968).

The Condemned of Altona, trans. Sylvia and George Leeson, in *Penguin Plays: Altona, Men without Shadows, The Flies* (London: Penguin, 1973).

Critique of Dialectical Reason Vol. 1, Theory of Practical Ensembles, trans. Alan Sheridan-Smith (London: Verso, 2004).

Critique of Dialectical Reason Vol. 2, The Intelligibility of History, trans. Alan Sheridan-Smith (London: Verso, 2004).

Dirty Hands (Crime Passionnel), trans. Kitty Black (London: Methuen, 1995).

Erostratus, in Sartre, *The Wall and Other Stories*, trans. Lloyd Alexander (New York: New Directions, 1988).

Existentialism and Humanism, trans. Philip Mairet (London: Methuen, 1993).

The Family Idiot, Vols. 1–5, trans. Carol Cosman (Chicago: University of Chicago Press, 1981–93).

The Flies, trans. Stuart Gilbert, in *Penguin Plays: Altona, Men without Shadows, The Flies* (London: Penguin, 1973).

The Freud Scenario, trans. Quintin Hoare (London: Verso, 2013).

Hope Now: The 1980 Interviews, with Benny Lévy, trans. Adrian Van Den Hoven (Chicago: University of Chicago Press, 1996).

The Imaginary: A Phenomenological Psychology of the Imagination, trans. Jonathan Webber (London and New York: Routledge, 2004).

Imagination: A Psychological Critique, trans. Forrest Williams (Ann Arbor: University of Michigan Press, 1979).

In Camera, trans. Stuart Gilbert, in *In Camera and Other Plays* (London: Penguin, 1990).

Intimacy, in Sartre, *The Wall and Other Stories*, trans. Lloyd Alexander (New York: New Directions, 1988).

Iron in the Soul, trans. David Caute (London: Penguin, 2004).

It's Right to Rebel (On a raison de se révolter), with Philippe Gavi and Pierre Victor (Paris: Gallimard, 1974).

Kean, trans. Kitty Black, in *Three Plays: Kean, Nekrassov, The Trojan Women* (London: Penguin, 1994).

The Last Chance: Roads of Freedom IV, trans. Craig Vasey (London and New York: Continuum, 2009).

Lucifer and the Lord, trans. Kitty Black, in *In Camera and Other Plays* (London: Penguin, 1990).

Men without Shadows, trans. Kitty Black, in *Altona, Men without Shadows, The Flies* (London: Penguin, 1973).

Nausea, trans. Robert Baldick (London: Penguin, 2000).

Nekrassov, trans. Sylvia and George Leeson, in *Three Plays: Kean, Nekrassov, The Trojan Women* (London: Penguin, 1994).

Notebooks for an Ethics, trans. David Pellauer (Chicago: University of Chicago Press, 1992).

The Reprieve, trans. Eric Sutton (London: Penguin, 2005).

The Respectful Prostitute (The Respectable Prostitute), trans. Kitty Black, in *In Camera and Other Plays* (London: Penguin, 1990).

The Room, in Sartre, *The Wall and Other Stories*, trans. Lloyd Alexander (New York: New Directions, 1988).

Saint Genet, Actor and Martyr, trans. Bernard Frechtman (New York: Pantheon, 1983).

Sartre on Theatre, ed. Michel Contat and Michel Rybalka, trans. Frank Jellinek (New York: Pantheon, 1976).

Search for A Method, trans. Hazel E. Barnes (New York: Vintage, 1968).

Situations, Vols. 1–7 (Paris: Gallimard 1947, 1948, 1949, 1964, 1965). *Situations*, Vols. 8–9: *Between Existentialism and Marxism*, trans. John Mathews (New York: Pantheon, 1974). *Situations*, Vol. 10: *Life/*

Situations, trans. Paul Auster and Lydia Davis (New York: Pantheon, 1977).

Sketch for a Theory of the Emotions, trans. Philip Mairet (London: Methuen, 1985).

The Transcendence of the Ego: A Sketch for a Phenomenological Description, trans. Andrew Brown (London and New York: Routledge, 2004).

The Trojan Women, trans. Ronald Duncan, in *Three Plays: Kean, Nekrassov, The Trojan Women* (London: Penguin, 1994).

The Wall, in Sartre, *The Wall and Other Stories*, trans. Lloyd Alexander (New York: New Directions, 1988).

War Diaries: Notebooks from a Phoney War, 1939–1940, trans. Quintin Hoare (London: Verso, 2000).

What is Literature?, trans. Bernard Frechtman (London and New York: Routledge, 2002).

Words, trans. Irene Clephane (London: Penguin, 2000).

Other Works Referred To

Aron, Raymond, *The Opium of the Intellectuals* (New Brunswick, NJ: Transaction, 2001).

Bergson, Henri, *Time and Free Will* (Boston, MA: Adamant, 2000).

Camus, Albert, *The Stranger (The Outsider)*, trans. Joseph Laredo (London: Penguin, 2000).

Camus, Albert, *The Rebel*, trans. Anthony Bower (London: Penguin, 2006).

Cocteau, Jean, *Les Enfants Terribles* (London: Vintage, 2011).

Cohen-Solal, Annie, *Jean-Paul Sartre: A Life*, trans. Anna Cancogni (New York: The New Press, 2005).

de Beauvoir, Simone, *Adieux: A Farewell to Sartre*, trans. Patrick O'Brian (New York: Pantheon, 1984).

de Beauvoir, Simone, *Force of Circumstance*, trans. Richard Howard (London: Penguin, 1987).

de Beauvoir, Simone, *Memoirs of a Dutiful Daughter*, trans. James Kirkup (London: Penguin, 2001).

de Beauvoir, Simone, 'Merleau-Ponty et le Pseudo-Sartrisme', *Les Temps Modernes* 10: 2072–122 (Paris: Éditions Julliard, 1955).

de Beauvoir, Simone, *The Prime of Life*, trans. Peter Green (London: Penguin, 2001).

de Beauvoir, Simone, *The Second Sex* (London: Vintage, 1997).

de Beauvoir, Simone, *She Came to Stay*, trans. Yvonne Moyse and Roger Senhouse (London and New York: Harper Perennial, 2006).

Ehrenburg, Ilya, *The Thaw*, trans. Manya Harari (London: Harvill, 1955).

Eliot, George, *The Mill on the Floss* (London: Penguin, 2003).

Fanon, Frantz, *The Wretched of the Earth*, preface by Jean-Paul Sartre, trans. Constance Farrington (London: Penguin, 2001).

Faulkner, William, *Light in August* (London: Vintage, 2000).

Flaubert, Gustave, *Madame Bovary*, trans. Geoffrey Wall (London: Penguin, 2003).

Freud, Sigmund, *The Interpretation of Dreams* (London: Wordsworth, 1997).

Hayman, Ronald, *Writing Against: A Biography of Sartre* (London: Weidenfeld & Nicolson, 1986).

Hegel, George Wilhelm Friedrich, *The Phenomenology of Spirit*, trans. J. B. Bailey (New York: Dover, 2003).

Heidegger, Martin, *Being and Time*, trans. John Macquarrie and Edward Robinson (Oxford: Blackwell, 1993).

Hume, David, *A Treatise of Human Nature*, ed. L. A. Selby-Bigge (Oxford: Oxford University Press, 1978).

Huston, John, *An Open Book* (London: Macmillan, 1981).

Kant, Immanuel, *Critique of Practical Reason*, trans. Mary Gregor (Cambridge: Cambridge University Press, 1997).

Koestler, Arthur, *Darkness at Noon* (London: Vintage, 2005).

Lagache, Daniel, *Verbal Hallucinations and Speech* (*Les hallucinations verbales, Oeuvres 1, 1932–46*) (Paris: Presses Universitaires de France, 1977).

Lévinas, Emmanuel, *The Theory of Intuition in Husserl's Phenomenology*, trans. Andre Orianne (Evanston, IL: Northwestern University Press, 1995).

Lukács, György, *Existentialism or Marxism?* (*Existentialisme ou marxisme?*) (Paris: Nagel, 1961).

Merleau-Ponty, Maurice, *Adventures of the Dialectic: Studies in Phenomenology and Existential Philosophy*, trans. Joseph J. Bien (Evanston, IL: Northwestern University Press, 1973).

Merleau-Ponty, Maurice, *Phenomenology of Perception*, trans. Colin Smith (London and New York: Routledge, 2002).

Murdoch, Iris, *Sartre: Romantic Rationalist* (London: Vintage, 1999).

Nietzsche, Friedrich, *Beyond Good and Evil: Prelude to a Philosophy of the Future*, trans. R. J. Hollingdale (London: Penguin, 2003).

Nizan, Paul, *Antoine Bloyé*, trans. Edmund Stevens (New York: Monthly Review Press, 1974).

Nizan, Paul, *Aden Arabie*, preface by Jean-Paul Sartre, trans. Joan Pinkham (New York: Columbia University Press, 1987).

Perrin, Marius, *Avec Sartre au Stalag XIID* (Paris: Delarge, 1980).

Rowley, Hazel, *Tête-à-Tête: The Lives and Loves of Simone de Beauvoir & Jean-Paul Sartre* (London: Vintage, 2007).

Schopenhauer, Arthur, *The World as Will and Representation Vol. 1 & 2*, trans. E. F. J. Payne (New York: Dover, 2000).

Solzhenitsyn, Aleksandr, *One Day in the Life of Ivan Denisovich,* trans. Ralph Parker (London: Penguin, 2000).

INDEX